Frommer's

New York City day BY day™

2nd Edition

by Alexis Lipsitz Flippin

Wiley Publishing, Inc.

Contents

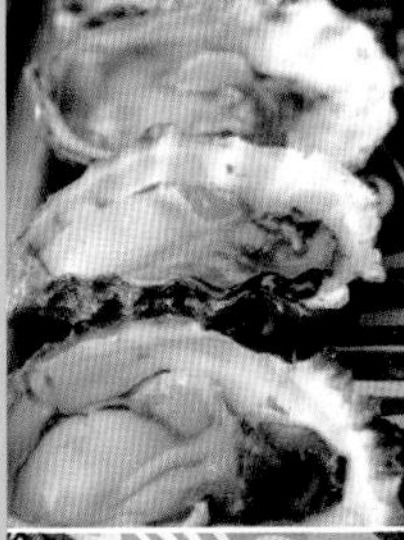
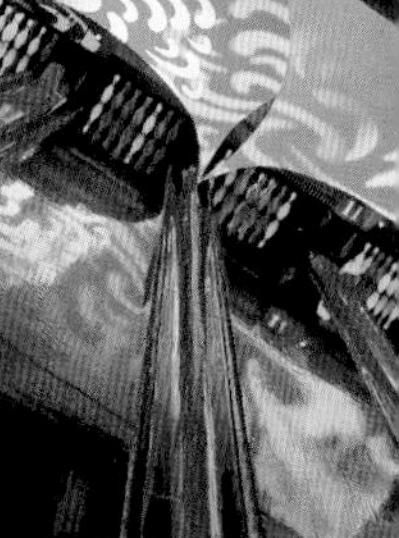

Published by:

Wiley Publishing, Inc.

111 River St.
Hoboken, NJ 07030-5774

ISBN 978-0-470-38434-3

Editor: Maureen Clarke
Production Editor: Jana M. Stefanciosa
Photo Editor: Richard Fox
Cartographer: Roberta Stockwell
Production by Wiley Indianapolis Composition Services

For information on our other products and services or to obtain technical support, please contact our Customer Care Department within the U.S. at 800/762-2974, outside the U.S. at 317/572-3993 or fax 317/572-4002.

Wiley also publishes its books in a variety of electronic formats. Some content that appears in print may not be available in electronic formats.

Manufactured in China

5 4 3

Letter from the Editorial Director

Organizing your time. That's what this guide is all about.

Other guides give you long lists of things to see and do and then expect you to fit the pieces together. The Day by Day guides are different. These guides tell you the best of everything, and then they show you how to see it *in the smartest, most time-efficient way.* Our authors have designed detailed itineraries organized by time, neighborhood, or special interest. And each tour comes with a bulleted map that takes you from stop to stop.

Hoping to explore the treasures at the Metropolitan Museum of Art, or to see some of Brooklyn's best neighborhoods and clubs? Planning a walk through Greenwich Village or Harlem, or just a whirlwind tour of the best that Manhattan has to offer? Whatever your interest or schedule, the Day by Days give you the smartest routes to follow. Not only do we take you to the top attractions, hotels, and restaurants, but we also help you access those special moments that locals get to experience—those "finds" that turn tourists into travelers.

The Day by Days are also your top choice if you're looking for one complete guide for all your travel needs. The best hotels and restaurants for every budget, the greatest shopping values, the wildest nightlife—it's all here.

Why should you trust our judgment? Because our authors personally visit each place they write about. They're an independent lot who say what they think and would never include places they wouldn't recommend to their best friends. They're also open to suggestions from readers. If you'd like to contact them, please send your comments our way at feedback@frommers.com, and we'll pass them on.

Enjoy your Day by Day guide—the most helpful travel companion you can buy. And have the trip of a lifetime.

Warm regards,

Kelly Regan

Kelly Regan, Editorial Director
Frommer's Travel Guides

About the Author

Alexis Lipsitz Flippin is a writer and editor who lives in New York City. She is the author of several Frommer's audio walking tours and the forthcoming *Frommer's Portable St. Maarten/St. Martin, Anguilla & St. Barts,* 2nd Edition.

An Additional Note

Please be advised that travel information is subject to change at any time—and this is especially true of prices. We therefore suggest that you write or call ahead for confirmation when making your travel plans. The authors, editors, and publisher cannot be held responsible for the experiences of readers while traveling. Your safety is important to us, however, so we encourage you to stay alert and be aware of your surroundings.

Star Ratings, Icons & Abbreviations

Every hotel, restaurant, and attraction listing in this guide has been ranked for quality, value, service, amenities, and special features using a **star-rating system.** Hotels, restaurants, attractions, shopping, and nightlife are rated on a scale of zero stars (recommended) to three stars (exceptional). In addition to the star-rating system, we also use a **kids icon** to point out the best bets for families. Within each tour, we recommend cafes, bars, or restaurants where you can take a break. Each of these stops appears in a shaded box marked with a coffee-cup-shaped bullet.

The following **abbreviations** are used for credit cards:

AE	American Express	DISC	Discover	V	Visa
DC	Diners Club	MC	MasterCard		

Frommers.com

Now that you have this guidebook to help you plan a great trip, visit our website at **www.frommers.com** for additional travel information on more than 4,000 destinations. We update features regularly to give you instant access to the most current trip-planning information available. At Frommers.com, you'll find scoops on the best airfares, lodging rates, and car rental bargains. You can even book your travel online through our reliable travel booking partners. Other popular features include:

- Online updates of our most popular guidebooks
- Vacation sweepstakes and contest giveaways
- Newsletters highlighting the hottest travel trends
- Podcasts, interactive maps, and up-to-the-minute events listings
- Opinionated blog entries by Arthur Frommer himself
- Online travel message boards with featured travel discussions

A Note on Prices

In the "Take a Break" and "Best Bets" sections of this book, we have used a system of dollar signs to show a range of costs for 1 night in a hotel (the price of a double-occupancy room) or the cost of an entree at a restaurant. Use the following table to decipher the dollar signs:

Cost	Hotels	Restaurants
$	under $100	under $10
$$	$100–$200	$10–$20
$$$	$200–$300	$20–$30
$$$$	$300–$400	$30–$40
$$$$$	over $400	over $40

An Invitation to the Reader

In researching this book, we discovered many wonderful places—hotels, restaurants, shops, and more. We're sure you'll find others. Please tell us about them, so we can share the information with your fellow travelers in upcoming editions. If you were disappointed with a recommendation, we'd love to know that, too. Please write to:

Frommer's New York City Day by Day, 2nd Edition
Wiley Publishing, Inc. • 111 River St. • Hoboken, NJ 07030-5774

15 Favorite **Moments**

15 Favorite Moments

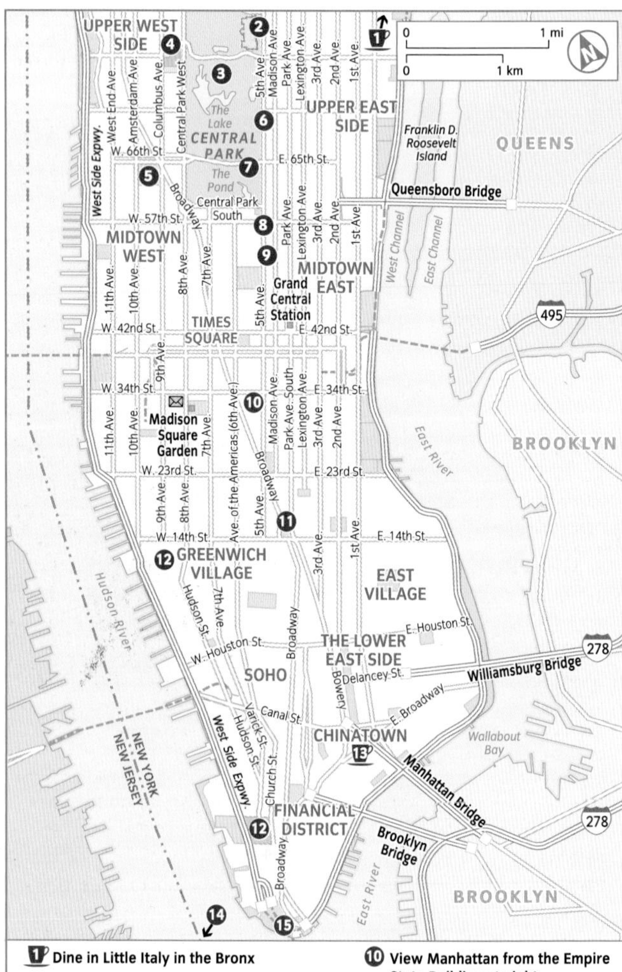

- 1 Dine in Little Italy in the Bronx
- 2 Say hello to Rembrandt at the Met.
- 3 Play in Central Park.
- 4 Stare up at the Barosaurus.
- 5 Dress up for the opera.
- 6 Feel like a Gilded Age millionaire.
- 7 Visit Gus the polar bear at the Central Park Zoo.
- 8 Window shop on Fifth Avenue.
- 9 Sip a cocktail at an über-NYC lounge.
- 10 View Manhattan from the Empire State Building at night.
- 11 Get a taste of the Greenmarket in Union Square.
- 12 Walk the storied streets of Greenwich Village.
- 13 Eat dim sum in Chinatown.
- 14 Relive the immigrant experience at Ellis Island.
- 15 Smell the sea at Battery Park.

Previous page: Rowers on the lake in Central Park.

Visitors often wonder how Manhattan residents put up with the city's crowds and frenetic pace—not to mention the tiny, cramped apartments. But when we're out exploring any of the 15 attractions below, we wouldn't be anywhere else. Every New Yorker has a list of favorite places to visit and things to see. Here's mine.

1 Dine in Little Italy in the Bronx. I like to stroll down Arthur Avenue and window-shop at the bakeries, cheese shops, and meat purveyors there. But what I love best is to order a big red-sauce-laden meal in one of the neighborhood's old-fashioned Italian restaurants. My pick? The legendary Dominick's. *See p 116.*

2 Say hello to Rembrandt at the Met. A self-portrait of the Dutch painter is one of thousands of masterpieces on view at the Metropolitan Museum of Art, the city's premier museum and one of the world's best. It's open until 9pm on Friday and Saturday nights, so soak up a little art and sip an evening cocktail on the elegant Great Hall Balcony Bar or in the Roof Garden if it's warm out. *See p 50.*

3 Play in Central Park. Manhattan's backyard is loved for its endless variety: undulating paths and greenswards, formal gardens, boat ponds, a castle, a puppet theater, an Egyptian obelisk, a lake, and even a storied carousel. *See p 102.*

4 Stare up at the Barosaurus. Yes, the largest free-standing mounted dinosaur in the world is impressive, but the American Museum of Natural History offers more than just giant reptile fossils. The adjacent Rose Center planetarium is spectacular during the day—and pure magic at night. *See p 58.*

5 Dress up for the opera. Even on casual Fridays New Yorkers like to get gussied up to see Metropolitan Opera productions at Lincoln Center (the sets alone are reason to visit). Opera not your bag? Simply cross the newly renovated plaza to see world-class performances in ballet, the symphony, and theater. *See p 144.*

The barosaurus skeleton at the American Museum of Natural History.

6 Feel like a Gilded Age millionaire. Take a walk in a robber baron's slippers and see priceless art in the bargain at steel magnate Henry Frick's Fifth Avenue mansion. The warm, elegant rooms are adorned with choice works by Rembrandt, El Greco, Gainsborough, and others, as well as original furnishings. *See p 25.*

7 Visit Gus the polar bear at the Central Park Zoo. This small-scale zoo is perfect for kids and adults in

The Gramercy Hotel's Jade Bar.

need of a relaxing break from big-city prowling. The animals at play include polar bears, penguins, and monkeys. *See p 105.*

❽ **Window-shop on Fifth Avenue.** Legendary stores such as Saks, Bergdorf Goodman, Tiffany & Co., Cartier, and Harry Winston are now rubbing shoulders with va-va-va-voom upstarts such as Gucci, Cavalli, and Versace. All vie hard for your attention. *See p 15.*

❾ **Sip a cocktail at an über-NYC lounge.** Choose an old standard such as the King Cole Lounge in the St. Regis or a new classic-in-the-making such as the Gramercy Hotel's Rose Bar or Jade Bar, and you'll see why the biggest star of *Sex and the City* is New York. *See p 128.*

❿ **View Manhattan from the Empire State Building at night.** The city that never sleeps begins to glitter at dusk, when millions of lights set it aglow. You won't see any stars in the New York sky, but you won't miss them with views like this. *See p 43.*

⓫ **Get a taste of the Greenmarket in Union Square.** Country comes to city 4 days a week year-round at New York's largest Greenmarket. Most of the excellent fresh produce, flowers, meats, and other artisanal food comes from small farmers in Long Island and New Jersey. Open Monday, Wednesday, Friday, and Saturday. *See p 18.*

⓬ **Walk the storied streets of Greenwich Village.** This historic, human-scale neighborhood affords serendipitous charms around every corner—from vintage brownstones to fabled watering holes. Many famous writers, artists, and poets of yesteryear called this former hamlet home. *See p 76.*

⓭ **Eat dim sum in Chinatown.** You can choose one of the big Hong Kong–style eateries with multiple floors and endless rolling carts of tasty, surprising morsels, or a smaller, less frenetic spot such as Ping's or the Oriental Garden. *See p 85.*

⓮ **Relive the immigrant experience at Ellis Island.** Whether or not your family entered America through Ellis Island, a visit here is extremely moving. The on-site museum does an excellent job of bringing the immigrant experience to life. *See p 65.*

⓯ **Smell the sea at Battery Park.** This is where Manhattan was born. Start at the yacht basin at the World Financial Center and head south. When you reach the southern tip of Manhattan, you get a magnificent view of the mouth of the mighty New York Harbor with big ships chugging into view. *See p 9, bullet* ❾.

1 The Best **Full-Day Tours**

The Best in One Day

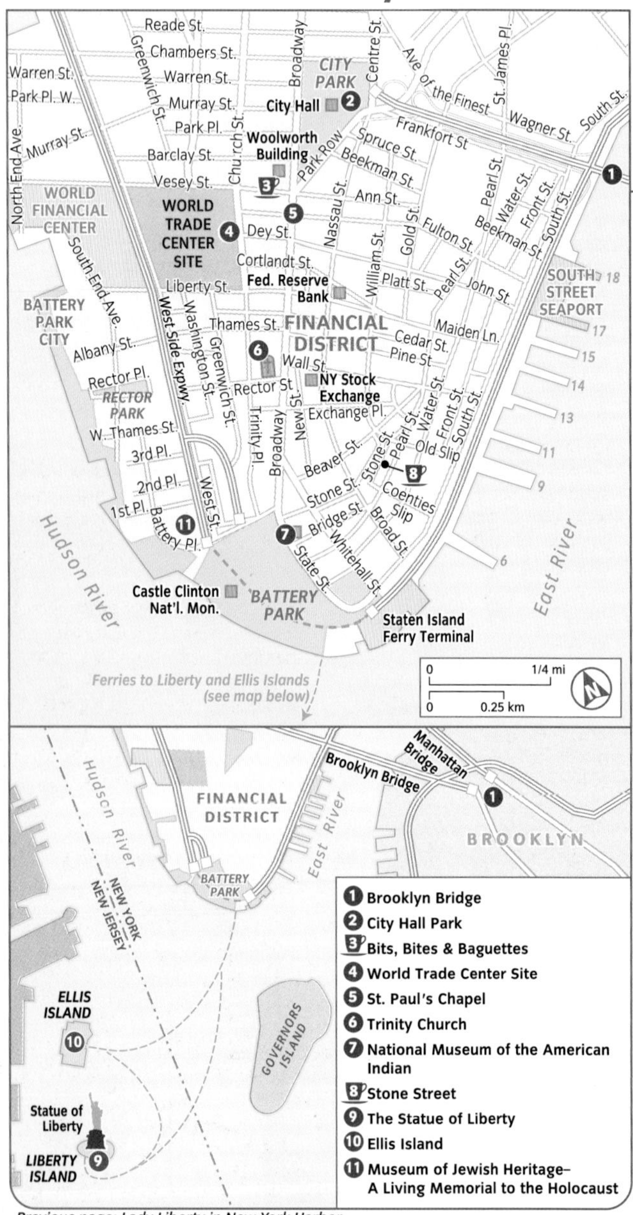

Previous page: Lady Liberty in New York Harbor.

The most wonderful—and maddening—thing about New York? The endless number of choices. To explore the city's beginnings, head first to Lower Manhattan, with its Dutch roots and cobblestoned streets. But this area of New York is not limited to centuries-old structures frozen in time; it's also the dynamic center of city government and world finance. For more details on southern Manhattan, see "Historic Downtown" on p. 64 in chapter 4. **START: Subway A or C to High Street in Brooklyn**

1 ★★ **Brooklyn Bridge.** For a glorious view of New York City, you can't beat the 30-minute walk across the Brooklyn Bridge. The celebrated suspension bridge is a wonder in itself, with its Gothic-inspired towers, Maine granite, and intricate web of steel cables. *See p 48. Subway: A/C to High St. in Brooklyn.*

2 **City Hall Park.** City Hall has been the seat of NYC government since 1812. Security concerns prevent visitors from touring inside, but you can get close enough to appreciate the handsome French Renaissance exterior, built from 1803 to 1811. Abraham Lincoln was laid in state in the soaring rotunda. Equally grand is the colossal Municipal Building (1 Centre St. at Chambers), built on the other side of Centre Street in 1915 by McKim, Mead, and White; it was the celebrated firm's first "skyscraper." Across Broadway at no. 233 is that temple of commerce known as the ★ **Woolworth Building.** Built from the proceeds of a nickel-and-dime empire in 1913, this neo-Gothic masterpiece is the work of Cass Gilbert. At press time, the public was not allowed inside the building. *City Hall Park (btwn. Broadway & Park Row).*

3 **Bits, Bites & Baguettes.** Grab a sandwich or one of the hearty salads. *22 Park Place (btwn. Church & Broadway). ☎ 212/374-1111. $.*

4 ★ **World Trade Center Site.** The Twin Towers once dominated the city's skyline, and visitors from around the world have made pilgrimages to the vast, gaping hole left after their destruction during the September 11, 2001, terrorist attacks. Today, it's a bustling

The Brooklyn Bridge and Manhattan skyline.

Founding Father Alexander Hamilton is buried at Trinity Church.

construction site with a small area devoted to the attacks and their aftermath. A Wall of Heroes lists the names of those who died that day. Daniel Libeskind's proposed 1,776-foot-tall (533m) **Freedom Tower** will eventually stand here, along with a permanent memorial entitled ***Reflecting Absence.*** A bird wing–like steel and glass canopy, designed by Catalan architect Santiago Calatrava, will shelter the nearby World Trade Center transportation hub and PATH station. Construction work is ongoing and is expected to last till 2015. The **Tribute WTC Visitor Center** (www.tributenyc.org), at 120 Liberty St. (at the site's south border), was created by the nonprofit September 11th Families' Association; it offers daily walking tours ($10), led by people whose lives were affected by the disaster. *Bounded by Church, Barclay, Liberty & West sts. ☎ 212/484-1222. www.wtc.com. Subway A/C to World Trade Center; N/R to Cortland St.*

5 ★ **St. Paul's Chapel.** This is Manhattan's only surviving pre-Revolutionary church, from 1766. Built to resemble London's St. Martin-in-the-Fields, with an elegant Georgian interior, the chapel was a refuge for rescue workers after September 11, and is home to the "Unwavering Spirit" exhibition, which chronicles 9/11 with artifacts and donations from around the world. The churchyard in back is filled with 18th- and 19th-century tombstones. ⌚ *45 min. 209 Broadway (at Fulton St.). ☎ 212/233-4164. Mon–Fri 10am–6pm; Sat 8am–3pm; Sun 7am–3pm. Free concerts Mon 1–2pm. www.saintpaulschapel.org. Subway: 2/3 to Park Place; 1/9/4/5/A to Fulton St./Broadway Nassau.*

6 ★★ **Trinity Church.** This lovely neo-Gothic marvel was consecrated in 1846 and is still active today. The main doors, modeled on the doors in Florence's Baptistery, are decorated with biblical scenes; inside are splendid stained-glass windows. Among those buried in the pretty churchyard are Alexander Hamilton and Robert Fulton. ⌚ *30 min. Broadway (at Wall St.). ☎ 212/602-0800. Mon–Fri 10am–6pm; Sat 8am–4pm; Sun 7am–4pm. www.trinitywallstreetorg. Subway: 4/5 to Wall St.*

7 ★★ kids **National Museum of the American Indian.** This Smithsonian Institution museum is a little-known New York treasure. The collection spans more than 10,000 years of Native heritage, housed in a glorious 1907 Beaux Arts building designed by Cass Gilbert. ⌚ *1 hr. 1 Bowling Green. ☎ 212/514-3700. www.americanindian.si.edu. Free. Daily 10am–5pm (Thurs till 8pm). Subway: 4/5 to Bowling Green; 1/9 to South Ferry.*

8 ★ **Stone Street.** This historic cobblestoned street is lined with restaurants. You might try **Adrienne's Pizzabar,** a new spot (with alfresco seating) that has gotten raves for its thin-crust square pizza.

54 Stone St. (btwn. William & Pearl sts.). ☎ 212/248-3838. $–$$.

9 ★ kids **The Statue of Liberty.** For the millions who arrived in New York by ship, Lady Liberty was their first glimpse of America. A gift from France to the United States, the statue was designed by sculptor Frédéric-Auguste Bartholdi and unveiled on October 28, 1886. The crown and torch are not accessible, but visitors can explore the Statue of Liberty Museum, peer into the inner structure through a glass ceiling near the base of the statue, and enjoy views from the observation deck. ***Tip:*** The Staten Island Ferry (a free 25-min. trip) provides spectacular skyline views of Manhattan and is a wonderful way to see the harbor. You'll pass by (though not stop at) the Statue of Liberty and Ellis Island. Check **www.siferry.com** for details. *1 hr. (ferry ride: 15 min.). On Liberty Island in New York Harbor. Buy tickets online or in Castle Clinton National Monument (see above). ☎ 212/363-3200 (general info). www.nps.gov/stli. Free admission; ferry ticket to Statue of Liberty & Ellis Island $12 adults, $10 seniors, $5 children 3–17 (☎ 877/523-9849; www.statuecruises.com). Daily 9am–4pm (last ferry departs around 3pm); extended hours in summer. Subway: 4/5 to Bowling Green; 1/9 to South Ferry.*

10 ★★★ kids **Ellis Island.** For 62 years (1892–1954), this was the main point of entry for newcomers to America. Today it's one of New York's most moving attractions—particularly for the 40% of Americans whose ancestors passed through the immigration center here. Among the points of interest: the **Immigration Museum,** which skillfully describes coming to America through the eyes of the immigrants; the **American Immigrant Wall of Honor,** which commemorates more than 500,000 immigrants and their families; and the **American Family Immigration Center,** where interactive exhibits can help you research your own family history. *90 min. (ferry ride: 10 min. from Liberty Island) ☎ 212/363-3200. www.nps.gov/elis or www.ellisisland.org. For tickets, see Statue of Liberty, above. Subway: 4/5 to Bowling Green; 1/9 to South Ferry.*

11 ★★ **Museum of Jewish Heritage—A Living Memorial to the Holocaust.** Dedicated to teaching people of all backgrounds about 20th-century Jewish life, this award-winning museum was designed in a six-sided shape to symbolize the Star of David and honor the six million Jews who died in the Holocaust. Inside are photos, artifacts, and moving accounts from survivors. A second-story stone garden—where each of the hollowed-out boulders has a tree growing out of it—overlooks New York Harbor. *90 min. 36 Battery Place. ☎ 646/437-4200. www.mjhnyc.org. Admission $10 adults, $7 seniors, $5 students, free for children 12 and under. Sun–Tues & Thurs 10am–5:45pm; Wed 10am–8pm; Fri & eves of Jewish holidays 10am–3pm. Subway: 4/5 to Bowling Green; 1/9 to South Ferry.*

Artifact at the National Museum of the American Indian.

The Best in Two Days

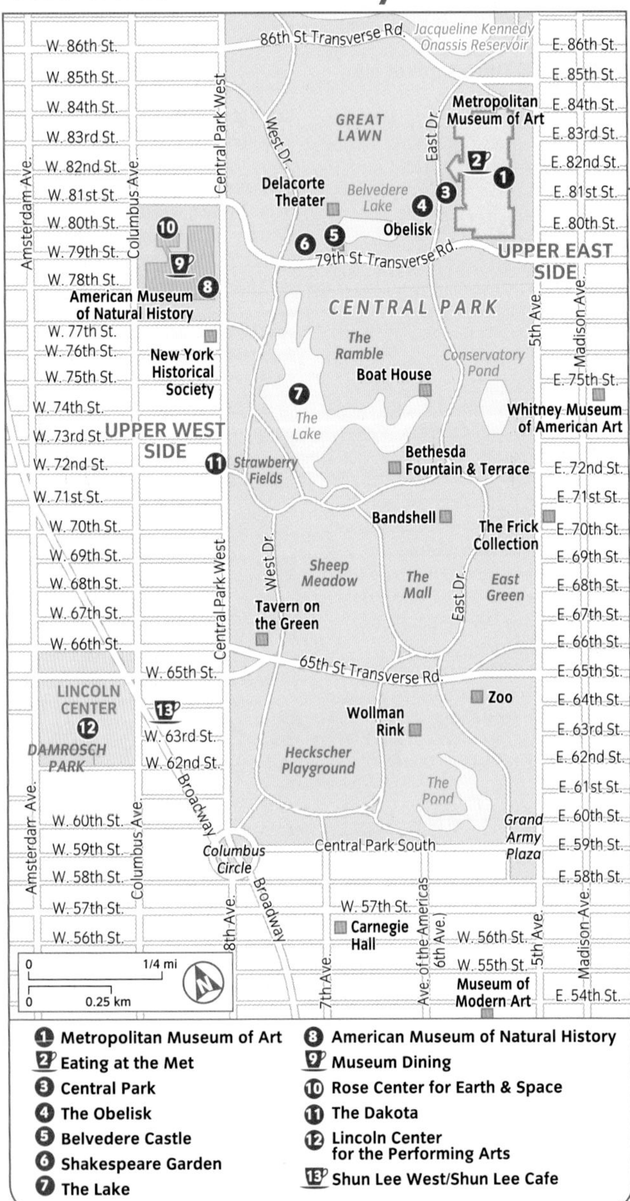

If Lower Manhattan is the city's historic heart, uptown is its artistic soul, as home of the Metropolitan Museum and Lincoln Center. It's also home to Central Park, an urban oasis that recharges body and mind. This part of town has a wealth of museums—most of them along Fifth Avenue. To avoid burnout, decide which ones you want to focus on before heading out. If you have kids in tow, don't miss the American Museum of Natural History. START: **Subway 4, 5, or 6 to 86th Street**

1 ★★★ kids **Metropolitan Museum of Art.** At 177,777 square yards (148,644 sq. m), this is the largest museum in the Western Hemisphere, attracting five million visitors annually. Nearly all the world's cultures through the ages are on display—from Egyptian mummies to ancient Greek statuary to Islamic carvings to Renaissance paintings to 20th-century decorative arts—and masterpieces are the rule. You could go once a week for a lifetime and still find something new on each visit. Everyone should see the **Temple of Dendur,** the jewel of the Egyptian collection. But let personal preference be your guide to the rest. My touchstones are the exceptional Rembrandts, Vermeers, and other Dutch master paintings. I also love the transplanted period rooms—from the elegant 18th-century bedroom from a Venetian castle to the warm and inviting 20th-century Frank Lloyd Wright living room. For a full tour of the Met, see p 50. *2½ hr. Fifth Ave. (at 82nd St.). ☎ 212/535-7710. www.metmuseum.org. Admission $20 adults, $5 seniors, $10 students, free for children under 12 with adult. Sun & Tues–Thurs 9:30am–5:30pm; Fri–Sat 9:30am–9pm. Closed Mon (except holiday Mon, like Labor Day). Subway: 4/5/6 to 86th St. Bus: M1/2/3/4.*

2 Eating at the Met. If you're visiting between May and October, check out the Roof Garden's casual **cafe/bar** ($) and breathtaking treetop view of Central Park. Year-round you can grab lunch at the ground-floor **cafeteria** ($) or at the elegant **Petrie Court Café** (☎ 212/570-3964; $$), which overlooks Central Park. On Friday and Saturday evenings, cocktails and appetizers are served at the **Balcony Bar** ($) overlooking the Great Hall.

3 ★★★ kids **Central Park.** Manhattanites may not have yards, but they do have this glorious swath of green. Designed by Frederick Law Olmsted and Calvert Vaux in the 1850s, the park is 2½ miles (4km) long (extending from 59th to 110th sts.) and a half-mile (.8km) wide (from Fifth Ave. to Central Park West). It encompasses a zoo, a carousel, two ice-skating rinks, restaurants, children's playgrounds,

The Metropolitan Museum's glass-walled gallery containing the Temple of Dendur.

even theaters. *See p 102 for a full tour.*

❹ **The Obelisk.** Also called Cleopatra's Needle, this 69-foot (21m) obelisk is reached by following the path leading west behind the Met. Originally erected in Heliopolis, Egypt around 1475 B.C., it was given to New York by the khedive of Egypt in 1880. Continue on the path to the **Great Lawn,** site of countless softball games, concerts, and peaceful political protests.

❺ ★ **Belvedere Castle.** Built by Calvert Vaux in 1869, this fanciful medieval-style fortress-in-miniature sits at the highest point in the park and affords sweeping views. The many birds that call this area home led to the creation of a bird-watching and educational center in the castle's ranger station. To get here, follow the path across East Drive and walk west.

❻ **Shakespeare Garden.** Next to Belvedere Castle, you'll find this garden where the only flowers and plants in evidence are those mentioned in the Bard's plays.

❼ ★★ **The Lake.** South of the garden, you'll cross the 79th Street Transverse Road to reach The Lake, with its perimeter pathway lined with weeping willows and Japanese cherry trees. The neo-Victorian Loeb Boathouse at the east end of the Lake rents rowboats and bicycles; on summer evenings, you can arrange gondola rides. Walk back up to the 79th Street Transverse Road and follow it west; it exits the park at 81st Street and Central Park West.

❽ ★★★ kids **American Museum of Natural History.** If you can get past the spectacular entrance—a **Barosaurus,** the world's largest freestanding dinosaur exhibit—you'll find plenty more to see. Founded in 1869, the AMNH houses the world's greatest natural science collection in a square-block group of buildings made of whimsical towers and turrets, pink granite, and red brick. The diversity of the holdings is astounding: some 36 million specimens, ranging from microscopic organisms to the world's largest cut gem, the **Brazilian Princess Topaz** (21,005 carats). If you only see one exhibit, make it the ★ **dinosaurs,** which take up the entire fourth floor. *2 hr. Central Park West (btwn. 77th & 81st sts.). ☎ 212/769-5100. www.amnh.org. Admission (includes entrance to Rose Center, below) $15 adults, $11 seniors & students, $8.50 children 2–12; Space Show (see below) & museum admission $22 adults, $17 seniors & students, $13 children under 12. Daily 10am–5:45pm (Rose*

T-Rex at the AMNH.

The Rose Center for Earth & Space, home of the Hayden Planetarium.

Center open Fri to 8:45pm). Subway: B/C to 81st St.

9 kids **Museum Dining.** The **Food Court** ($) has a kid-friendly selection of pizzas, hot entrees, sandwiches—and even down-home barbecue from five different regions of the country. The **Starlight Café** ($) features sandwiches, chicken nuggets, hot dogs, and fresh fruit or Dippin' Dots ice cream treats.

10 ★★ kids **Rose Center for Earth & Space.** Attached to the American Museum of Natural History, this four-story sphere "floating" in a glass square is astonishing. Even if you're suffering from museum overload, the Rose Center will lift your spirits. The center's Hayden Planetarium features a spectacular new space show, "Cosmic Collisions," narrated by Robert Redford (every half-hour 10:30am–4:30pm; from 11am Wed).

11 **The Dakota.** With its dark trim and dramatic gables, dormers, and oriel windows, this 1884 apartment house is one of the city's most legendary landmarks. Its most famous resident, John Lennon, was gunned down next to the entrance on December 8, 1980; Yoko Ono still lives here. *1 W. 72nd St. (at Central Park West). Subway: 1/2/3/4 to 72nd St.*

12 ★★ **Lincoln Center for the Performing Arts.** New York has countless performing arts venues, but none so multifaceted as Lincoln Center—presenting world-class opera, ballet, dramatic theater, jazz, symphonies, and more. After a long day on your feet, relax on the outdoor plaza in front of the fountains. At Christmas the light displays are lovely, and on summer evenings the plaza becomes an outdoor dance party. *See p 140.*

13 **Shun Lee West/Shun Lee Cafe.** Whenever I attend a performance at Lincoln Center, I head to this "haute Chinese" restaurant afterward for delicious and beautifully prepared Chinese dishes. I love the drama of the space, sheathed in black lacquer. Grand Marnier prawns are rich and decadent, as is the Heavenly Sea Bass Filet, cooked in a rice wine sauce. Its more casual and less expensive cafe counterpart just next door serves dim sum and other offerings. *43 W. 65th St. (btwn. Columbus Ave. & Central Park West).* ☎ *212/769-3888 $$–$$$.*

The Best in Three Days

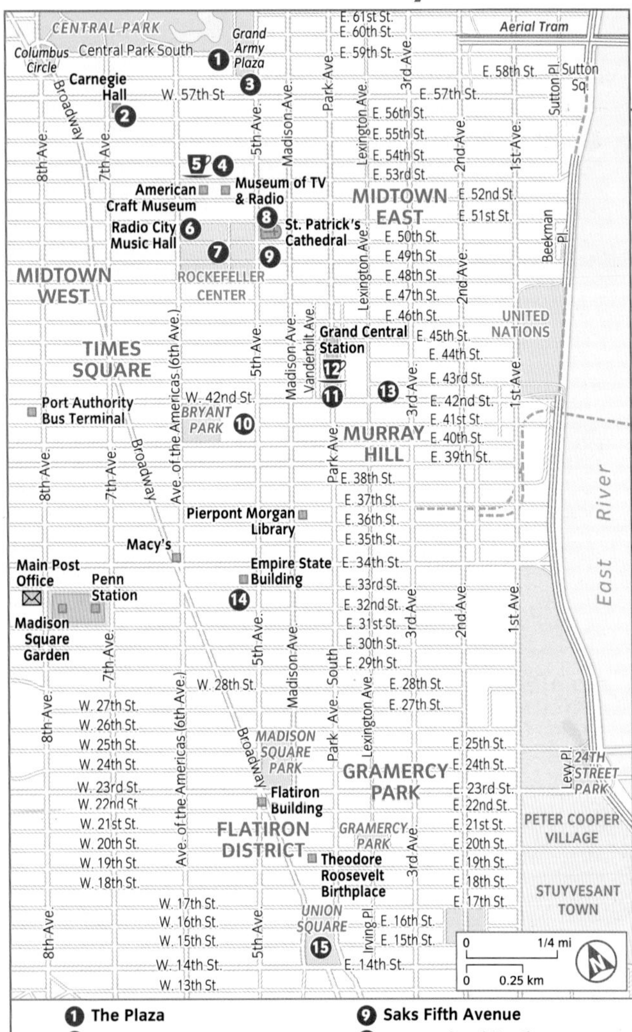

1. The Plaza
2. Carnegie Hall
3. Fifth Avenue
4. Museum of Modern Art
5. Cafe 2
6. Radio City Music Hall
7. Rockefeller Center
8. St. Patrick's Cathedral
9. Saks Fifth Avenue
10. New York Public Library
11. Grand Central Terminal
12. Grand Central food court
13. Chrysler Building
14. Empire State Building
15. Union Square Greenmarket

You've discovered downtown and uptown, so now it's time to hit midtown—the city's business and commercial center. But it's not all about corporate skyscrapers and designer shops; this tour will also introduce you to many quintessential New York landmarks. START: **Subway N, R, or W to Fifth Avenue/59th Street**

1 ★ **The Plaza.** There's no denying the glamour of the Big Apple's most famous hotel, reopened in 2008 after a glitzy 2-year, $400-million renovation. This 1907 landmark French Renaissance palace has hosted royalty, celebrities, and a legion of honeymooners. *768 Fifth Ave. (at Central Park South). ☎ 888/850-0909. www.fairmont.com/theplaza. Subway: N/R/W to Fifth Ave./59th St.* *See p 38.*

2 ★ **Carnegie Hall.** How do you get to Carnegie Hall? Practice, practice, practice. Perhaps the world's most famous performance space, Carnegie Hall features everything from orchestral classics to solo sitar. The **Isaac Stern Auditorium,** the 2,804-seat main hall, welcomes visiting orchestras from around the world. There's also the intimate 268-seat **Weill Recital Hall,** and the ornate underground 600-seat **Zankel Hall.** Tickets for the 1-hour tours are available at the box office. *1 hr. (for tour). 881 Seventh Ave. (at 56th St.). ☎ 212/247-7800, or 212/903-9765 for tour information. www.carnegiehall.org. Tours cost $10 adults, $7 students & seniors, and $3 children under 12 and run Mon–Fri 11:30am, 2pm & 3pm; Sat 11:30am & 12:30pm; Sun 12:30pm. Subway: A/B/C/D/1/9 to Columbus Circle; N/Q/R/W to 57th St./Seventh Ave.*

3 ★★ **Fifth Avenue.** New York's most famous shopping artery starts at the southeast corner of Central Park at 59th Street. Some landmarks to note: **FAO Schwarz,** at no. 767 (58th St.), the city's top toy emporium; **Tiffany & Co.,** at no. 727 (btwn. 56th & 57th sts.), with its stainless-steel doors and Atlas clock; gilded **Trump Tower,** at no. 725 (56th St.), with a seven-story waterfall and pinkish granite walls; **Henri Bendel,** at no. 712 (btwn. 55th & 56th sts.), a whimsical department store with vintage Lalique art-glass windows; **Takashimaya,** at no. 693 (btwn.

Shoppers on Fifth Avenue near Bergdorf Goodman.

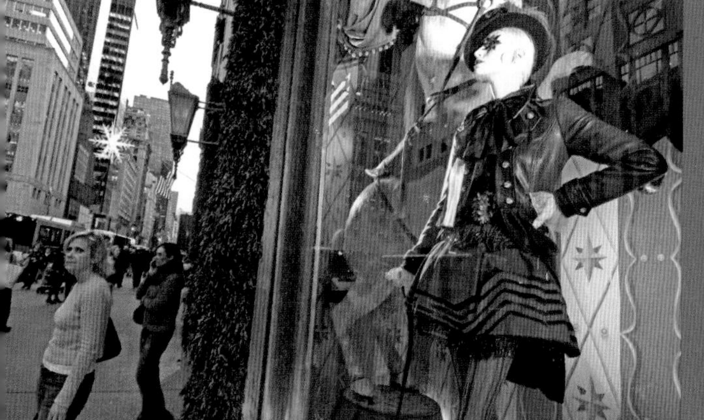

54th & 55th sts.); and at 754 (at 57th St.) **Bergdorf Goodman.** *Subway: N/R/W to Fifth Ave./59th St.*

4 ★★★ Museum of Modern Art. MoMA houses the world's greatest collection of painting and sculpture from the late 19th century to the present—from Monet's *Water Lilies* and Klimt's *The Kiss* to 20th-century masterworks by Frida Kahlo and Jasper Johns to contemporary pieces by Richard Serra and Chuck Close. Add to that a vast collection of modern drawings, photos, architectural models and modern furniture, iconic design objects ranging from tableware to sports cars, and film and video. After a massive 3-year, $650-million renovation project—under the guidance of Japanese architect Yoshio Taniguchi in 2004, it's twice as big and, many critics contend, better. Paul Goldberger, writing in *The New Yorker,* said "The old building looks better than it has in half a century, both inside and out. *2 hr. 11 W. 53rd St. (btwn. Fifth & Sixth aves.). ☎ 212/708-9400. www.moma.org. Admission $20 adults, $16 seniors, $12 students, kids 16 & under free when accompanied by an adult. Sat–Mon & Wed–Thurs 10:30am–5:30pm; Fri 10:30am–8pm. Subway: E/V to Fifth Ave./53rd St.; B/D/F to 47th–50th sts.*

The Rockefeller Center skating rink.

The door to St. Patrick's Cathedral.

5 Cafe 2. On the second floor of MoMA, this cafeteria-style restaurant serves rustic Italian cuisine. Rest your feet and enjoy pastas, panini, *salumi,* soups, and salads. *$–$$.*

6 ★★★ Radio City Music Hall. Designed by Donald Deskey and opened in 1932, this sumptuous Art Deco classic is the world's largest indoor theater, with 6,000 seats. Long known for its Rockettes revues and popular Christmas show, Radio City also has a stellar history as a venue for movie premieres (more than 700 films have opened here since 1933). The "powder rooms" are some of the swankiest in town. *1260 Sixth Ave. (at 50th St.). ☎ 212/247-4777. www.radiocity.com. 1-hr. Stage Door Tour is daily 11am to 3pm (extended hours Nov 15–Dec 30). Tickets $17 adults, $14 seniors,*

$10 children 12 & under. Subway: B/D/F/V to 47th–50th sts./Rockefeller Center.

7 ★★★ Rockefeller Center. A prime example of civic optimism expressed in soaring architecture, Rock Center was built mainly in the 1930s. Designated a National Historic Landmark in 1988, it's now the world's largest privately owned business-and-entertainment center, with 18 buildings on 21acres. The **GE Building,** also known as **30 Rock,** at 30 Rockefeller Plaza, is a 70-story showpiece towering over the plaza; walk through the granite-and-marble lobby lined with handsome murals by Spanish painter José Maria Sert (1874–1945). The mammoth Rockefeller Christmas tree is traditionally placed in the plaza fronting 30 Rock, overlooking the famous skating rink. *Bounded by 48th & 51th sts. & Fifth & Sixth aves. Subway: B/D/F/V to 47th–50th sts./Rockefeller Center.*

8 ★★ St. Patrick's Cathedral. This Gothic white-marble-and-stone wonder is the largest Roman Catholic cathedral in the United States. Designed by James Renwick, begun in 1859, and consecrated in 1879, St. Patrick's wasn't completed until 1906. You can pop in between services to get a look at the impressive interior. The St. Michael and St. Louis altar came from Tiffany & Co. (also on Fifth Ave.), while the St. Elizabeth altar—honoring Mother Elizabeth Ann Seton, the first American-born saint—was designed by Paolo Medici of Rome. *15 min. Fifth Ave. (btwn. 50th & 51st sts.). ☎ 212/753-2261. www.saintpatrickscathedral.org. Free admission. Daily 6:30am–8:45pm. Subway: B/D/F/V to 47th–50th sts./ Rockefeller Center.*

9 Saks Fifth Avenue. At this quintessential New York luxury retailer, even the elaborate window displays are a treat. *611 Fifth Ave. (at 50th St.) ☎ 212/753-4000. www.saksfifthavenue.com. Subway: B/D/F/V to 47th–50th sts./Rockefeller Center.*

10 ★ New York Public Library. The lions *Patience* and *Fortitude* stand guard outside the grand Fifth Avenue entrance of the library, designed by Carrère & Hastings in 1911. It's one of the country's finest examples of Beaux Arts architecture. Sadly, architect John Mervin Carrère never got to enjoy the fruits of his labor; he was killed in a taxi accident 2 months before the library dedication. The majestic white-marble structure is filled with Corinthian columns and allegorical statues. Always peculiarly interesting, special exhibits inside have run the gamut, from Imperial Russia to "400 Years of Milton." *Fifth Ave. (btwn. 42nd & 40th sts.). ☎ 212/ 340-0849. www.nypl.org. Open Mon & Thurs–Sat 11am–6pm; Tues–Wed 10am–7:30pm, Sun 1–5pm. Subway: B/D/F/V to 42nd St.*

11 ★★ Grand Central Terminal. Another Beaux Arts beauty. The highlight is the vast, imposing main concourse, where high windows allow sunlight to pour onto

Marble lions guard the New York Public Library.

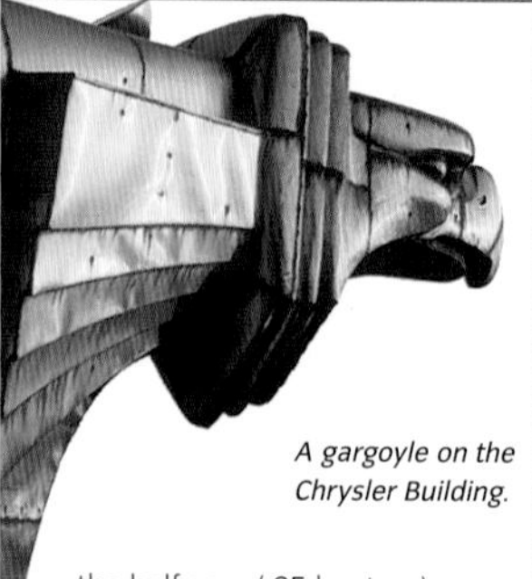

A gargoyle on the Chrysler Building.

the half-acre (.25-hectare) Tennessee-marble floor. Everything gleams, from the brass clock over the central kiosk to the gold- and nickel-plated chandeliers piercing the side archways. The breathtaking ***Sky Ceiling*** depicts the constellations of the winter sky above New York. *42nd St. & Park Ave. ☎ 212/340-2210. www.grand centralterminal.com. Subway: 4/5/6/7/S to 42nd St.*

12 ★ Grand Central food court. I know people who, like me, go way out of their way to eat on the lower level at Grand Central. From hearty Mexican (Zócalo) to deli (Mendy's) to top-notch soup (Hale & Hearty), Indian (Spice), and pizza (Two Boots), the choices are delicious and fast, and the seating plentiful. *$–$$.*

13 ★★★ Chrysler Building. Built as the Chrysler Corporation headquarters in 1930, this is New York's most romantic Art Deco masterpiece and, for many New Yorkers, its most endearing visual touchstone. It's especially dramatic at night, when lights glitter through triangular openings in its steely crown. The marble-clad lobby is a hymn to Art Deco, with a mural on the ceiling that was rediscovered in 1999. *405 Lexington Ave. (btwn. 42nd & 43rd sts.). Subway: 4/5/6 to Grand Central.*

14 ★★ Empire State Building. King Kong climbed it in 1933. A plane slammed into it in 1945. After September 11, 2001, the Empire State regained its status as New York City's tallest building. Through it all, it has remained one of the city's favorite landmarks. Completed in 1931, the limestone and stainless steel Art Deco dazzler climbs 103 stories (1,454 ft./436m). The best views are from the 86th- and 102nd-floor observatories, but you may prefer the former, from which you can walk onto an outer windswept deck. From here the citywide panorama is electric. ◷ *1 hr. 350 Fifth Ave. (at 34th St.). ☎ 212/736-3100. www.esbnyc.com. Observatory admission (86th floor) $19 adults, $17 seniors & children 12–17, $13 children 6–11, free for children under 6. Express pass: $45. 102nd floor Observatory: $15 extra. Buy & print tickets in advance online to avoid lines. Observatories open daily 8am–2am; last elevator goes up at 1:15am. Subway: 6 to 33rd St.; B/D/F/V to 34th St.*

15 ★★ Union Square Greenmarket. At Manhattan's largest green market, you'll find fresh produce from upstate and New Jersey farms, fish just off the boat from Long Island, artisanal cheeses and home-cured meats, plants, and organic herbs and spices. I've seen celebrated chefs arrive here with wheelbarrows in tow. *In Union Sq. ☎ 212/477-3220. www.cenyc.org. Open year-round Mon, Wed, Fri–Sat during daylight hours. Subway: 4/5/6/N/Q/R/W to Union Sq.* ●

2 Special-Interest Tours

Romantic New York

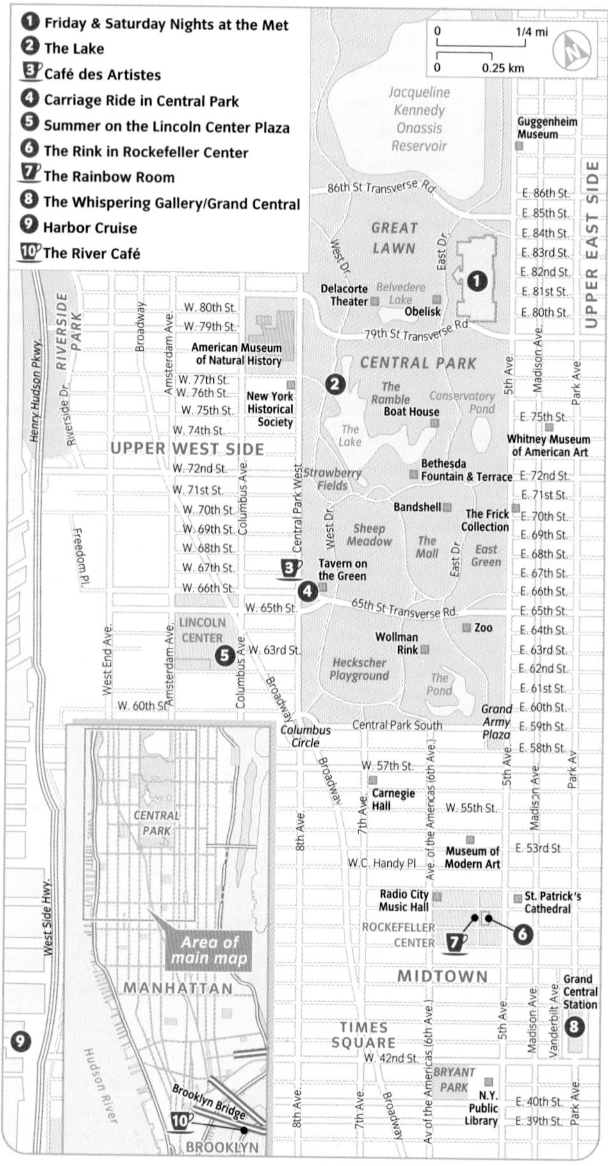
1 Friday & Saturday Nights at the Met
2 The Lake
3 Café des Artistes
4 Carriage Ride in Central Park
5 Summer on the Lincoln Center Plaza
6 The Rink in Rockefeller Center
7 The Rainbow Room
8 The Whispering Gallery/Grand Central
9 Harbor Cruise
10 The River Café
Jacqueline Kennedy Onassis Reservoir
Guggenheim Museum
86th St Transverse Rd.
GREAT LAWN
Delacorte Theater
Belvedere Lake
Obelisk
79th St Transverse Rd.
American Museum of Natural History
CENTRAL PARK
New York Historical Society
The Ramble
Conservatory Pond
Boat House
The Lake
Whitney Museum of American Art
UPPER WEST SIDE
UPPER EAST SIDE
RIVERSIDE PARK
Strawberry Fields
Bethesda Fountain & Terrace
Bandshell
The Frick Collection
Sheep Meadow
The Mall
East Green
Tavern on the Green
65th St Transverse Rd.
Zoo
LINCOLN CENTER
Wollman Rink
Heckscher Playground
The Pond
Grand Army Plaza
Columbus Circle
Central Park South
Carnegie Hall
Museum of Modern Art
Radio City Music Hall
St. Patrick's Cathedral
ROCKEFELLER CENTER
MIDTOWN
Grand Central Station
TIMES SQUARE
BRYANT PARK
N.Y. Public Library
Area of main map
MANHATTAN
Hudson River
Brooklyn Bridge
BROOKLYN
Henry Hudson Pkwy.
West Side Hwy.

Previous page: The Empire State Building seen through the Manhattan Bridge.

New York is revered for its high-energy, never-say-die attitude. But to my mind, the city harbors a romantic streak as wide as the Hudson River. This tour introduces you to places that are best discovered as a twosome. START: **Subway 6 to 79th or 86th Street**

1 ★★ Friday and Saturday Nights at the Met. The city's premier museum stays open until 9pm on weekend nights. It's a lovely time to visit—quieter, with fewer visitors. You'll have some rooms almost all to yourself (and the Met security team, of course). You can combine some leisurely gallery hopping with cocktails in the Balcony Bar overlooking the Great Hall. When the weather warms, rendezvous for drinks on the Roof Garden with spectacular views of Central Park and the skyline that surrounds it. To the west, the tip of a real Egyptian obelisk rises above the park tree line. Dating from about 1500 B.C., it was a gift from the Egyptian government in the late 19th century. Its name alone, Cleopatra's Needle, conjures up ageless romance. ***Roof Garden open May to late autumn.*** ***See p 50.***

2 ★★ The Lake. Ella Fitzgerald sang "I love the rowing on Central Park Lake" in "The Lady Is a Tramp," and when you see the shimmering waters edged by weeping willows and Japanese cherry trees, you'll understand why it inspired songwriters Rodgers and Hart. The green banks along the man-made lake slope gently toward the water and make for an ideal picnic spot. You can rent a rowboat for two at the neo-Victorian Loeb Boathouse at the east end of the lake. The boathouse also has a seasonal outside bar with terrace seating overlooking the lake. It's a pleasant place to enjoy a glass of wine, but it can get quite crowded in the early evening. ***Midpark from 71st to 78th sts.***

3 FireBird. This jewel box of a restaurant on Times Square's Restaurant Row is an homage to the opulent decadence of czarist Russia. For sheer romance, head upstairs to the parlor for a cocktail

In a world of their own, on the Lake in Central Park, a couple rows near Calvert Vaux's graceful cast iron Bow Bridge.

and a sampling of Russian delicacies—you'll feel like royalty inside a gilded Fabergé egg. *365 W. 46th St. (btwn 8th and 9th aves.). ☎ 212/586-0244. www.firebirdrestaurant.com. $$$-$$$$. Subway: 1/2/3/9/N/R/A/C/E to Times Square.*

4 Carriage Ride in Central Park. Yes, it sounds cheesy, but it's actually a lot of fun, not to mention romantic. It's particularly memorable after a snowfall, when the park is hushed, and you can snuggle under a heavy blanket. Rides run roughly $40 for 20 minutes. To continue the tour, tell the driver to drop you off on Central Park South near Sixth Avenue, and then sit back and enjoy the scenery—and the company. You can find a carriage on Central Park South (near Seventh Ave.) or catch one at Tavern on the Green on the west side of the park at 68th Street (one or two are generally pulled up outside).

Midsummer Night's Swing at Lincoln Center.

5 Summer on the Lincoln Center Plaza. On a warm summer night, grab your partner and dance with romantic abandon during "Midsummer Night Swing," the sexy dance party on Josie Robertson Plaza. Every night is a different dance theme, from salsa to swing to ballroom. The fountains and floodlights of the plaza are particularly seductive at dusk. Go to **www.lincolncenter.org** for the latest information.

6 ★★ The Rink in Rockefeller Center. A romantic winter rendezvous on the ice-skating rink in the center's Lower Plaza is clichéd, I know, but few are unmoved by a swirl around the rink—especially during the holidays, with the spectacular Rock Center Christmas tree glittering from above. Avoid crowds by going early or late. Don't skate? Have a drink in the Sea Grill—which directly faces the rink—and watch the action. *Lower Plaza, Rockefeller Center (btwn. 49th and 50th sts). ☎ 212/332-7654. Admission $10–$14 adults, $7.50–$8.50 senior and children under 11. Mid-Oct to mid-Apr; call for hours.* *See p 17.*

7 Le Gigot. In these challenging times, sometimes the best recipe for romance is a warm, intimate spot where candles flicker seductively. At this classic little Provençal *boîte* in the West Village, you can dine on bouillabaisse or a hearty cassoulet. Look around; you're not the only ones on a romantic rendezvous. *18 Cornelia St. (btwn Bleecker and West 4th St.). ☎ 212/627-3737. www.legigotrestaurant.com. $$$. Subway: A/B/C/D/E/F/V to West 4th St.*

Under the Brooklyn Bridge, with twinkling views of New York Harbor, River Café is one of the city's most enchanting spots for dinner à deux.

8 The Whispering Gallery. Not only is the tiled Gustavino ceiling outside the Grand Central Oyster Bar beautiful, but it creates an acoustical phenomenon. Stand facing one of the pillars with your loved one facing the one directly opposite and whisper sweet nothings. You'll be able to hear one another—and no one else can listen in. *Grand Central Station, 42nd St. & Park Ave. ☎ 212/340-2210. www.grandcentralterminal.com. Subway: 4/5/6 to 42nd St./Grand Central.*

9 ★★ Harbor Cruise. Whether you're on a simple spin around the island or an elegant dinner cruise, seeing Manhattan from the water is a thrill. That old reliable, **Circle Line** (www.circleline42.com), has the most options, from 2-hour harbor cruises to summer live-music cruises. Circle Line leaves from Pier 83 (W. 42nd St.). **Bateaux New York** (www.bateauxnewyork.com) runs dinner cruises in sleek glass boats to the accompaniment of a jazz quintet. It leaves from Pier 61, at Chelsea Piers (W. 23rd St.)

10 The River Café. Often named the most romantic spot in New York, the River Café sits on the Brooklyn waterfront practically underneath the Brooklyn Bridge, with magnificent views of Manhattan. Go at twilight as the lights of downtown begin to flicker on. Though the food at restaurants with views is usually not great, you won't be disappointed by the fare here. Even if you don't come for dinner, you can sit on the terrace, sip a cocktail, and drink in the views. *1 Water St., Brooklyn. ☎ 718/522-5200. www.rivercafe.com. $$$–$$$$*

Power Brokers: The Robber Barons & Their Descendants

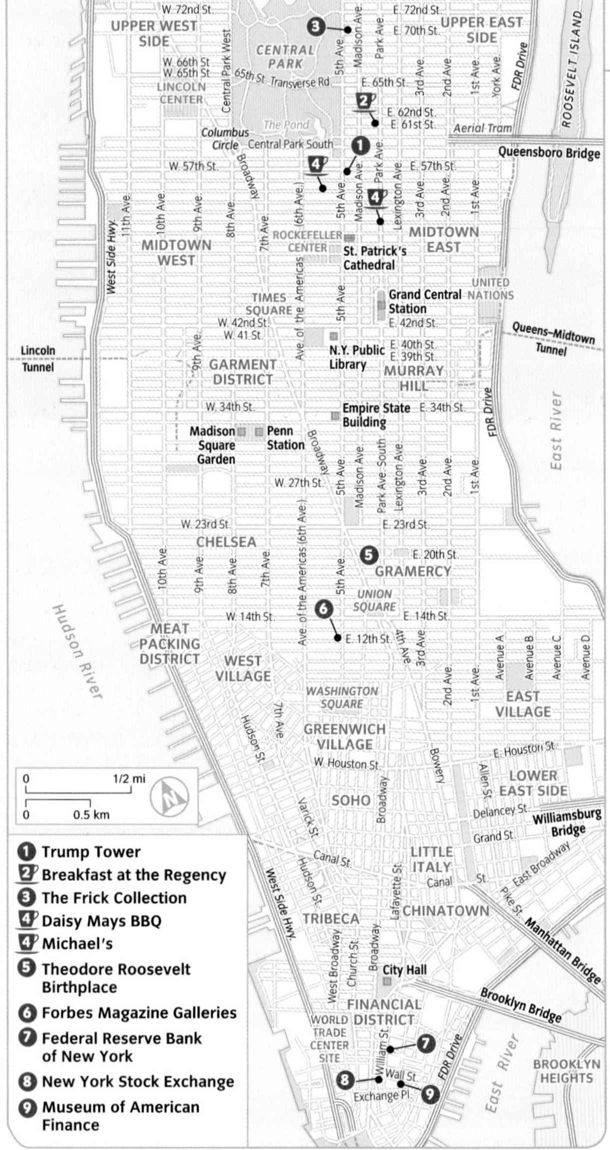

The city has long been a mecca for ambitious types, from artists to mercenaries—and some things never change. The robber barons of the 19th century, men such as Henry Clay Frick and J. P. Morgan, thrived here. Their modern-day counterparts include such power titans as residents Donald Trump and Mike Bloomberg. START: **Subway B, F, or V to Fifth Avenue and 57th Street**

❶ **Trump Tower.** This place is definitely not your average shopping mall. Bold and brassy, the gold signage on this 1983 building practically screams "Look at me!" Step inside to view the six-story mirrored atrium and the waterfall cascading down a pink-granite wall. Admire the glitzy displays of luxury shops such as Cartier and Asprey of London as you glide up the escalators. *725 Fifth Ave. (btwn. 56th & 57th sts.). ☎ 212/832-2000. Subway: B/D/F/V to 57th St.*

❷ ★ **Breakfast at the Regency.** According to local lore, this is where the term "power breakfast" was coined. Come before 8am to see tycoons and politicians table-hopping, back-slapping, and making deals aplenty. You may not recognize some of the big players (many prefer to keep a low profile), but semifamous faces do appear. If you're a fan of Sunday morning "talking head" programs, you'll be in heaven. If you want to be guaranteed a seat, make a reservation. *540 Park Ave. (at 61st St.). ☎ 212/759-4100. www.loewshotels.com. $$–$$$.*

Trump Tower on Fifth Avenue.

❸ ★★ **The Frick Collection.** Industrialist Henry Clay Frick, who controlled the steel industry in Pittsburgh at the turn of the 20th century, began collecting art after he made his first million. Architects Carrère & Hastings built this palatial French neoclassical mansion in 1914 to house both Frick's family and his art (Frick chose to live in Manhattan instead of his native Pennsylvania, legend has it, to avoid the soot from the steel mills). This living testament to New York's Gilded Age is graced with paintings from Frick's collection: works by Titian, Gainsborough, Rembrandt,Turner, Vermeer, El Greco, and Goya. A highlight is the Fragonard Room, which contains the sensual rococo series *The Progress of Love*. The house is particularly stunning dressed in Christmas finery. *◷ 90 min. 1 E. 70th St. (at Fifth Ave.). ☎ 212/288-0700. www.frick.org. Admission $15 adults, $10 seniors, $5 students. Children under 10 not admitted; children under 16 must be accompanied by an adult. Tues–Sat 10am–6pm; Sun 11–5pm. Closed Mon & all major holidays. Subway: 6 to 68th St. Bus: M1/2/3/4.*

The Fragonard Room at the Frick.

4 ★ **Power Lunch.** The New York media elite lunches at **Michael's** (24 W. 55th St., btwn. Fifth and Sixth aves.; ☎ 212/767-0555; $$$–$$$$), a spacious spot in a landmark building—and we're talking everybody, from Barbara Walters to Bill Clinton. As *Vanity Fair* columnist Michael Wolff put it, "Michael's is as close as I've ever come to my dream of living in the Manhattan of movies." You know your place in the pecking order when you are seated in this power palace—even though the fresh flowers, pretty paintings, sunny service, and California cuisine work to soften the blow. If you want to spend a little less, grab lunch to go from a food cart such as **Daisy Mays BBQ** (52nd St. and Park Ave.; $), which dishes out some of New York's best barbecue.

5 ★ **Theodore Roosevelt Birthplace.** America's 26th president was born and raised here (the original house was destroyed in 1916 then faithfully reconstructed in 1923). It was decorated by Roosevelt's wife and sisters with many original furnishings. The reconstructed house contains five period rooms, two museum galleries, and a bookstore. Roosevelt was the nemesis of the robber barons. Known as the "Trust Buster," he broke up monopolies in industries such as railroads and steel to protect the public interest. 🕘 *45 min. 28 E. 20th St. (btwn. Broadway & Park Ave. South).* ☎ *212/260-1616. www.nps.gov/thrb. Admission $3. Tues–Sat 9am–5pm. Subway: 6 to 23rd St.*

6 ★ kids **Forbes Magazine Galleries.** The late magnate Malcolm Forbes was a passionate collector. Toy soldiers (10,000 or so), early edition Monopoly boards, and toy boats (over 500) are the highlights here. (The real stars of the Forbes collection, 12 Fabergé Imperial Eggs,

More than 10,000 miniature figures are on view at the Forbes Galleries.

were sold, fittingly, to a Russian tycoon in 2004.) Changing exhibits have included a selection of letters written by first ladies, jeweled flowers and fruit by Cartier, and historically accurate miniature rooms. *45 min. You can book a free tour in advance. 62 Fifth Ave. (at 12th St.). 212/206-5548. www.forbesgalleries.com. Free admission; children under 16 must be accompanied by an adult. Tues–Wed & Fri–Sat 10am–4pm. Subway: 4/5/6 to 14th St.*

7 **Federal Reserve Bank of New York.** This is where they keep the gold—$90 billion of it. It rests 50 feet (15m) below sea level. The 60-minute tours are free, but you need to book at least 5 days ahead—and because the tours are so popular, you should try to book at least a month in advance. *1 hr. 33 Liberty St. (btwn. William and Nassau sts.). To schedule a tour, call 212/720-6130 or e-mail frbnytours@ny.frb.org. www.newyorkfed.org. Subway: 4/5 to Wall St.*

8 **New York Stock Exchange.** The serious action is here on Wall Street, a narrow lane dating from the 18th century. At its heart is the NYSE, the world's largest securities exchange. The NYSE came into being in 1792, when merchants met daily under a nearby buttonwood tree to trade U.S. bonds that had funded the Revolutionary War. In 1903 traders moved into this Beaux Arts building designed by George Post. The NYSE is still surrounded by

The New York Stock Exchange.

heavy security and is not open to the public. *20 Broad St. (btwn. Wall St. & Exchange Place). 212/656-3000. www.nyse.com.*

The "Charging Bull" statue, symbol of Wall Street.

9 ★ **Museum of American Finance.** This museum explores the country's free-market traditions and spirit of entrepreneurship. It is housed in its new home at 48 Wall St., a landmark Benjamin Morris–designed building from the late 1920s, with major exhibitions filling the building's grand mezzanine. *45 min. 48 Wall St. (at William St.) 212/908-4100. www.financialhistory.org. Admission $8 adults, $5 seniors/students. Tues–Sat 10am–4pm. Subway: 4/5/2/3 to Wall St.*

New York **with Kids**

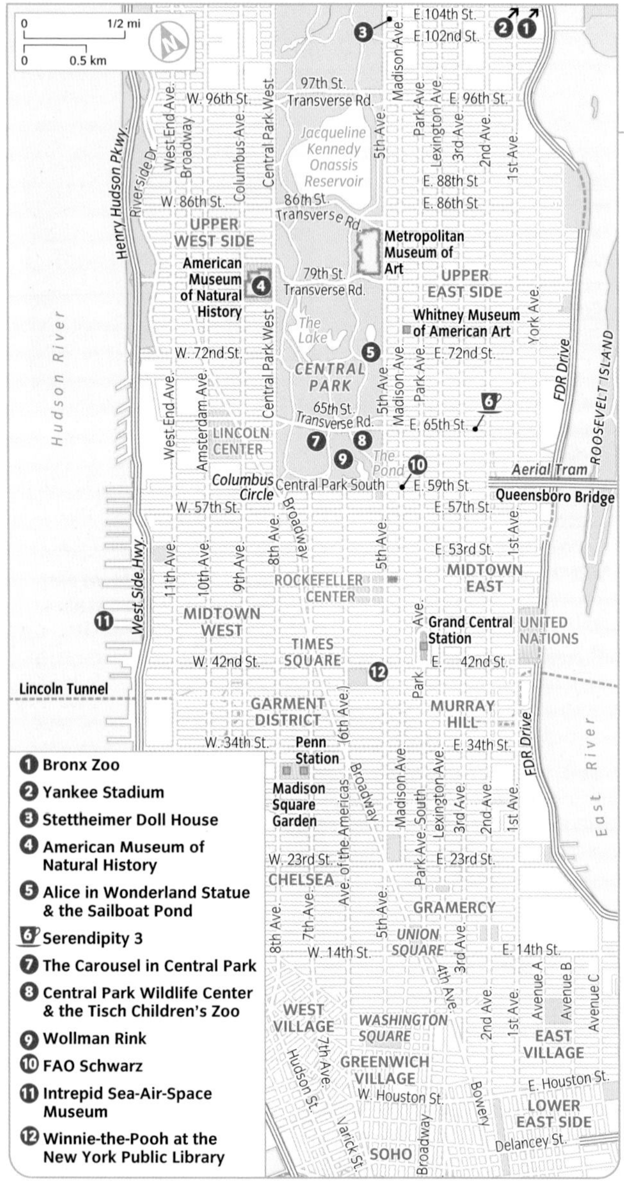
0 1/2 mi
0 0.5 km
E. 104th St.
E. 102nd St.
97th St. Transverse Rd.
W. 96th St.
E. 96th St.
Jacqueline Kennedy Onassis Reservoir
E. 88th St
W. 86th St.
86th St. Transverse Rd.
E. 86th St
UPPER WEST SIDE
Metropolitan Museum of Art
American Museum of Natural History
79th St. Transverse Rd.
UPPER EAST SIDE
The Lake
Whitney Museum of American Art
W. 72nd St.
E. 72nd St.
CENTRAL PARK
65th St. Transverse Rd.
E. 65th St.
LINCOLN CENTER
The Pond
Aerial Tram
ROOSEVELT ISLAND
Columbus Circle
Central Park South
E. 59th St.
W. 57th St.
E. 57th St.
Queensboro Bridge
E. 53rd St.
MIDTOWN EAST
ROCKEFELLER CENTER
MIDTOWN WEST
Grand Central Station
UNITED NATIONS
TIMES SQUARE
W. 42nd St.
E. 42nd St.
Lincoln Tunnel
GARMENT DISTRICT
MURRAY HILL
W. 34th St.
Penn Station
E. 34th St.
Madison Square Garden
W. 23rd St.
E. 23rd St.
CHELSEA
GRAMERCY
UNION SQUARE
W. 14th St.
E. 14th St.
WEST VILLAGE
WASHINGTON SQUARE
GREENWICH VILLAGE
EAST VILLAGE
W. Houston St.
E. Houston St.
LOWER EAST SIDE
Delancey St.
SOHO
Hudson River
East River
Henry Hudson Pkwy.
Riverside Dr.
West Side Hwy.
West End Ave.
Broadway
Columbus Ave.
Central Park West
Amsterdam Ave.
11th Ave.
10th Ave.
9th Ave.
8th Ave.
7th Ave.
Ave. of the Americas (6th Ave.)
5th Ave.
Madison Ave.
Park Ave.
Park Ave. South
Lexington Ave.
3rd Ave.
2nd Ave.
1st Ave.
York Ave.
FDR Drive
4th Ave.
Avenue A
Avenue B
Avenue C
Hudson St.
Varick St.
Bowery
1 Bronx Zoo
2 Yankee Stadium
3 Stettheimer Doll House
4 American Museum of Natural History
5 Alice in Wonderland Statue & the Sailboat Pond
6 Serendipity 3
7 The Carousel in Central Park
8 Central Park Wildlife Center & the Tisch Children's Zoo
9 Wollman Rink
10 FAO Schwarz
11 Intrepid Sea-Air-Space Museum
12 Winnie-the-Pooh at the New York Public Library

Beneath its noise, grit, and air of jaded cynicism, New York City is extremely kid-friendly. It opens its arms to kids of all ages, with some of the top children's attractions in the country, magical kid-centric holidays, and a world of treats for the eyes, ears, and tummy. What kid can resist? START: **Subway 2/5 to East Tremont Avenue/West Farms Square**

1 ★★★ kids **Bronx Zoo.** The largest urban wildlife conservation facility in America, the Bronx Zoo has some 4,000 animals roaming 265 acres (106 hectares). It's hard to believe that you're actually in the Bronx as you watch lions, zebras, and gazelles roam the African Plains, a re-created savanna. Don't miss Tiger Mountain, featuring Siberian tigers, or the Congo Gorilla Forest, where 23 lowland gorillas, assorted monkeys, and other species live in a 6½-acre (2.6-hectare) African rain forest environment. *4–5 hr. Fordham Rd. and Bronx River Pkwy. ☎ 718/652-8400. www.bronxzoo.com. Mon–Fri 10am–5pm, Sat–Sun 10am–5:30pm (extended summer & holiday hours). Admission $14 adults, $13 seniors, $11 children 3–12, kids 2 and under free. Subway: 2/5 to E. Tremont Ave./West Farms Sq.*

2 ★★★ kids **Yankee Stadium.** I can't think of a better way to spend a warm early summer afternoon with the family than taking in a baseball game at Yankee Stadium—the new Yankee Stadium, that is, right next door, scheduled to open in time for the 2009 season. You can take a subway right to the stadium or—even better—a NY Waterway ferry from several departure points (www.nywaterway.com). *4 hr. Yankee Stadium in the Bronx. ☎ 718/293-6000. www.yankees.com. Tickets $8–$55. Subway: B, D, 4 to 161st St.*

3 ★★★ kids **Stettheimer Doll House.** This rare, remarkable dollhouse in the Museum of the City of New York was the creation of Carrie Walter Stettheimer, a theater set designer who, with her two equally talented sisters, entertained the city's avant-garde artist community in the 1920s. Among the exquisite furnishings are period wallpaper, paper lampshades, and an art gallery featuring original miniatures of famous works such as Marcel Duchamp's *Nude Descending a Staircase*. The museum has more vintage dollhouses and timeless toys on display. *15 min.*

The Stettheimer Doll House at the Museum of the City of New York.

Museum of the City of New York, 120 Fifth Ave. (103rd St.). ☎ 212/534-1672. www.mcny.org. Tues–Sun 10am–5pm. Admission $9 adults, $5 students & seniors, free for children 12 and under. Subway: 6 to 103rd St.

4 ★★★ kids American Museum of Natural History. One word: ★ **dinosaurs,** which devour the entrance hall and take up the entire fourth floor. Not to mention diamonds as big as the Ritz, and more. *See p 58.*

5 ★★ kids Alice in Wonderland Statue & the Sailboat Pond. Every time I pass this 1959 bronze statue of Alice sitting on a giant mushroom, I see kids clambering all over it. It's catnip to the little ones. The Sailboat Pond, officially called Conservatory Water, is an ornamental pond where kids can sail miniature boats or watch radio-powered model yachts compete in racing regattas. *Central Park, east side from 72nd to 75th sts.*

6 kids Serendipity 3. Even the most hardened soul will melt at this whimsical East Side dessert palace, where the ice cream sundaes are legendary. It also has great kid-friendly lunch and dinner menus; try the "Shake, Batter & Bowl": half a chicken, fried and oven-roasted, and french fries. *225 E. 69th St. (btwn. Second & Third aves.). ☎ 212/838-3531. www.serendipity3.com. $$.*

Skaters on Wollman Rink.

7 ★★ kids The Carousel in Central Park. A quarter of a million children ride these vintage hand-carved horses every year. You can even arrange a birthday party for your kid here. *Midpark at 64th St. ☎ 212/879-0244.* *See p 104.*

8 ★★ kids Central Park Wildlife Center & the Tisch Children's Zoo. Better known as the Central Park Zoo, the Wildlife Center dates from the mid-19th century, when caged animals on loan from circuses and other outlets were put on display near the Arsenal. The current zoo was built in 1988 to replace a 1934 WPA-built structure. Today the zoo's 5½ acres (2.2 hectares) house more than 400 animals, among them sea lions, polar bears, and penguins. In the small **Tisch Children's Zoo,** kids can feed and pet tame farm animals. Check out the **Delacorte Clock,** with six dancing animals designed by the Italian sculptor Andrea Spadini. *East side & 65th St.* *See p 105.*

9 kids Wollman Rink. The small ice-skating rink at Rockefeller Center is right in the center of midtown action, but this much bigger rink in Central Park is built for stretching out and perfecting your moves. Plus, it has views of skyscrapers along Central Park South. In the summer it's transformed into the Victoria Gardens Amusement Park, which has rides for young children. *East side btwn. 62nd & 63rd sts.* *See p 105.*

Holiday Magic

It's no wonder the city is inundated with families during Thanksgiving and Christmas vacations—few places celebrate the holidays with such glitter and gusto. On Thanksgiving Day, the **Macy's Day Parade** is a family favorite; find yourself a perch along the parade route or, if you're smart, a hotel room with a view of the festivities. Join the locals the night before for what's become a street party around the Museum of Natural History to watch the inflation of the giant parade balloons. At Christmastime, head for the ever-popular holiday revue at Radio City Music Hall, the **Christmas Spectacular** (☎ 212/307-1000; www.radiocity.com; tickets $40–$140). In the Bronx, the New York Botanical Gardens is the site for the wonderful **Holiday Train Show,** where vintage model trains zip around architectural reproductions of well-known New York landmarks and historic buildings—all made entirely out of plant materials (☎ 718/817-8700; www.nybg.org; $20 adults, $7 children 2–12, free children under 2). Take the 15-minute Metro-North Railroad from Grand Central to the Botanical Gardens stop. Both the Radio City show and the train show run from November through early January.

⑩ ★★ kids FAO Schwarz. Remember Tom Hanks dancing on the piano in *Big*? This legendary toy store looks different than it did in the film (thanks to a 2004 renovation), but the "Dance-On Piano," a giant musical keyboard mat, is still here (it's on the second floor). Look for humongous stuffed animals on the first floor; dolls, crafts, trains, and toys on the second floor; and a lower level devoted to babies and toddlers. *767 Fifth Ave. (at 59th St.). ☎ 212/644-9400. www.fao.com. Subway: N/R/W to Fifth Ave. & 59th St.*

⑪ ★ kids Intrepid Sea-Air-Space Museum. ***Note:*** Following a 2-year refurbishment and restoration, the Intrepid was scheduled to reopen on Pier 86 in November 2008. The aircraft carrier known as the "Fighting I" served the U.S. Navy for 31 years, suffering bomb attacks, kamikaze strikes, and a torpedo shot. In 1982 it opened as a sea, air, and space museum on the New York waterfront. You can crawl inside a wooden sub from the American Revolution; inspect a nuclear missile submarine; or enter the cockpit of an A–6 Intruder and manipulate the controls. 🕒 *1½ hr. Summers are crowded; get here early or buy tickets online. Pier 86, 12th Ave. & 46th St. ☎ 212/245-0072. www.intrepidmuseum.org. Apr–Sept Mon–Fri 10am–5pm, Sat–Sun 10am–6pm; Oct–Mar Tues–Sun 10am–5pm. Bus: M42 to 12th St & Hudson Ave.; Subway: 1/2/3/7/9/A/C/E/S to 42th St./Times Sq.*

⑫ ★★ kids Winnie-the-Pooh at the New York Public Library. The real Winnie-the-Pooh bear, the little stuffed animal owned and cherished by Christopher Robin Milne, is on display in the main branch's Humanities and Social Sciences Library, along with Eeyore, Piglet, Kanga, and Tigger. *See p 17.*

Literary Gotham

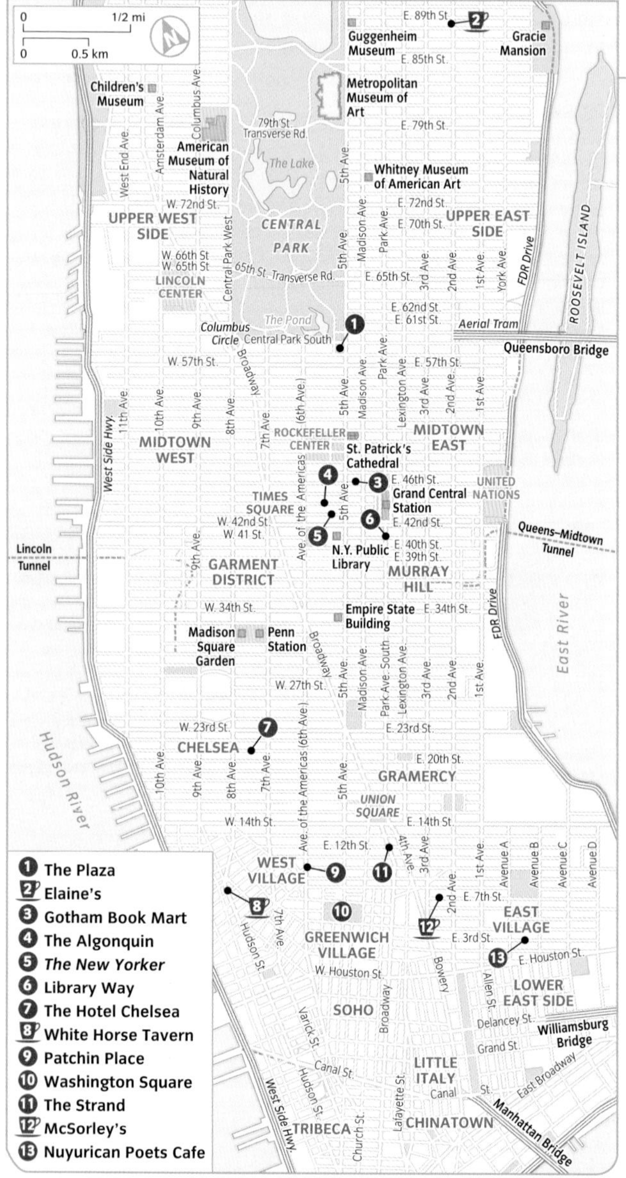

Long a city of writers, New York is a treasure trove of sites that honor authors, streets named for storytellers, and bookstores where you can find their works. Here are some of the most inspired literary haunts. START: **Subway N or R to Fifth Avenue**

1 ★★ The Plaza. Eloise lived here, of course; the celebrated children's book heroine won the hotel "Literary Landmark" status in 1998. Eloise was written in 1955 by performer Kay Thompson during her stay at the Plaza, and the new owners of the hotel promise that the famous portrait of the mischievous little girl will be displayed in the renovated lobby. In the 1920s, Scott and Zelda Fitzgerald, the toast of the literary world at the time, made a splash in their New York "debut" when they frolicked in the fountain out front. *See p 15.*

2 ★ Elaine's. A watering hole for the boldfaced literati in the second half of the 20th century, this atmospheric Upper East Side saloon/Italian restaurant is still presided over by Elaine Kaufman. According to A. E. Hotchner in *Everyone Comes to Elaine's,* it became more or less a "writers' club" during its heyday in the 1960s. On any given night, you could expect to see George Plimpton, David Halberstam, Gay Talese, and Norman Mailer—as well as assorted celebs and colorful characters. *1703 Second Ave. (btwn. 88th & 89th sts.). ☎ 212/534-8114. $$$.*

3 ★★ Gotham Book Mart. This bookstore contains a gallery and an estimated half-million volumes (both in and out of print) focusing on the arts. The gallery features up-and-coming artists and photographers, but it has also hung works by biggies such as Andy Warhol. Fans of quirky author-illustrator Edward Gorey will find much to love here. The store (in its original 47th St. location) opened in 1920, and habitués have included W. H. Auden, Anaïs Nin, e. e. cummings, Marianne Moore, J. D. Salinger, Arthur Miller, Tennessee Williams, T. S. Eliot, Ezra Pound, and several cats. *16 E. 46th St. (btwn. Madison & Fifth aves.). ☎ 212/719-4448. Subway: B/D/F/V to 47th–50th St. Rockefeller Center.*

Oscar night at Elaine's.

A Vicious Circle—*a painting of the Algonquin Round Table regulars, by Natalie Ascencios.*

4 ★ The Algonquin. In the 1920s, this was where notable literati, including James Thurber and the acid-tongued Dorothy Parker, met to drink and trade bons mots at the so-called Round Table. The table still has a place of honor, but be warned: It's rectangular. The richly appointed lobby is an atmospheric spot for a drink or snack. *59 W. 44th St. (btwn. Fifth & Sixth aves.). ☎ 212/ 840-6800. www.algonquinhotel.com. Subway: B/D/F/V to 42nd St.*

5 *The New Yorker.* America's most celebrated literary magazine came into being at the Algonquin Round Table, just a block away from its former office space here. Over the decades it has featured writers such as E. B. White, James Thurber, John Cheever, John Updike, and Calvin Trillin, and you'll find their names and others on a plaque. (Today *The New Yorker* offices are in the Condé Nast building at 4 Times Sq.) *25 W. 43rd St. (btwn. Fifth & Sixth aves.). Subway: B/D/F/V to 42nd St.*

6 ★ Library Way. Along 41st Street between Park and Fifth, you'll see bronze plaques embedded in the sidewalk. There are 96 in total, and all feature quotations from literature or poetry. Walking west along this street leads you to the New York Public Library. *41st St. (btwn. Park & Fifth aves.). Subway: B/D/F/V to 42nd St.*

7 The Hotel Chelsea. As Janis Joplin once said, "A lot of funky things happen at the Chelsea." Billed as "a rest stop for rare individuals," this legendary 12-story brick building maintains a distinct boho flair, from its lobby of abstract expressionist art (by artists who lived here in the 1950s and '60s) to its colorful history as a haven for creative, offbeat, even extremist types. Built in 1884, the Chelsea became a hotel in 1905 where artists and writers were encouraged to stay indefinitely. Among the writers who did: Thomas Wolfe, Dylan Thomas, O. Henry, Arthur Miller, and Sam Shepard (with

Outside the Chelsea Hotel.

his then-lover Patti Smith). Artists are still the main residents, but you can stay too, in one of the hotel rooms—and no two are alike. If you're staying elsewhere, feel free to stop in the lobby for a look around. *222 W. 23rd St. (btwn. Seventh & Eighth aves.) ☎ 212/243-3700. www.hotelchelsea.com. Subway: 1/9/A/C to 23rd St.*

8 White Horse Tavern. This atmospheric 1880 wood-frame bar was where writers such as Jack Kerouac, James Baldwin, Norman Mailer, and the Welsh poet Dylan Thomas threw down a few. Thomas, in fact, basically drank himself to death here in November 1953 at the tender age of 39. Order a newfangled burger, wash it down with a cold ale, and toast to the celebrated ghosts around you. *567 Hudson St. (at 11th St.) ☎ 212/243-9260. Cash only. Daily 11am–3am. Subway: 1 to Christopher St.*

9 Patchin Place. The sweet little cobblestone mews tucked off 6th Avenue were at one time a serious literary enclave. The poet e e cummings lived at no. 4 from 1923 to 1962. The reclusive writer Djuna Barnes lived at no. 5 for 40 years. Journalist John Reed and his paramour Louise Bryant lived here while he wrote *Ten Days that Shook the World*. (The lefty magazine he wrote for, *The Masses*, was located a couple of blocks away at 91 Greenwich Ave.) *Patchin Place (off 10th St. and 6th Ave.). Subway: A/B/C/D/F/E/V to W. 4th St.*

10 Washington Square. The literary history of New York is filled with references to this fabled downtown neighborhood—and why not? It's where many great writers grew up or chose to live. Novelist Henry James was born at 21 Washington Place in

The Washington Square arch.

1843 and later described the neighborhood in his memorable 1880 book *Washington Square* (later made into the heralded play and movie *The Heiress*). Edith Wharton, whose novels evoked the genteel days when Washington Square was where the aristocracy lived and ruled New York society, stayed briefly with her mother at 7 Washington Sq. N. Willa Cather lived at both 60 Washington Sq. S. and 82 Washington Place. *Washington Sq. Park. See also p 77. Subway: A/B/C/D/F/E/V to W. 4th St.*

11 ★ The Strand. You can spend hours browsing the "18 miles" of books crammed into the high, narrow shelves of this 1927 institution. *See p 95.*

12 McSorley's. This working 1854 saloon was immortalized by *New Yorker* writer Joseph Mitchell in "McSorley's Wonderful Saloon," found in his classic collection of true New York tales *Up in the Old Hotel and Other Stories*. *15 E. 7th St. ☎ 212/474-9148. www.mcsorleysnewyork.com. Mon–Sat 11am–1am; Sun 1pm–1am. Subway: 6 to Astor Place or N/R to 8th St.*

13 Nuyurican Poets Cafe. What started out more than 30 years ago as the "living room salon" of East Village writer and poet Miguel Algarín has become a celebrated arts enterprise and a forum for up-and-coming poets, writers, playwrights, musicians, and comedians. Weekly poetry "slams" are held Friday nights. *236 E. 3rd St. (btwn. aves. B & C). ☎ 212/505-8183. www.nuyorican.org. Subway: A/B/C/D/F/E/V to W. 4th St.*

Celluloid City: NY on Film & TV

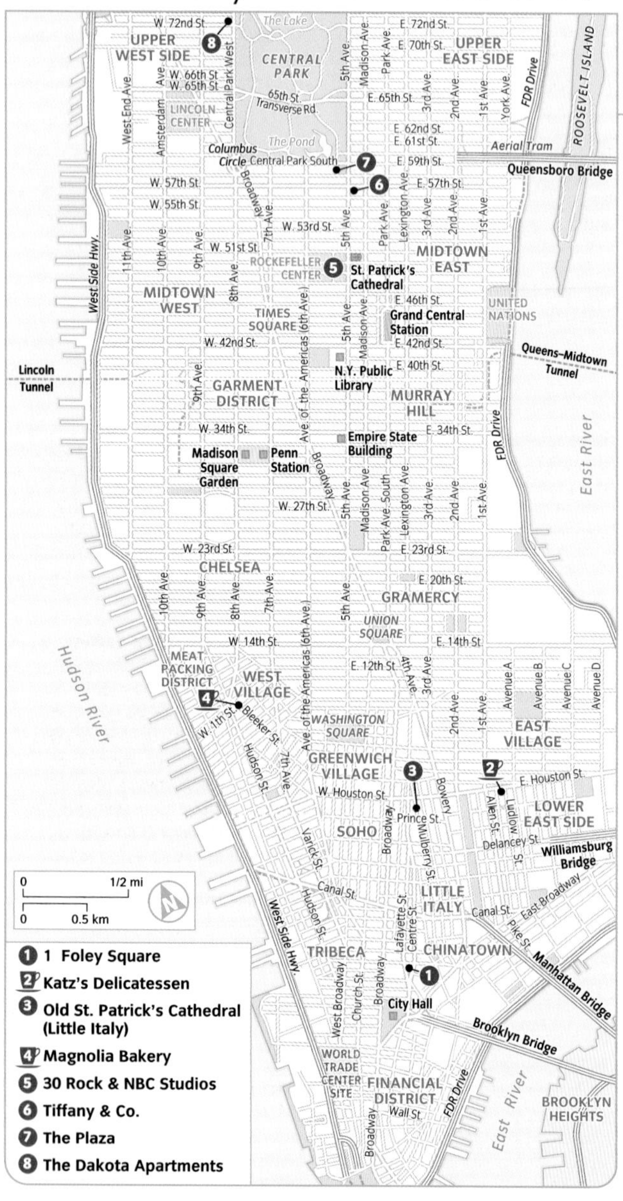

From Marilyn Monroe exposed atop a subway grate to the gleaming windows of Tiffany & Co., images of New York are ubiquitous on film. Even if you've never visited the city, you may feel as though you know it already—but there's nothing like seeing the original. START: **Subway 4, 5, or 6 to Brooklyn Bridge/City Hall**

1 ★ **Foley Square.** It's hard to believe that this dignified urban landscape was once a fetid swamp and the center of one of the city's most notorious slums. Today, with its ring of colonnaded courthouse buildings, Foley Square is one of the most-filmed places in the five boroughs. The long-running TV series *Law & Order* beats a path up and down the courthouse steps. The exterior of the 1913 **NY State Supreme Court Building** (60 Centre St.) is also where Kris Kringle goes on trial in *Miracle on 34th Street* (the original) and where Henry Fonda is seen at the end of *Twelve Angry Men*. ***Bounded by Centre, Worth & Lafayette sts. Subway: 4/5/6 to Brooklyn Bridge/City Hall.***

Law & Order *filming in front of the courthouse.*

2 ★★ **Katz's Delicatessen.** Although Katz's is one of the city's best Jewish delis, movie lovers may know it better as the site of Meg Ryan's, ahem, performance in *When Harry Met Sally*. It's an out-of-the-way stop, so make the most of it by grabbing a snack (or an early lunch) here. Served with New York attitude, Katz's offerings are first rate: matzo ball and chicken noodle soups, potato knishes, cheese blintzes, egg creams, beef hot dogs, hot pastrami on rye, and more. ***205 E. Houston St. (at Ludlow St.). ☎ 212/254-2246. www.katzdeli.com. $–$$. Subway: 6 to Bleecker St.; F to Second Ave.***

3 **Old St. Patrick's Cathedral, Little Italy.** The famous baptism scene in *The Godfather* (where Michael Corleone's rivals are murdered while his son is baptized) was shot in the impressive interiors of Old St. Patrick's Cathedral (ca. 1815), the original St. Patrick's (it also made it into *Godfather III)*. Its churchyard was also featured in a key scene between Robert De Niro and Harvey Keitel in *Mean Streets*. ***260–264 Mulberry St. (btwn. E. Houston & Prince sts.).***

4 ★ **Magnolia Bakery.** What draws the crowds to this old-fashioned dessert shop? Cupcakes, hundreds of 'em—but only a dozen per customer, please. It's quite a scene, with lines around the block and constant tour-bus activity, many carrying busloads of fans on the

ever-popular *Sex and the City* tours: This was a setting for a scene in the HBO series; the bakery was also featured in *The Devil Wears Prada*. ***401 Bleecker St. (at 11th St.). ☎ 212/462-2573. $.***

5 ★★ 30 Rock & NBC Studios. This 1930s Art Deco wonder is a vision from the outside—and you'll probably recognize the exterior if you're a fan of NBC's sitcom *30 Rock*—but the tour of NBC studios will give you an up-close perspective on some of the shows filmed within. Starting at the NBC History Theater—which covers the network's early radio days—the tour takes you to the studio where *Saturday Night Live* has been filmed since 1975, as well as to the studio homes of *Late Night With Conan O'Brien*, *Dateline NBC*, and *Nightly News*. As you listen to the NBC page conducting your tour, keep in mind that

Sarah Jessica Parker shoots a promo for Sex and the City *under the Brooklyn Bridge.*

The entrance to the Museum of Television & Radio.

Regis Philbin, Ted Koppel, and Kate Jackson all started out as pages here. If you get here on a weekday between 7 and 10am, you can join the big outdoor party that watches the taping of the *Today* show. ***70 min. Tour reservations recommended. 30 Rockefeller Plaza (at 49th St.). ☎ 212/664-7174. www.nbcuniversal store.com. Adults $19, seniors & children 6–12 $16 (no children under 6 admitted). Tours daily on the half-hour from 8:30am–4:30pm (9:30am–5:30pm Fri–Sat; 9:30am–4:30pm Sun). Subway: B/D/F/V to 47th–50th sts./ Rockefeller Center.***

6 ★★ Tiffany & Co. Who can forget the image of the sublime Audrey Hepburn ogling jewels in *Breakfast at Tiffany's*? ***727 Fifth Ave. (btwn. 56th & 57th sts.). ☎ 212/ 755-8000. Subway: E/V to Fifth Ave./ 53rd St.***

7 ★ The Plaza. The Plaza has played a part in countless films, including as background for the final, poignant scene between Barbra Streisand and Robert Redford in *The Way We Were* (a scene lovingly recreated following Big's engagement

Sex and the City: The Movie

Some have said that the brightest star of the wildly popular HBO series *Sex and the City* was New York. Few places have been so lovingly, so romantically, so *exhaustively* documented on celluloid—a good deal of it on location, from the real-time mean streets of the Big Apple rather than the pristine confines of a stage set. In *Sex and the City: The Movie,* Carrie, Samantha, Charlotte, and Miranda got up to their same old tricks. Clothes again figure prominently, with scenes shot at **Diane von Furstenberg**'s new flagship store in the Meat-Packing District (874 Washington St.). The girls hang out as usual in fabulous spots: **Buddakan** (75 Ninth Ave.); **Bryant Park Hotel** (40 W. 40th St.); **Raoul's** (180 Prince St.); **Four Seasons Hotel** (57 E. 57th St.). And fans don't seem to be tiring of the fab four femmes yet; the proliferation of *Sex and the City* tours attests to their continued popularity (try the "Sex and the City Hotspots Tour" with **On Location Tours;** www.sceneontv.com; $42).

party on TV's *Sex and the City*). Dudley Moore, as Arthur, famously boozed it up over dinner at the Plaza with a hooker. Eloise, the fictional little girl who lived at the Plaza, was the hotel's first famous "resident," and naturally, *Eloise at the Plaza* was filmed here. *767 Fifth Ave. (at 59th St.). ☎ 212/644-9400. www.fao.com. Subway: N/R/W to Fifth Ave. & 59th St.*

8 The Dakota Apartments. This 1884 apartment house, with its dramatic gables, dormers, and oriel windows, was the setting for Roman Polanski's psychological horror film *Rosemary's Baby.* In the movie, the Dakota is referred to as the Bramford, inhabited by a coven of witches. *1 W. 72nd St. (at Central Park West). Bus: M7 to 72nd St. & Amsterdam Ave. Subway: 1/2/3/9 to 72nd St.*

The Dakota Building was the setting for the horror classic Rosemary's Baby.

New York's Greatest Buildings

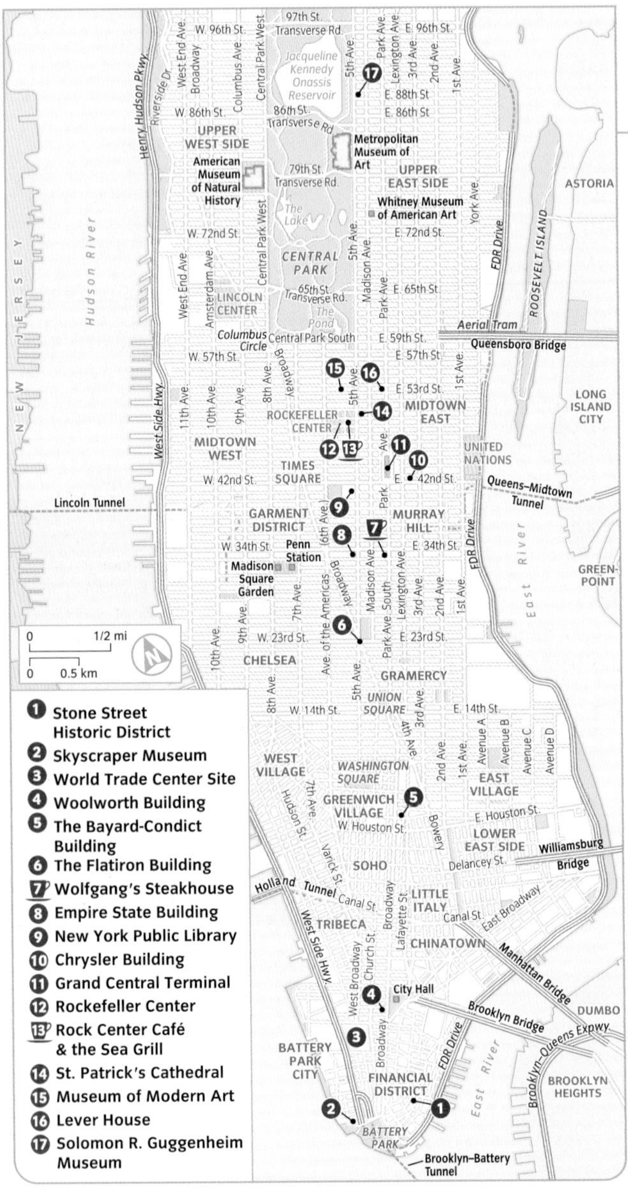

Manhattan's muscular, steel-and-concrete skyline is many things: a wonderfully eclectic architectural landscape; a visual metaphor for the dynamism of America's largest city, perpetually in flux; and a stunning, three-dimensional historical record of how the Big Apple has grown—and grown up—over the years. START: **Subway 2 or 3 to Wall Street**

1 ★ Stone Street Historic District. This narrow, winding street is a find, dating from the Dutch West India Company in the 1640s. The 15 existing brick structures lying in the shadow of Wall Street's canyons were built soon after the Great Fire of 1835 leveled the heavily commercial neighborhood. The Dutch-style facades trace the old cobblestone street, now home to attractive little restaurants, cafes, and bars. *Bounded by Pearl St., Hanover Sq., S. William St., & Coenties Alley. Subway: 2/3 to Wall St.*

2 ★ Skyscraper Museum. Wowed by New York's sheer verticality? Learn more about the technology, culture, and muscle behind it all at this small museum. Housed in the same building as Ritz-Carlton Battery Park, it contains two galleries: one dedicated to the evolution of Manhattan's skyline, the other to changing shows. *1 hr. 2 West St. (museum entrance faces Battery Place). 212/968-1961. www.skyscraper.org. Admission $5 adults, $2.50 seniors & students. Wed–Sun noon–6pm. Subway: 1/9 to Rector St; 4/5 to Bowling Green.*

The Woolworth Building.

3 ★ World Trade Center Site. The enormity of the tragedy that occurred on September 11 is driven home by the sight of the massive "bathtub" that once held the twin towers, and literally kept the Hudson River at bay. *See p 7.*

4 Woolworth Building. The irony, of course, is that this masterpiece was built from the profits of a nickel-and-dime empire. Architect Cass Gilbert designed it in 1913, and the neo-Gothic facade set a new standard for architectural grandeur. What made F. W. Woolworth proudest? The fact that he paid cash for the project. *233 Broadway.* *See p. 7, bullet 2.*

5 The Bayard-Condict Building. Renowned Chicago architect Louis Sullivan was Frank Lloyd Wright's boss and, some say, mentor. The only building he designed in New York is hidden down a nondescript NoHo street. It's a beaut, nonetheless: Constructed from 1897 to 1899, the 13-story building is a confection of a skyscraper, with fanciful terra-cotta decoration and ornamental friezes. *65 Bleecker St. (btwn. Broadway & Lafayette St.). Subway: 6 to Bleecker St.*

6 The Flatiron Building. This triangular masterpiece was one of the first skyscrapers. One of the city's most distinctive silhouettes, its wedge shape was the solution to a problem—filling the triangular property created by the intersection of Fifth Avenue and Broadway. Built in 1902 and fronted with limestone and terra cotta (not iron), the Flatiron measures only 6 feet (1.8m) across at its narrow end. So called for its resemblance to the laundry appliance, it was originally named the Fuller Building, then later "Burnham's Folly" because people were certain that architect Daniel Burnham's 21-story structure would fall down. There's no observation deck, and the building mainly houses publishing offices, but there are a few shops on the ground floor. The surrounding neighborhood has taken its name—the Flatiron District, home to a bevy of smart restaurants and shops. ***175 Fifth Ave. (at 23rd St.). Subway: R to 23rd St.***

The Flatiron Building.

7 Wolfgang's Steakhouse. Come here for a meal as bold as the architecture you're viewing. In a stunning historic space on the first floor of the old Vanderbilt Hotel, a 40-year waitstaff veteran of Peter Luger's storied Brooklyn steakhouse opened his own meat palace in 2004. The great Raphael Gustavino tiled the vaulted ceilings around 1910. ***4 Park Ave. (at 33rd St.).*** ☎ ***212/889-3369. $$$$.***

The Main Reading Room at the library.

8 ★★ Empire State Building. It has 103 stories, 6,500 windows, 73 elevators, 70 miles (113km) of water pipes, and 1,860 steps from bottom to top. The limestone-and-stainless-steel Art Deco icon has been synonymous with the Manhattan skyline since its completion in 1931. The lobby alone is worth the trip, with its shimmering metal-relief sculptures and rosy marble floors. The Empire State Building glows every night, bathed in colored floodlights to commemorate holidays or significant events—red, white, and blue for Independence Day; green for St. Patrick's Day; red, black, and green for Martin Luther King Day; blue and white for Hanukkah; and lavender and white for Gay Pride Day. *1 hr. 350 Fifth Ave. (at 34th St.). 212/736-3100. www.esbnyc.com. Observatory admission (86th floor) $19 adults, $17 seniors & children 12–17, $13 children 6–11, free for children under 6. Express pass: $45. 102nd floor Observatory: $15 extra. Buy & print tickets in advance online to avoid lines. Observatories open daily 8am–2am; last elevator goes up at 1:15am. Subway: 6 to 33rd St.; B/D/F/V to 34th St.*

9 ★ New York Public Library. This monumental Beaux Arts structure is glorious inside and out—and it's a model of utility to boot, with almost two million cardholders. The Main Reading Room, restored in 1998, is all soaring space and burnished oak. The sculpted lions out front are festooned with garlands during the Christmas season. Out back is one of Manhattan's prettiest green spaces, Bryant Park—a great warm-weather spot for a bag lunch. *Fifth Ave. (btwn. 42nd & 40th sts.). 212/661-7220. www.nypl.org. Open Tues–Wed & Sat 11am–6pm; Thurs–Fri 10am–6pm; Sun 1–5pm. Subway: B/D/F/V to 42nd St.*

10 ★ Chrysler Building. This 1930 Art Deco masterpiece was designed to be the world's tallest building—which it was, if only for a year. In the race against other New York architects to build the tallest building of the era, William Van Alen secretly added a stainless-steel spire inside the fire shaft, hoisting it into place only after his competitors thought his building was completed. *405 Lexington Ave. (at 42nd St.). Subway: 4/5/6 to Grand Central.*

11 ★ Grand Central Terminal. This magnificent public space is also an engineering wonder. The "elevated circumferential plaza," as it was called in 1913, leads Park Avenue around the building. The network of trains—subway and commuter—that passes through here is vast, but even more impressive is the "bridge" over the tracks, designed to support a cluster of skyscrapers. The main concourse was restored to its original glory in 1998; the *Sky Ceiling* depicts the constellations of the winter sky above New York. They're lit with 59 stars surrounded by dazzling 24-karat gold. Emitting light fed through fiber-optic

The Chrysler Building's Art Deco spire.

The sky ceiling at Grand Central.

cables, the stars in their intensities roughly replicate the magnitude of the actual stars as seen from Earth. Look carefully and you'll see a patch near one corner left unrestored as a reminder of the neglect this splendid masterpiece once endured. *42nd St. & Park Ave. ☎ 212/340-2210. www.grand centralterminal.com. Subway: 4/5/6/7/S to 42nd St.*

⓬ ★ **Rockefeller Center.** Rock Center was erected mainly in the 1930s, when the city was mired in the Depression and in thrall to Art Deco—the latter expressed both in the building's architecture and in the art commissioned to decorate it. The focal point is the 1933 **GE Building** at 30 Rockefeller Plaza, one of the city's most impressive buildings. The entrance sculpture, *Wisdom, Light and Sound,* by Lee Lawrie, is an Art Deco masterpiece, as is the artist's *Atlas,* at the entrance court of the International Building. The sunken plaza in front of 30 Rock is overseen by the gilded statue of ***Prometheus,*** by Paul Manship. *Bounded by 48th & 51st sts. & Fifth & Sixth aves. Subway: B/D/F/V to 47th-50th sts./Rockefeller Center.*

You won't go hungry in Rockefeller Center. In the 13 **dining and shopping concourse** ($) downstairs at 30 Rock, you can pick up light meals of soup, salads, and sandwiches. If you prefer a nice sit-down lunch (and don't mind spending more), the pleasant dining rooms in the **Rock Center Café** *(20 W. 50th St., btwn. Fifth & Sixth aves.; ☎ 212/332-7620; $$)* and the **Sea Grill** *(19 W. 49th, btwn. 5th & 6th aves.; same phone; $$)* both face the famed skating rink.

⓮ ★★ **St. Patrick's Cathedral.** Hundreds of daily visitors and worshippers stream in and out of this massive Gothic cathedral. Dedicated in 1879, the 2,200-seat structure has stained-glass windows made by artisans from Chartres, France. For those interested in visiting when the Archbishop of New York conducts services, Cardinal Egan usually presides over Mass at 10am on Sundays and on holidays. *See p 17.*

⓯ ★★ **Museum of Modern Art.** The MoMA boasts the world's greatest collection of painting and sculpture from the late 19th century to the present, but its newly renovated home—transformed under the guidance of Japanese architect Yoshio Taniguchi—now encompasses 630,000 square feet (58,529 sq. m), spread over six floors. Its highlight is a 110-foot-tall (33m) atrium, which diffuses natural light throughout. ⌚ *2 hr. 11 W. 53rd St. (btwn. Fifth & Sixth aves.).* ☎ *212/708-9400. www.moma.org. Admission $20 adults, $16 seniors, $12 students, free for kids 16 & under when accompanied by an adult. Sat–Mon & Wed–Thurs 10:30am–5:30pm; Fri 10:30am–8pm. Subway: E/V to Fifth Ave./53rd St.; B/D/F to 47th-50th sts.*

⑯ ★ **Lever House.** Built in 1952, this High Modern hymn to glass has undergone a spiffy renovation that restored its original sparkle. The clean-lined, relatively small skyscraper was the first in New York to employ the "curtain wall" design philosophy, with a brilliant blue-green glass facade. The bottom level is a public space. *400 Park Ave. (btwn. 53rd & 54th sts.). Subway: 6 to Lexington Ave.*

⑰ ★ **Solomon R. Guggenheim Museum.** Frank Lloyd Wright's only New York edifice—built in 1959—is a brilliant feat of architecture. The Babylonian-style "inverted ziggurat" has been compared to a wedding cake or a nautilus shell, but it is full of life and movement. Just forget your fantasies about roller-skating down the ramp of the rotunda. ⌚ *1 hr. 1071 Fifth Ave. (at 89th St.).* ☎ *212/423-3500. www.guggenheim.org. Admission $18 adults, $15 seniors & students, free for children under 12. Sat–Wed 10am–5:45pm; Fri 10am–7:45pm. Subway: 4/5/6 to 86th St. Bus: M1/2/3/4.*

Frank Lloyd Wright's Guggenheim Museum.

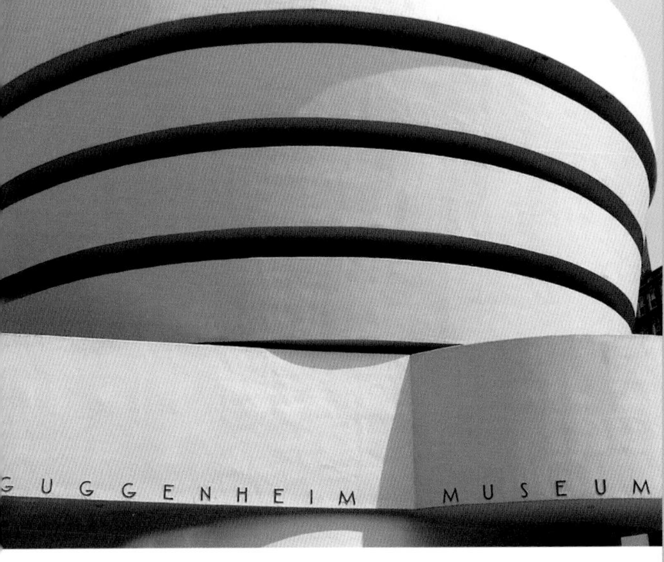

NYC Free & Dirt-Cheap

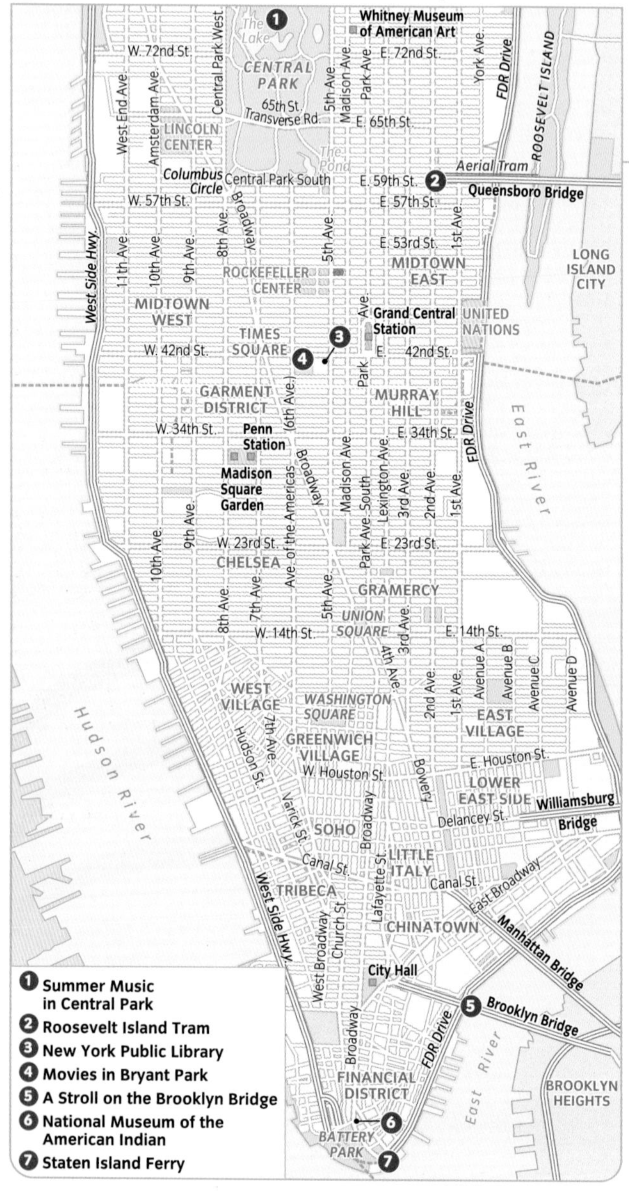

Seeing the sights in New York is often just a matter of turning a corner. I've watched "ballet aerialists" dangling from the Stock Exchange, brass bands wailing in Chinatown street funerals, and wall-to-wall hot dogs showing off during Dachshund Day in Washington Square Park—and I didn't pay a penny for any of it. Here are some free (or dirt-cheap) ways to savor the Big Apple. START: **Subway 6 to 77th or 86th Street**

❶ ★★ **Summer Music in Central Park.** The **New York Philharmonic** plays free evening concerts on the Great Lawn (midpark 79th–85th sts.; http://nyphil.org). Nearby, **Shakespeare in the Park** features free, star-studded Public Theater productions of a Shakespeare classic in June at the Delacorte Theater (southwest corner of the Great Lawn, midpark at 80th St.; www.publictheater.org).

❷ ★★ **Roosevelt Island Tram.** Roosevelt Island residents who ride the tram back and forth to Manhattan every day are privy to one of New York's best-kept secrets: The view from the tram is one of the city's most dramatic. Each way is only 4 minutes long. Look down the East River, and you'll see four bridges (Queensboro, Williamsburg, Manhattan, and Brooklyn). *Second Ave. & 59th St. Fare $2. Subway: 4/5/6/N/R/W to 59th St.*

❸ ★★★ **New York Public Library.** This magnificent Beaux Arts building, worth a trip in itself, has permanent and temporary exhibitions plus a nice gift shop in the lobby. Oh, and it's all free. *See p 43.*

The view is free from the Brooklyn Bridge.

TV Tapings

It's free but not easy to be an audience member on New York–based talk shows such as The *Late Show with David Letterman, the Colbert Report, the Daily Show,* and *Late Night with Conan O'Brien*. The catch is ordering tickets far in advance. Check the "ticket request" section on each show's website and specify how many tickets you want and your preferred dates. Or consult the convention and visitors bureau (☎ 212/484-1222; www.nycvisit.com).

A scene from Hamlet *performed in Central Park.*

4 ★ Movies in Bryant Park. During most of the year, Bryant Park is a peaceful oasis of green, just behind the New York Public Library. In summer, Bryant Park hosts its Summer Film Festival featuring classic-movie screenings on Monday evenings at dusk. The lawn opens at 5pm for blankets and picnics. *Bordered by 40th and 42nd sts. & Fifth and Sixth aves.* ☎ *212/512-5700. www.bryantpark.org. Subway: B/D/F/V to 42nd St.*

The Staten Island Ferry.

5 ★★ A Stroll on the Brooklyn Bridge. This 1883 neo-Gothic icon is as awe-inspiring up close as it is from afar. A stroll across will take 20 to 40 minutes. A sidewalk entrance to the bridge on Park Row leads to the pedestrian walkway above the traffic. Stay to the right while you walk; cyclists use the left lane. *Entrance across from City Hall Park on Park row. Subway: 4/5/6/N to Brooklyn Bridge/City Hall.*

6 ★★ kids National Museum of the American Indian. This Smithsonian Institution museum houses a fabulous collection of artifacts in one of the city's most impressive buildings. And it's free! *See p 57.*

7 ★★ Staten Island Ferry. The free 25-minute ride takes you past the Statue of Liberty and Ellis Island. *Whitehall Ferry Terminal.* ☎ *718/727-2508. www.siferry.com.*

3 New York **Museums**

The Met & the Cloisters

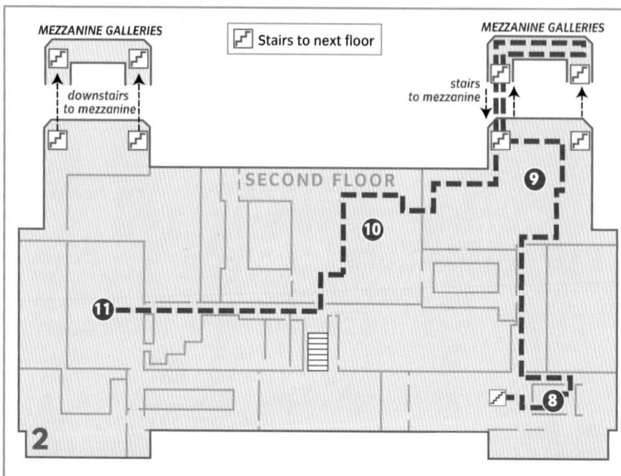

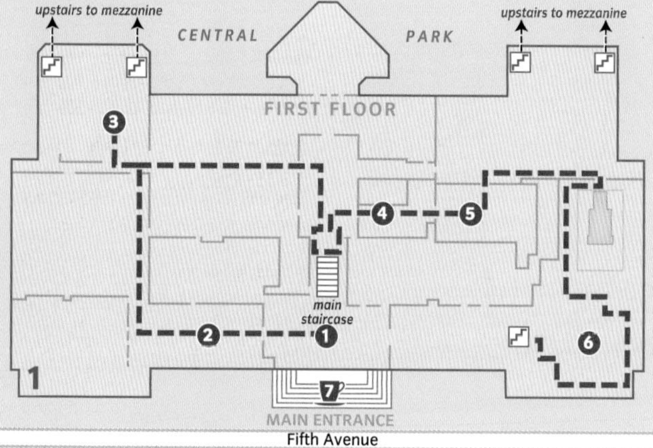

1. **The Great Hall**
2. **Greek & Roman Galleries**
3. **Modern Art Wing**
4. **European Sculpture & Decorative Arts**
5. **Arms & Armor**
6. **Egyptian Art**
7. **Lunch at the Met**
8. **Asian Art**
9. **American Wing**
10. **European Paintings: Old Masters**
11. **European Paintings: 19th & Early 20th Centuries**

Previous page: The Hayden Planetarium.

In 1866 a group of New Yorkers decided their hometown needed a museum that would function as a living encyclopedia of world art. Today the Metropolitan Museum of Art & the Cloisters fulfills that promise with a collection of more than two million objects dating from the Paleolithic period (that is, the Stone Age) to the early 21st century (that is, now). START: **Subway 4, 5, or 6 to 86th Street**

1 The Great Hall. The main entrance to the Met makes all who enter feel like royalty. With its soaring ceilings, elegant balconies, and restrained use of Greco-Roman motifs, it's a fine example of neoclassical architecture. The massive sprays of fresh flowers have been a tradition here since 1969. *3–4 hr. If you're in a rush, skip the main entrance on 82nd & enter through 81st St. The least crowded times are Fri & Sat nights or right at opening time. Fifth Ave. & 82nd St. ☎ 212/535-7710. www.metmuseum.org. Admission $20 adults, $5 seniors, $10 students, free for children under 12 with adult. Sun & Tues–Thurs 9:30am–5:30pm; Fri–Sat 9:30am–9pm. Closed Mon (except holiday Mon, such as Labor Day, and the like). Subway: 4/5/6 to 86th St. Bus: M1/2/3/4.*

2 ★★★ Greek & Roman Galleries. The big news at the Met is the completion of the new Greek and Roman galleries after 15 years of painstaking construction. Some 3,700 people per day have visited these spectacular rooms since their opening in 2007. The centerpiece is the **Leon Levy and Shelby White Court,** a dramatic peristyle area rich with Hellenistic and Roman art. Among its treasures is a massive statue of ***Hercules*** with a lion skin draped heroically over his arm. In the galleries visitors can see **Roman frescoes** long buried under ash after a volcanic eruption; exquisite **gold serpentine armbands;** and the **"Black Bedroom,"** reputedly made for a villa built by a close friend of the Emperor Augustus.

3 ★ Modern Art Wing. Head through the galleries of the Arts of Africa, Oceania, and the Americas to get to the Modern Art Wing, which is full of blockbuster works. Must-sees include Pablo Picasso's ***Gertrude Stein,*** Jackson Pollock's ***Autumn Rhythm,*** and Edward Hopper's ***The Lighthouse at Two Lights.*** If you need a jolt of energy, seek out Charles Demuth's 1928 ***The Figure 5 in Gold,*** a smashing iconic American image that radiates frenetic movement and was a big influence on the Pop artists of the 1950s.

4 European Sculpture & Decorative Arts. These galleries are filled with period rooms that include a handsome **bedroom** from an

The Met's Great Hall.

18th-century Venetian palace, a mid-18th-century **Tapestry Room** from an English country estate, and the astonishing **Studiolo** (study) from the Ducal Palace in Gubbio. The walls of this small Renaissance study are covered in elaborate wood panels inlaid with thousands of pieces of wood to give the illusion of a room lined with cabinets containing books, musical instruments, and scientific tools.

5 ★ kids **Arms & Armor.** The full sets of European armor in the courtyard are dazzling, but make sure you pop into the smaller galleries that surround the court. Here you'll find such curiosities as ceremonial saddles carved from bone and pistols inlaid with semiprecious stones. A Turkish saber created in 1876 for the investiture of an Ottoman sultan (who had a nervous breakdown before the ceremony and was deposed) is a miracle of sparkling diamonds, smooth-as-ice jade, and rich gold work.

6 ★★★ kids **Egyptian Art.** The **Temple of Dendur,** built in 15 B.C., is arguably the most famous object at the Met. Inside, you'll find graffiti from Victorian-era travelers. For a glimpse of daily life in ancient Egypt, check out the 13 wooden models from the **tomb of Meketre.** These models represent Meketre's earthly wealth that is to be taken with him into the afterlife. They show his bakery, his dairy, his beer-producing facility, and boats.

7 **Lunch at the Met.** Year-round you can grab a good, filling lunch at the ground-floor **cafeteria** ($)—it even has kids' meals. If it's a nice day, head outside the main entrance and get a snack from one of the carts ($) on the plaza. The food won't be gourmet, but eating a pretzel or hot dog while people-watching from the steps of the museum is a quintessential New York experience. For other dining options, see p 11, bullet 2.

8 ★ **Asian Art.** The **Astor Court,** a Chinese scholar's garden based on a Ming Dynasty design, is a great place for a little R&R. The principle of yin and yang, or opposites, gives this space its sense of harmony and tranquillity. The Japanese galleries are filled with delicate scrolls, screens, kimonos, and tapestries. Don't miss the **Japanese tearoom/study room.**

9 ★★ **American Wing.** ***Note:*** This wing of the museum is closed until 2010, although works from the Department of American Paintings and Sculpture are on view in the **Henry R. Luce Center for the Study of American Art** and other galleries. This light-filled section of the Met is a museum inside a museum. The Hudson River Valley paintings are extraordinary in their scope, from the grandeur of Frederick Church's ***The Heart of the Andes*** to the delicate and refined ***Lake George*** by John Kensett. Head into the opposite gallery with the iconic ***Washington Crossing the Delaware*** by Emanuel Leutze. On the mezzanine level, you'll find John Singer Sargent's ***Madame X,*** Winslow Homer's ***Northeaster,*** and Mary Cassatt's ***Lady at the Tea Table.*** Take the stairs to ground level to check out ***Frank Lloyd Wright's Living Room*** from the Little House. It's a wonderful example of

The Temple of Dendur dates to 15 B.C.

Francisco de Goya's Portrait of Don Manuel.

his Prairie Style, with the focus on open space and the dramatic horizontal lines that make you feel close to the earth.

⑩ ★★ **European Paintings: Old Masters.** To get to these galleries, cross the Engelhard Court and go up the elegant Louis Sullivan staircase to the second level. As you open the door into the European paintings galleries, you'll come face to face with Rembrandt's ***Aristotle with a Bust of Homer.*** Other highlights include Jan Vermeer's ***Young Woman with a Water Jug,*** El Greco's ***Portrait of a Cardinal,*** Diego Velázquez's ***Juan de Pareja,*** Francisco Goya's ***Don Manuel,*** Fra Filippo Lippi's ***Portrait of Man and Woman at the Casement,*** Pieter Bruegel's ***The Harvesters,*** Titian's ***Venus and Adonis,*** and Duccio's ***Madonna and Child.***

⑪ ★★★ **European Paintings: 19th & Early 20th Centuries.** One of the most popular sections in the museum, these galleries have been newly renovated and expanded. Here you can compare Gustave Courbet's controversial and explicitly sexual ***Woman with a Parrot*** with a more discreet version by Edouard Manet. You can watch the emergence of Claude Monet's loose, painterly style from his tightly composed ***Garden at Sainte-Adresse*** to the practically abstract ***Poplars.*** Finally, take a look at Paul Cézanne's ***Still Life with Apples and Pears*** with its funky perspectives and innovative use of color to get a feel for the radical changes in painting that developed in the 20th century.

The Cloisters

If you still have energy after visiting the Met, hop on the M4 bus at Madison and 83rd Street and head up to **The Cloisters** (☎ 212/923-3700). This museum devoted to medieval art and architecture is a branch of the Met, but it feels like a world apart. In Fort Tryon Park overlooking the Hudson, the building incorporates elements from five medieval cloisters in France, Spain, and Italy.

Besides the Cloisters' magnificent setting and extraordinary architecture, it would be worth coming just to see ***The Unicorn Tapestries,*** a series of seven tapestries depicting a sometimes brutal hunt that ends with the resurrection of the unicorn enclosed in a garden under a pomegranate tree. Robert Campin's ***Annunciation altarpiece*** is another memorable work. Filled with genre details, it depicts the Virgin Mary in a medieval Dutch setting.

Note: The last stop on the M4 is directly in front of The Cloisters. The ride takes 1 hour. Admission is free with same-day Met button.

The Best Small Museums

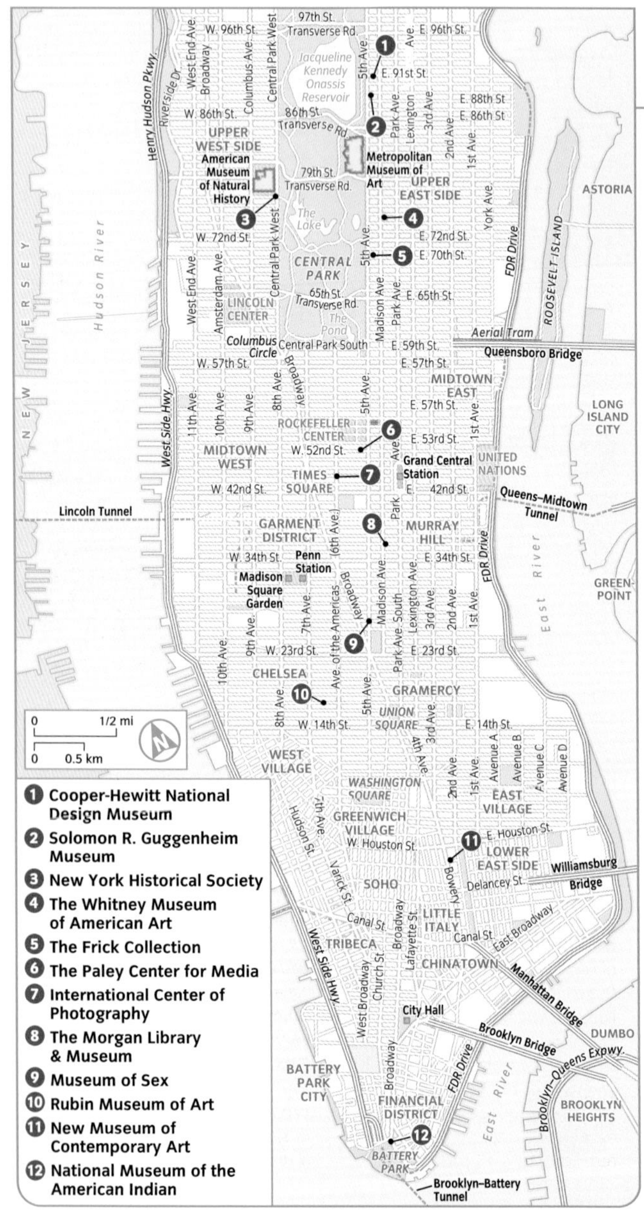

Few cities can match New York in the breadth and depth of its museum collections. Sure, the big boys are here—the Met, MoMa, and the Natural History museum—but world-class treasures await in the smaller collections as well. Here are some of the best to get you started. START: **Subway 6 to 103rd Street**

1 ★★ Cooper-Hewitt National Design Museum. This richly appointed 64-room mansion, with sumptuous oak paneling and a truly grand staircase (one, a critic noted, "you could drive a Sherman tank up"), was steel industrialist Andrew Carnegie's private home. After a $20-million renovation in 1974, the house became part of the Smithsonian Institution, with 11,000 square feet (1,022 sq. m) of gallery space devoted to industrial design, drawings, textiles, wall coverings, books, and prints. You'll see woven silk from 13th-century Europe, Chinese hand-painted wallpaper, and a rare Michelangelo scribble. Spend time in the garden, an idyllic oasis—Carnegie deliberately built his home farther north than his contemporaries in order to have room to create this spectacular, private space. Steal a kiss in the lovely glass conservatory—you won't be the first. *1½–2 hr. 2 E. 91st St. (at Fifth Ave.). ☎ 212/849-8400. www.ndm.si.edu. Admission $15 adults, $10 seniors & students, free for children under 12. Tues–Thurs 10am–5pm; Fri 10am–9pm; Sat 10am–6pm; Sun noon–5pm. Subway: 4/5/6 to 86th St.*

2 ★★ Solomon R. Guggenheim Museum. One of the largest of New York's small museums, the Guggenheim holds a wide-ranging collection of modern art, from an 1867 landscape by Camille Pissaro to important works by Picasso, Wassili Kandinsky, and Amedeo Modigliani. The recently restored building is a Frank Lloyd Wright masterpiece. *See p 45, bullet* 17.

The Smithsonian's Cooper-Hewitt National Design Museum in the former home of Andrew Carnegie.

3 ★★ New York Historical Society. The New York Historical Society is a major repository of American history, culture, and art, with a special focus on New York. Where else can you find a collection that includes Tiffany lamps, vintage dollhouses, Audubon watercolors, life and death masks of prominent Americans, and even George Washington's camp bed? *1½ hr. 2 W. 77th St. (at Central Park West). ☎ 212/873-3400. www.nyhistory.org. Admission $10 adults, $7 seniors, $6 students, free for children 12 & under. Tues–Sat 10am–6pm (till*

The Frick Collection.

8pm Fri); Sun 11am–5:45pm. Bus: M79. Subway: 1/9 to 79th St.

❹ ★★ **The Whitney Museum of American Art.** This museum was built around Gertrude Vanderbilt Whitney's collection of 20th-century art, including works by Edward Hopper, Jasper Johns, and Georgia O'Keefe. The original museum was established in 1931 near Vanderbilt's home in Greenwich Village. It has been in its present home, a concrete-and-granite structure designed by architect Marcel Breuer, since 1966. The collection includes provocative 21st-century pieces, many of them shown in the trend-setting Whitney Biennial, an exhibition of cutting-edge works by up-and-coming artists. *2–3 hr. 945 Madison Ave. (at 75th St.). ☎ 800/WHIT-NEY (800/944-8639). www.whitney.org. Admission $15 adults, $10 seniors & students, free children under 12. Wed–Thurs & Sat–Sun 11am–6pm, Fri 1–9pm. Subway: 6 to 77th St.*

❺ ★★★ **The Frick Collection.** If you want to see how Gilded Age millionaires lived, don't miss the Frick. It's said that steel titan Henry Clay Frick commissioned this marble mansion to make his fellow industrialist Andrew Carnegie's home "look like a miner's shack." The collection is first-rate, with works by Rembrandt, Goya, Vermeer, James McNeill Whistler, Jean Baptiste Camille Corot, and Frederick Turner. *90 min. See p 25, bullet ❸.*

❻ ★ kids **The Paley Center for Media.** Formerly known as the Museum of Television & Radio, this interactive museum is irresistible fun. You can see performances by great personalities past and present—from Milton Berle to Jerry Seinfeld—or do your own computer search of the museum's 140,000 choices for shows you half-remember from childhood. History buffs can revisit great moments such as the dismantling of the Berlin Wall. *1–3 hr., depending on the shows you pick. Call in advance to make a reservation. 25 W. 52nd St. (btwn. Fifth & Sixth aves.). ☎ 212/621-6600. www.mtr.org. Admission $10 adults, $8 seniors & students, $5 children under 13. Tues–Sun noon–6pm (Thurs until 8pm, Fri theater programs until 9pm). Subway: B/D/F/V to 47th–50th sts.*

❼ ★ **International Center of Photography.** A "must see" for any photography buff, the ICP is one of the world's premier educators, collectors, and exhibitors of photographic art. The collection includes 50,000-plus prints with an emphasis on contemporary photographic works, but with a respectable collection of historically important photographers as well. *1133 Sixth Ave. (at 43rd St.). ☎ 212/857-0000. www.icp.org. Admission $12 adults, $8 seniors and students, under 12 free. Tues–Thurs and Sat–Sun 10am–6pm; Fri 10am–8pm. Subway: B, D, F, V to 42nd St.*

❽ ★★ **The Morgan Library & Museum.** Reopened in 2006 after a major expansion by architect Renzo Piano, this Italian Renaissance–style mansion—once the private library of financier Pierpont Morgan—boasts one of the best collections of rare books and manuscripts in the world. Look for the autographed manuscript of a Mozart symphony, early children's books, a chalk drawing by Peter Paul Rubens, and the ornate illustrations in medieval and Renaissance manuscripts. 🕘 *2 hr. 29 E. 36th St. (btwn. Park & Madison aves.). ☎ 212/685-0610. www.themorgan.org. Admission $12 adults, $8 seniors & students, free children 12 and under. Tues–Thurs 10:30am–5pm; Fri 10:30am–9pm; Sat 10am–6pm; Sun 11am–6pm. Subway: B/D/F/N/Q/R/V to 34th St.*

9 ★ Museum of Sex. When this museum opened, it managed to cause a stir even among hard-bitten New Yorkers. Among the collections are early sex films, artifacts from burlesque theaters, S&M displays, painted nudes, and even blow-up dolls. 🕘 *1 hr. 233 Fifth Ave. (at 27th St.). ☎ 866/MOSEX-NYC (667-3969). www.museumofsex.com. Admission $15 adults, $14 students & seniors. No one under 18 admitted. Sun–Fri 11am–6:30pm; Sat 11am–8pm. Subway: N/R to 28th St.*

10 ★★ Rubin Museum of Art. New York must have some good karma: In October 2004 it scored this stunning collection of Himalayan art. In the former Chelsea outpost of Barneys, the Rubin Museum features sculptures, paintings, and textiles. Great gift shop, too. 🕘 *90 min. 150 W. 17th St. (btwn. Sixth & Seventh aves.). ☎ 212/620-5000. www.rmanyc.org. Admission $10 adults, $7 seniors, students, artists & neighbors, free for children under 12. Mon & Thurs 11am–5pm; Wed 11am–7pm; Fri 11am–10pm; Sat–Sun 11am–6pm. Subway: 1/9 to 18th St.*

11 ★ New Museum of Contemporary Art. In its new digs since 2007, the seven-story New Museum of Contemporary Art, designed by Tokyo–based architects Kazuyo Sejima and Ryue Nishizawa, rises above the tenements of the Lower East Side like boxes haphazardly piled upon one another. The offbeat exterior reflects the character of the exhibitions inside by new and emerging artists. *235 Bowery (at Prince St.) ☎ 212/219-1222. www.newmuseum.org. Admission: $12 adult, $8 Senior, $6 student, 18 and under free; free for all Thurs 7–10pm. Wed noon–6pm; Thurs–Fri noon–10pm; Sat–Sun noon–6pm. Subway: 6 to Spring St; N, R to Prince St.*

12 ★★ kids National Museum of the American Indian. Long before European colonists arrived, the North and South American continents were the sole domain of Native Indian tribes and an abundant assortment of fauna. But once settlers arrived, the saga of the American Indian's rapid decline began. Guns and disease took their toll, but here in New York, it took a simple trade to ultimately displace the natives: In 1626, regional tribes sold Manhattan Island to the Dutch West India Company for 60 guilders. This museum's collection spans more than 10,000 years of North and South America's pre-European history. *See p 8, bullet 7.*

American Museum of **Natural History**

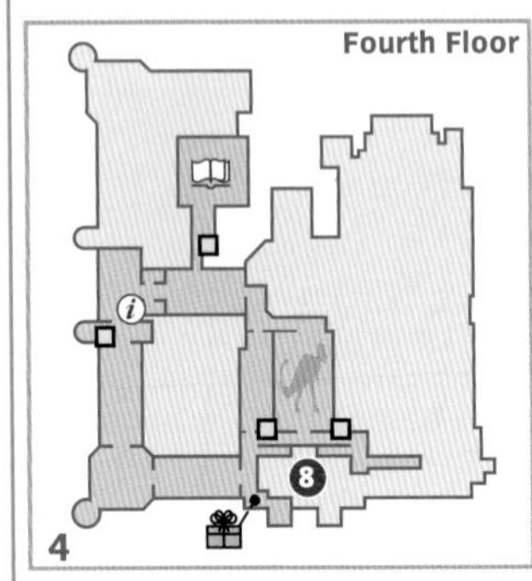

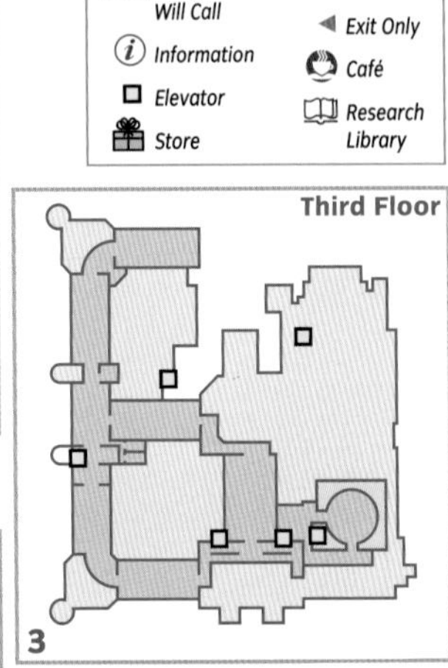

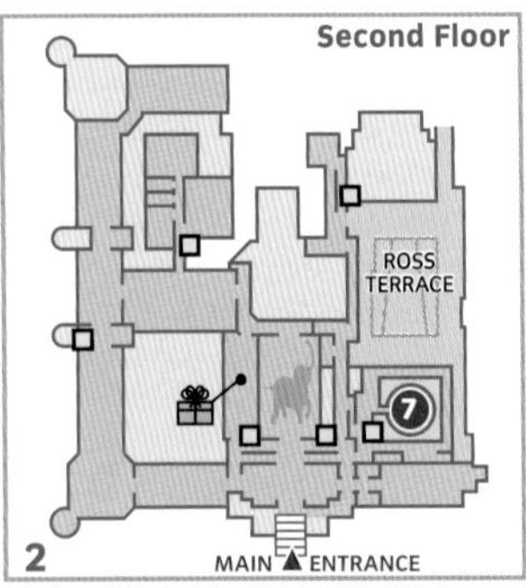

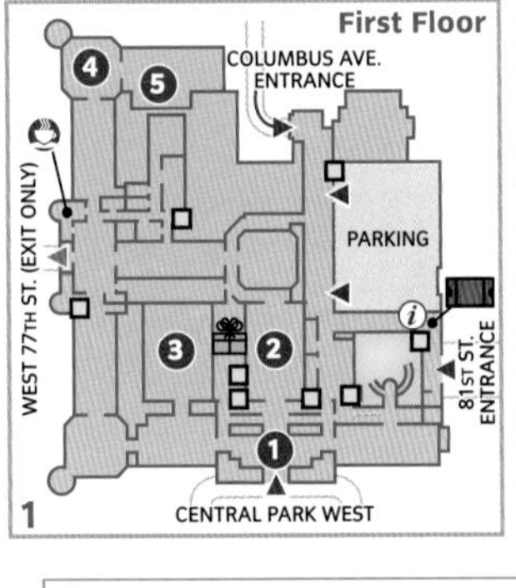

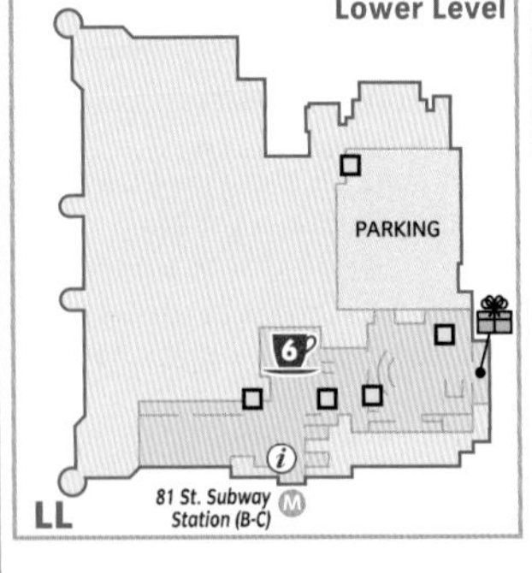

1. Theodore Roosevelt Memorial Hall
2. North American Mammals
3. Millstein Hall of Ocean Life
4. Ross Hall of Meteorites
5. Morgan Memorial Hall of Gems
6. Museum Food Court
7. Rose Center for Earth & Science/ Hayden Planetarium
8. Koch Dinosaur Wing

It's got dinosaurs, meteorites, and giant sapphires—and that's just for starters. The American Museum of Natural History has one of the most diverse and thrilling collections in the world—four floors of nature's wonders for the intrepid explorer in all of us. It's delicious fun for all ages. START: **Subway 1 or 9 to 231st Street and then bus Bx7 or Bx10 to 252nd Street**

❶ ★★ **Theodore Roosevelt Memorial Hall.** The sight of a giant *Barosaurus* fossil in this soaring entrance rotunda provides a smashing first course to the rest of your visit. *4 hr. Central Park West (btwn. 77th & 81st sts.). 212/769-5100. www.amnh.org. Admission (includes entrance to Rose Center, below) $15 adults, $11 seniors & students, $8.50 children 2–12; Space Show (see below) & museum admission $22 adults, $17 seniors & students, $13 children under 12. Daily 10am–5:45pm (Rose Center open Fri to 8:45pm). Subway: B/C to 81st St.*

❷ ★★ **North American Mammals.** One of the museum's popular Habitat Group Dioramas, where skillfully mounted animals are shown in lifelike reproductions of their natural habitats. In one diorama, an Alaskan brown bear, the world's largest living carnivore, rears up on its hind legs.

❸ ★★ **Millstein Hall of Ocean Life.** This newly restored room on the first floor explores life in the deep blue sea, with lighted fish dioramas and a spectacular replica of a giant blue whale overhead.

❹ ★★ **Ross Hall of Meteorites.** On display is a 34-ton meteorite, which is merely a fragment of a massive meteorite that scientists estimate weighed around 200 tons.

❺ ★ **Morgan Memorial Hall of Gems.** This collection of precious gems includes the biggest sapphire ever found, the 563-carat Star of India.

6 **Museum Food Court.** Sustenance for the whole family, including barbecue, panini, and sandwiches. *Lower Level. $–$$.*

❼ ★★★ **Rose Center for Earth & Space/Hayden Planetarium.** A sphere inside a seven-story glass cube holds the Hayden Planetarium, where you can take a virtual ride through the Milky Way. Prepare to be blown away by the literally earth-shaking short film *Cosmic Collisions*, narrated by Robert Redford, about the violent beginnings of the universe. Buy your tickets in advance for the Space Show in order to guarantee admission (they're available online).

❽ ★★★ **Koch Dinosaur Wing.** The fourth floor contains the largest collection of real dinosaur fossils in the world. Among the treasures is the ***Tyrannosaurus rex***, with 6-inch-long teeth, and the first ***Velociraptor*** skull ever found.

Travel Tip

I recommend buying tickets in advance for a specific IMAX film or special exhibition, such as the Butterfly Conservatory. The museum excels at special exhibitions, so check to see what will be on while you're in town in case any advance planning is required. (From October through May, for example, the magical **Butterfly Conservatory**, a walk-in enclosure housing nearly 500 free-flying tropical butterflies, has developed into a museum staple that's not to be missed in season.)

The Museum of Modern Art

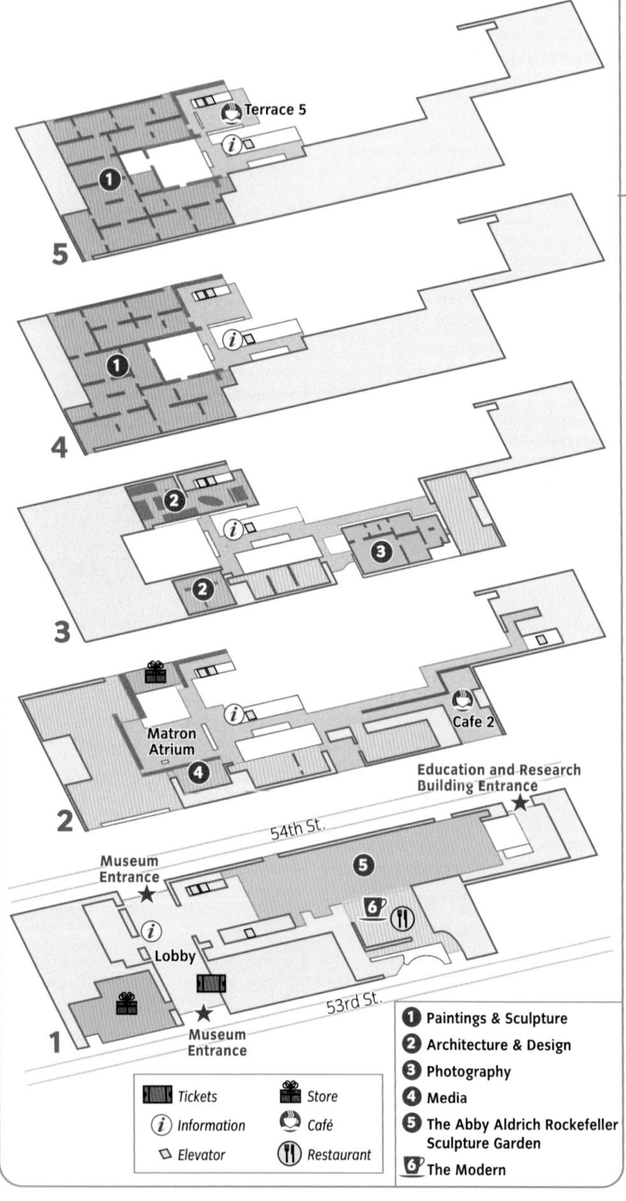
Terrace 5
5
4
3
2
1
Matron Atrium
Cafe 2
Education and Research Building Entrance
54th St.
Museum Entrance
Lobby
53rd St.
Museum Entrance
Tickets
Information
Elevator
Store
Café
Restaurant
1 Paintings & Sculpture
2 Architecture & Design
3 Photography
4 Media
5 The Abby Aldrich Rockefeller Sculpture Garden
6 The Modern

For the best in modern painting and sculpture from the late 19th century to the present, head straight to MoMa, as it's affectionately known. The 2006 renovation by Yoshio Taniguchi highlights space and light, with open rooms, high ceilings, and gardens. It's a beautiful work of architecture and an enhancing complement to the art within—a vast repository of drawings, photographs, architectural models and modern furniture, iconic design objects ranging from tableware to sports cars, and film and video. START: **Subway B, D, or F to 47th–50th streets**

Tip

In 2008, MoMA installed a museum-wide Wi-Fi network so that visitors can access a mobile Web site on handheld devices with HTML browsers (which basically means Apple's iPhone and iPod Touch). They can then upload audio tours and commentary; content is available in eight languages and in specialized versions for children, teenagers, and the visually impaired.

1 ★★★ Paintings & Sculpture. Start your tour at the top: on the fourth and fifth floors. Among the museum treasures are Vincent van Gogh's ***The Starry Night,*** Paul Cézanne's ***The Bather,*** Picasso's ***Les Demoiselles d'Avignon,*** and Henri Rousseau's ***The Sleeping Gypsy.*** Look for celebrated works by Henri Matisse, Paul Gauguin, Marc Chagall, Edward Hopper, René Magritte, Willem de Kooning, Mark Rothko, Barnett Newman, Frank Stella, and Jackson Pollock. *3 hr. 11 W. 53rd St. (btwn. Fifth & Sixth aves.). 212/708-9400. www.moma.org. Admission $20 adults, $16 seniors, $12 students, kids 16 & under free when accompanied by an adult. Sat–Mon & Wed–Thurs 10:30am–5:30pm; Fri 10:30am–8pm. Subway: E/V to Fifth Ave./53rd St.; B/D/F to 47th–50th sts.*

2 ★★ Architecture & Design. The third floor contains some 28,000 works that perhaps more than any other collection reflect the form-follows-function elegance and dynamism of the era. Here are Eames chairs, Frank Lloyd Wright windows, a 1908 Peter Behrens fan, and even smartly designed ball bearings.

3 ★★ Photography. MoMa started collecting photographs in 1930, well before most people considered photography an art form. This stunning collection on the third floor holds important works by Walker Evans, Man Ray, and Cindy

The Museum of Modern Art.

P.S. 1 Contemporary Art Center

If you're interested in new work that's too cutting-edge for most museums, this MoMA affiliate is worth the trip one stop outside Manhattan, in Queens. Originally a public school, P.S. 1 is the world's largest institution exhibiting contemporary art from America and abroad. Expect an array of works by artists ranging from Jack Smith to Julian Schnabel and large-scale exhibitions by artists such as James Turrell. 22–25 Jackson Ave. (at 46th Ave.), Long Island City, Queens. ☎ **718/784-2084.** www.ps1.org. Suggested admission $5 adults, $2 seniors and students. Thurs–Mon noon–6pm. Subway: E, V to 23rd St./Ely Ave.; 7 to 45th Rd./Court House Sq.

Sherman, as well as mid-19th-century albumen silver prints from glass-plate negatives.

❹ ★ **Media.** This collection on the second floor covers some 50 years of works in media, from moving-image installations and short films to pieces that combine avant-garde performance art and video.

❺ ★★ **The Abby Aldrich Rockefeller Sculpture Garden.** This landscaped outdoor space (originally designed by architect Philip Johnson) is home to works of sculpture from the museum collection. Look for Pablo Picasso's whimsical ***She-Goat*** (1950) and Alberto Giacometti's ***Tall Figure III*** (1960), as well as installations by contemporary artists such as Richard Serra.

❻ ★★ **The Modern.** Whether you're here for lunch, dinner, or a cocktail, this is one museum restaurant that is a destination in itself. It's sleek and fabulous, and it overlooks the Sculpture Garden. ***The Museum of Modern Art. 9 W. 53rd St. (btwn. Fifth and Sixth aves.). ☎ 212/333-1220. www.themodernnyc.com. $$$.*** ●

4 The Best Neighborhood Walks

Historic Downtown

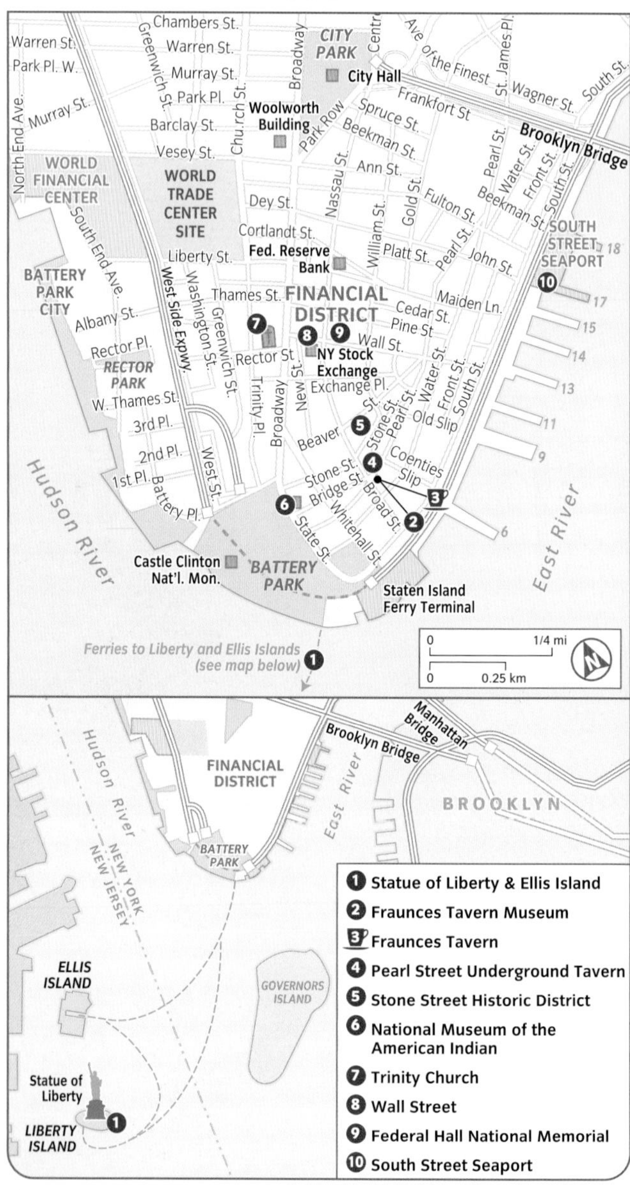

Previous page: Autumn in the West Village.

The southern tip of Manhattan is where the action began some 400 years ago. This area includes 17th-century cobblestone alleyways, the seaport where 18th-century commerce helped build the city, historic landmarks of the American Revolution, and the canyons of Wall Street, constructed in outsize Deco style in the early 20th century. START: **Subway 4 or 5 to Bowling Green**

1 ★★★ kids Statue of Liberty & Ellis Island. Annie Moore, an Irish teenager, celebrated her 15th birthday on January 1, 1892, as the first person to pass through Ellis Island, America's main point of entry for immigrants from 1892 to 1954. For Annie and the 12 million immigrants who subsequently entered the U.S. through Ellis Island, Lady Liberty was likely their first glimpse of America. The statue was slated to commemorate 100 years of American independence in 1876. But it wasn't until 1886 that the statue was finally dedicated on U.S. soil. On Liberty Island, you can explore the **Statue of Liberty Museum,** peer into the inner structure through a glass ceiling near the base of the statue, and enjoy views from the observation deck atop a 16-story pedestal. On Ellis Island, you can take self-guided or ranger tours of the immigration complex and view exhibits at the **Ellis Island Immigration Museum,** in the main building. *2 ½ hr.* *See p 9, bullet 9.*

2 ★ Fraunces Tavern Museum. It was here that George Washington bade farewell to his officers at the end of the American Revolution with these words: "With a heart full of love and gratitude I now take leave of you. I most devoutly wish that your latter days may be as prosperous and happy as your former ones have been glorious and honorable." This 1907 building is an exact replica of the original 1717 tavern. The museum has period rooms, art and artifacts (including a lock of Washington's hair and one of his false teeth), and temporary exhibits. *45 min. 54 Pearl St. (near Broad St.). 212/425-1778. www.fraunces tavernmuseum.org. Admission $4 adults, $3 seniors & students, free for children under 6. Mon–Sat noon–5pm. Subway: R/W to Whitehall St.; 4/5 to Bowling Green; 1/9 to South Ferry.*

The Fraunces Tavern Museum.

3 Fraunces Tavern. Housed in the museum of the same name, Fraunces Tavern has changed since Washington dined here, but still offers a taste of history. Enjoy soup, sandwiches, and salads. *54 Pearl St. (near Broad St.). 212/425-1776. $–$$.*

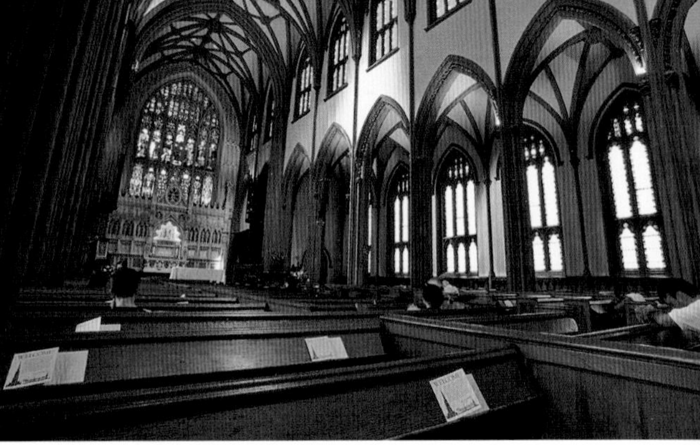

The Interior of Trinity Church.

4 ★ Pearl Street Underground Tavern. Little is left of 17th-century New York, but an excavation in 1979 led to the discovery of the foundation of Lovelace's Tavern, built in 1670. In an ingenious move, the underground excavation was left in place—as was an early-18th-century cistern—and the street above it was replaced with glass, so that anyone walking by can look down and see the old foundation and artifacts. *Pearl St. at Coenties Alley. Subway: R/W to Whitehall St.; 4/5 to Bowling Green, 1/9 to South Ferry.*

5 ★★ Stone Street Historic District. This 17th-century cobblestone alley has become a dynamic contemporary enclave, with simmering restaurants, bars, and a heralded pizzeria. *Bounded by Pearl St., Hanover Sq., S. William St. & Coenties Alley.* *See p 41.*

6 ★★ kids National Museum of the American Indian. Long before European colonists arrived, the North and South American continents were the sole domain of Native Indian tribes and an abundant assortment of fauna. But once settlers arrived, the saga of the American Indian's rapid decline began. Guns and disease took their toll, but here in New York, it took a simple trade to ultimately displace the natives: In 1626, regional tribes sold Manhattan Island to the Dutch West India Company for 60 guilders. This museum's collection spans more than 10,000 years of North and South America's pre-European history. What's more, admission is free. *See p 57, bullet* 12.

7 ★★ Trinity Church. Alexander Hamilton is buried in the church's south cemetery. The original building was erected in 1698, though the present structure dates to 1846. *See p 8, bullet* 6.

8 ★★★ Wall Street. The street synonymous with high finance began, literally, as a 12-foot-high (3.6m) wooden wall built to keep out the British. Today it's home to some of the city's most impressive architecture, much of it skyscraping Art Deco artifacts from the city's Jazz Age heyday. Check out **One Wall Street,** the Bank of New York building, built in 1931, a tiered limestone tribute to Art Deco. In 1920, a bomb exploded in front of financier J. P. Morgan's 1913 headquarters, the neoclassical **23 Wall Street** (the Morgan Guaranty Trust Building), killing 33 people; it was said to be the work of anarchists. For a nanosecond, the tallest building in the world was **40 Wall St.,** a Deco beauty built in 1930 but soon overtaken in height by the Chrysler Building. The sumptuous Merchants' Exchange (now Cipriani Wall Street) at **55 Wall St.** was built from 1836 to 1842 but was added onto by McKim, Meade and White in 1907.

9 ★★ **Federal Hall National Memorial.** This majestic structure is one of Wall Street's most recognizable monuments. On this site the First Congress met and the Bill of Rights was written. It was also where George Washington was inaugurated, on April 30, 1789. The capital moved to Philadelphia in 1790, and the original Federal Hall was torn down in 1812. The Memorial was built in 1842, and in 1883 the statue of George Washington was placed on the steps. It's directly across from the New York Stock Exchange. *15 min. 26 Wall St. (btwn. Nassau & William sts.).*

South Street Seaport's Historic District.

212/825-6888. www.nps.gov/feha. Free admission. Mon–Fri 9am–5pm. Subway: 2/34/5/6 to Wall St.

10 kids **South Street Seaport.** Dating from the 18th century, this landmark historic district on the East River encompasses 11 square blocks of buildings, a maritime museum, several piers, shops, and restaurants. Although today the Seaport is shamelessly commercial and touristy (the biggest draw is Pier 17, a barge converted into a mall with The Gap, Coach, Abercrombie & Fitch, and other chain stores), visible reminders of the city's vibrant shipping past abound. Rows of ships once lined South Street, doing business with the various warehouses in the neighborhood. Much of the **Schermerhorn Row** block (2–18 Fulton St.) has remained intact since its beginnings in 1811. The **South Street Seaport Museum** boasts paintings and prints, ship models, and temporary exhibitions; and several historic ships, including the 1911 four-masted **Peking,** are berthed at piers 15, 16, and 17. *1½–2 hr. At Water & South sts. www.southstreetseaport.com. Museum visitor center is at 12 Fulton St. 212/732-8257. www.southstseaport.org. Museum admission $10 adults, $8 seniors & students, $5 children 5–12, free for children under 5. Museum Apr–Oct Tues–Sun 10am–6pm; Nov–Mar Fri–Sun 10am–5pm. Subway: 2/3/4/5/J/Z/M to Fulton St.; A/C to Broadway-Nassau.*

Historic Harlem

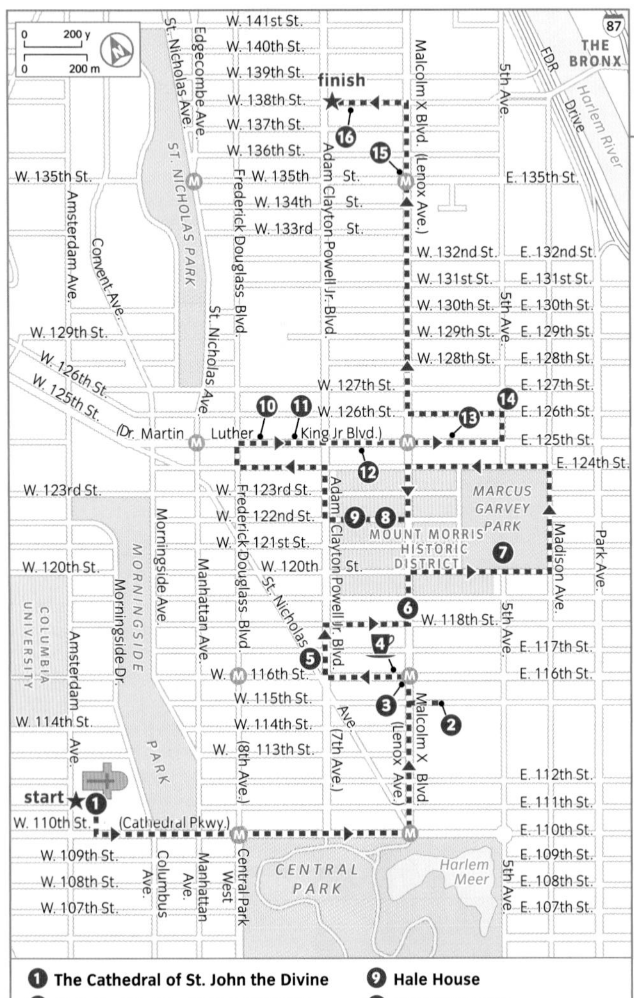

1. The Cathedral of St. John the Divine
2. Malcolm Shabazz Harlem Market
3. Masjid Malcolm Shabazz Mosque
4. Amy Ruth's
5. Minton's Playhouse
6. Mount Morris Park Historic District
7. Marcus Garvey Park
8. Doctors' Row
9. Hale House
10. Apollo Theater
11. Victoria Theater
12. Studio Museum in Harlem
13. 55 W. 125th St
14. A Great Day in Harlem
15. Schomburg Center for Research in Black Culture
16. Abyssinian Baptist Church

It wasn't until the mid–19th century that Nieuw Amsterdam and Nieuw Harlem—the two towns the Dutch founded on the island of Manhattan—became one. Largely shaped by African Americans who came north in large numbers after the Civil War and again after the end of World War I, Harlem has retained its own distinct character. START: **Subway 1 or 9 to 110th Street**

1 ★★★ The Cathedral of St. John the Divine. Although it's in Morningside Heights, the mother church of New York's Episcopal diocese makes a good starting point for your walk. A work in progress, its size alone is breathtaking—once completed, it will be the largest Gothic-style cathedral in the world. And you could walk around studying the elaborate stained-glass windows for hours. The land was purchased in 1887, the cornerstone was laid in 1892, and the choir was finally installed in 1911. Work stopped with the advent of World War II, then resumed in 1979. St. John the Divine houses fantastic art treasures in its thematic chapels (dedicated to sports, poetry, and firefighting, among other subjects). Above the choir, the 17th-century **Barberini Tapestries** depict scenes from the life of Christ. The tremendous rose window is composed of 10,000 pieces of colored glass. *90 min. 1047 Amsterdam Ave. (btwn. 111th & 112th sts.). 212/316-7490. www.stjohndivine.org. Public tours $5 adults; $4 students & seniors. Mon–Sat 7am–6pm; Sun 7am–7pm. Subway: 1/9 to 110th St.*

Stained-glass at St. John the Divine.

2 ★ Malcolm Shabazz Harlem Market. At this colorful outdoor bazaar, tiny shops and stalls hawk West African crafts and local souvenirs. You'll also find hair-braiding booths and African-style clothing. *52 W. 115th St. (btwn. Lenox & Fifth aves.). 212/987-8131. Daily 10am–8pm. Bus: M4. Subway: 2/3 to 115th St.*

3 Masjid Malcolm Shabazz Mosque. In a former life, this religious center was the Lenox Casino. After Malcolm X was assassinated in 1965, it was redesigned as a mosque; the building was thoroughly renovated to incorporate aspects of Middle Eastern architecture, topped off by an aluminum dome. *102 W. 116th St. (Lenox Ave.). 212/662-2200. Open daily 9am–5pm.*

4 ★★ Amy Ruth's. This cozy restaurant serves seriously good Southern soul food. *113 W. 116th St. (btwn. Lenox Ave. & Adam Clayton Powell Blvd.). 212/280-8779. www.amyruthsharlem.com. $–$$.*

5 ★★ Minton's Playhouse. Thirty years after the club was shuttered, the jaunty neon sign glitters once again at this legendary 1930s jazz club where bebop was born.

Brownstones in the Mount Morris Park Historic District.

Here Charlie Parker, Miles Davis, house pianist Thelonious Monk, and other budding greats jammed late into the night. *208 W. 118th St. (btwn. St. Nicholas Ave. & Adam Clayton Powell, Jr., Blvd.)* ☎ *212/864-8346. www.uptownatmintons.com.*

6 ★★ **Mount Morris Park Historic District.** Mount Morris' impressive collection of 19th- and 20th-century row houses and brownstones was built for wealthy white merchants. The homes were built in various styles, from Romanesque Revival to Queen Anne, and many have been restored to their former glory. *Bounded by 119th St., 124th St., Lenox Ave. & Mount Morris Park West.*

7 ★ **Marcus Garvey Park.** This rocky outcropping is one of the highest natural points on Manhattan (firefighters built a watchtower here in 1865, which you can still climb for a fantastic view). The park was renamed in 1973 in honor of black nationalist leader Marcus Garvey, but locals call it Mount Morris Park. *120th St. & Mount Morris Park West.*

8 ★★★ **Doctors' Row.** This stretch of row houses dates from the late 1800s. My favorites are nos. 133 through 143, which were built by architect Francis H. Kimball; these are the most beautiful surviving Queen Anne–style houses in the entire city. *122nd St. & Lenox Ave.*

9 **Hale House.** Established in 1969 by Mother Clara Hale to aid drug-addicted infants and their mothers, this residence now also shelters HIV-infected mothers and their babies. Hale died in 1992, but 4 years later, sculptor Robert Berks memorialized her in a sculpture surrounded by etched bronze plaques of children. *152 W. 122nd St. (btwn. Seventh Ave. & Malcolm X Blvd.).* ☎ *212/663-0700.*

10 ★★★ **Apollo Theater.** This legendary theater has featured them all—Bessie Smith, Count Basie, Billie Holiday, Louis Armstrong, Dizzy Gillespie, Duke Ellington, Charlie "Bird" Parker, Nat "King" Cole, Marvin Gaye, Aretha Franklin, B.B. King, and more. "Amateur Night at the Apollo" launched the careers of Ella Fitzgerald, James Brown, Lauryn Hill, and the Jackson 5. Tours are available only to groups of 20 or more and must be booked well in advance, but you can still pay to attend Amateur Night and other performances. See the website for details. *253 W. 125th St. (Frederick Douglass Blvd.).* ☎ *212/531-5300. www.apollotheater.com.*

11 **Victoria Theater.** At press time, plans to redevelop this elegant and long-shuttered 1911 movie palace as a towering mixed-use complex had run into opposition from community activists, who argued that the historic theater should be restored intact. Included in the plans is a space to house the permanent home of the **Jazz Museum of Harlem** (www.jazzmuseuminharlem.org). *235–237 W. 125th St. (btwn. Seventh & Eighth aves.)*

⓬ ★ **Studio Museum in Harlem.** Since 1968 the SMH has been devoted to collecting, preserving, and promoting 19th- and 20th-century African-American art as well as traditional African art and artifacts. 🕘 *90 min. 144 W. 125th St. (btwn. Lenox Ave. & Adam Clayton Powell, Jr., Blvd.).* ☎ *212/864-4500. www.studiomuseum.org. Admission $7 adults, $3 seniors & students, free for children under 12. Sun & Wed–Fri noon–6pm; Sat 10am–6pm. Subway: 2/3/A/B/C/D to 125th St.*

⓭ **55 W. 125th St.** This office building gained instant fame in 2001 when former president Bill Clinton moved in.

Harlem's Abyssinian Baptist Church.

⓮ **A Great Day in Harlem.** On the steps of a brownstone in 1958, Art Kane, a photographer for *Esquire,* took a black-and-white photograph of 57 assembled jazz greats, including Count Basie, Coleman Hawkins, Charles Mingus, Thelonious Monk, Lester Young, and Mary Lou Williams. An Academy Award–nominated documentary based on the gathering, *A Great Day in Harlem,* was released in 1994. *17 E. 126th St. (btwn. Park & Madison aves.).*

⓯ ★★★ **Schomburg Center for Research in Black Culture.** This national research library has more than five million items documenting the experiences of African-American people around the world. The collections include manuscripts and rare books, moving image and recorded sound, art and artifacts, and photographs and prints. Entry is free. 🕘 *45 min. 515 Malcolm X Blvd. (btwn. 135th & 136th sts.).* ☎ *212/491-2200. www.nypl.org. Free admission. Mon–Wed noon–8pm; Thurs–Fri 11am–6pm; Sat 10am–5pm.*

⓰ **Abyssinian Baptist Church.** This Baptist church is Harlem's most famous. Its congregation first gathered downtown in 1808, when a group of African Americans and Ethiopians withdrew from the First Baptist Church to protest its segregated seating policy. The congregation grew here in 1922 under the leadership of Adam Clayton Powell, Sr. (his son was the preacher, activist, and congressman for whom the nearby boulevard was named). You can join the crowds that gather for Abyssinian's Sunday services at 9am and 11am, presided over by the Rev. Calvin O. Butts. 🕘 *20 min. 132 W. Odell Clark Place (formerly 138th St., btwn. Malcolm X Blvd. & Adam Clayton Powell Jr. Blvd.).* ☎ *212/862-7474. www.abyssinian.org.*

Chelsea for Art Lovers

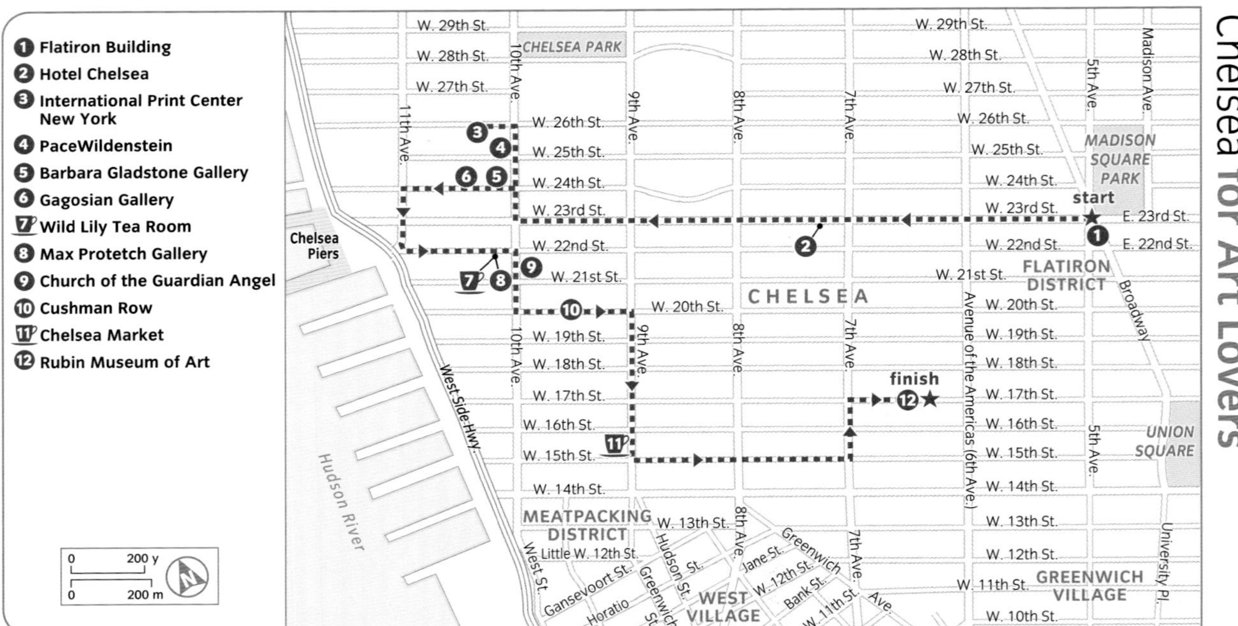

In the '80s, New York's art scene was all about SoHo and the East Village, but for a decade now the best place to browse commercial galleries has been the Chelsea Art District, in the rough-hewn western edges of the neighborhood amid industrial lofts, garages, and repair shops. It's where you'll find the densest concentration of galleries and art-world denizens. START: **Subway N or R to 23rd Street**

1 ★ Flatiron Building. The Flatiron's triangular shape wasn't chosen for aesthetic reasons—it was simply the only way to fill the intersections of Fifth Avenue, 23rd Street, and Broadway. That happy accident in 1902 created one of the city's most recognizable buildings, and one of the first skyscrapers anywhere. There's no observation deck, so what you see from the street is what you get. *175 Fifth Ave. (Broadway). Subway: N/R to 23rd St.*

2 Hotel Chelsea. Want some local flavor? Step into the lobby of the Chelsea, which is both a hotel and residential apartments. The hotel prides itself on the colorful coterie that passes through its doors. Over the years that has included artists such as Claes Oldenburg, Jackson Pollack, and Jim Dine. Plaques at the entrance honor the many writers who also lived here: Mark Twain, O. Henry, Dylan Thomas, Thomas Wolfe, and more. Note the delicate wrought-iron balconies extending along the facade of this 12-story brick building. *See p 34, bullet 7.*

Paintings in the lobby of the Hotel Chelsea.

3 ★ International Print Center New York. This nonprofit gallery was founded in 2000 to exhibit and promote art prints in a

A Donald Judd and Josef Albers show at PaceWildenstein Gallery.

A Damien Hirst exhibition at Gagosian.

range of media. The core of the IPCNY's program is a quarterly New Prints exhibition, which has featured the works of some 800 artists. *526 W. 26th St. (btwn. 10th & 11th aves.). ☎ 212/989-5090. www.ipcny.org. Tues–Sat 11am–6pm.*

❹ **PaceWildenstein.** This massive space is deliberately shorn of decoration so as not to detract from the dramatic paintings and sculptures it showcases. It's one of the neighborhood's best-known galleries, so expect to see the work of major artists living and dead—from Kiki Smith and Chuck Close to Alexander Calder (1898–1976) and Mark Rothko (1903–1970). *534 W. 25th St. (btwn. 10th & 11th aves.). ☎ 212/929-7000. www.pacewildenstein.com. Tues–Sat 10am–6pm.*

❺ ★★ **Barbara Gladstone Gallery.** Gladstone's sizable roster of American and European artists includes famous names such as German artist Rosemarie Trockel and Matthew Barney (creator of the ***Cremaster*** cycle and father of singer Björk's daughter Isadora). A second location has opened at 530 W. 21st St. *515 W. 24th St. (btwn. 10th & 11th aves.). ☎ 212/206-9300. www.gladstonegallery.com. Tues–Sat 10am–6pm.*

❻ ★★ **Gagosian Gallery.** This is a must-see. Most of Chelsea's galleries aren't large enough to hold more than one major exhibition at a time, but the Gagosian is an exception. Past shows have included works by neoexpressionist Julian Schnabel, sculptor Richard Serra, and British artist Damien Hirst—he of the sharks in formaldehyde and diamond-encrusted skulls. *555 W. 24th St. (btwn. 10th & 11th aves.). ☎ 212/741-1111. www.gagosian.com. Tues–Sat 10am–6pm.*

❼ ★ **Wild Lily Tea Room.** This Taiwainese-inspired oasis is an ideal spot for a pot of tea or light fare such as steamed dumplings, scones, and pastries. The tearoom displays paintings and ceramics by local artists. *511 W. 22nd St. (at 10th Ave.). ☎ 212/691-2258. www.wildlilytearoom.com. $.*

❽ ★ **Max Protetch Gallery.** This gallery specializes in architectural drawings and functional sculpture. Previous exhibits have included works by architects such as Rem Koolhaas, Michael Graves, and the legendary Frank Lloyd Wright. *511 W. 22nd St. (at 10th Ave.). ☎ 212/633-6999. www.maxprotetch.com. Tues–Sat 10am–6pm.*

❾ **Church of the Guardian Angel.** This brick-and-limestone example of Romanesque architecture

Visiting Chelsea Piers

All this art and history got your blood going? It may be time to hit the links. Yes, at the massive Chelsea Piers sports complex, you can drive golf balls out over the Hudson River (caught by a giant net, of course) to your heart's content. The views aren't bad either. The complex also has a bowling alley, batting cages, two sundecks, and basketball courts. *23rd St. & Hudson River.* ☎ *212/336-6400. www.chelseapiers.com. $25: 90 balls (peak), 147 balls (off-peak); club rentals $4. Oct–Mar 6:30am–11pm; Apr–Sept 6:30am–midnight. Bus: M23; subway: C/E to 23rd St.*

was built in 1931. At that time it was known as the Shine Church of the Sea because of its proximity to the Chelsea piers (the real ones, not the entertainment center). ***193 10th Ave. (btwn. 21st & 22nd sts.).*** ☎ ***212/929-5966. Mass Sat 5pm, Sun 9am & noon.***

⑩ ★ **Cushman Row.** In the late 1830s, much of Chelsea's real estate was developed by a merchant named Don Alonzo Cushman. His little empire included the stunning Greek Revival houses on West 20th Street between Ninth and Tenth avenues. The houses from no. 406 to no. 418 are better known as Cushman Row (there's a little plaque at no. 412 in tribute). ***20th St. (btwn. 9th & 10th aves.).***

11 **Chelsea Market.** Fast food doesn't get any better than what's served at this ingeniously restored biscuit factory. Here you have your choice of delicious quick repasts, from sweet (Fat Witch Bakery) to savory (Cleaver Company). ***75 Ninth Ave. (btwn. 15th & 16th sts.). www.chelseamarket.com. $–$$.***

⑫ ★★ **Rubin Museum of Art.** You've checked out some contemporary galleries; now it's time to enjoy some historic gems. This noncommercial gallery of Himalayan art joined the Chelsea art scene in 2004. ***See p 57, bullet*** ⑩.

Max Protetch Gallery often shows architectural drawings.

Greenwich Village

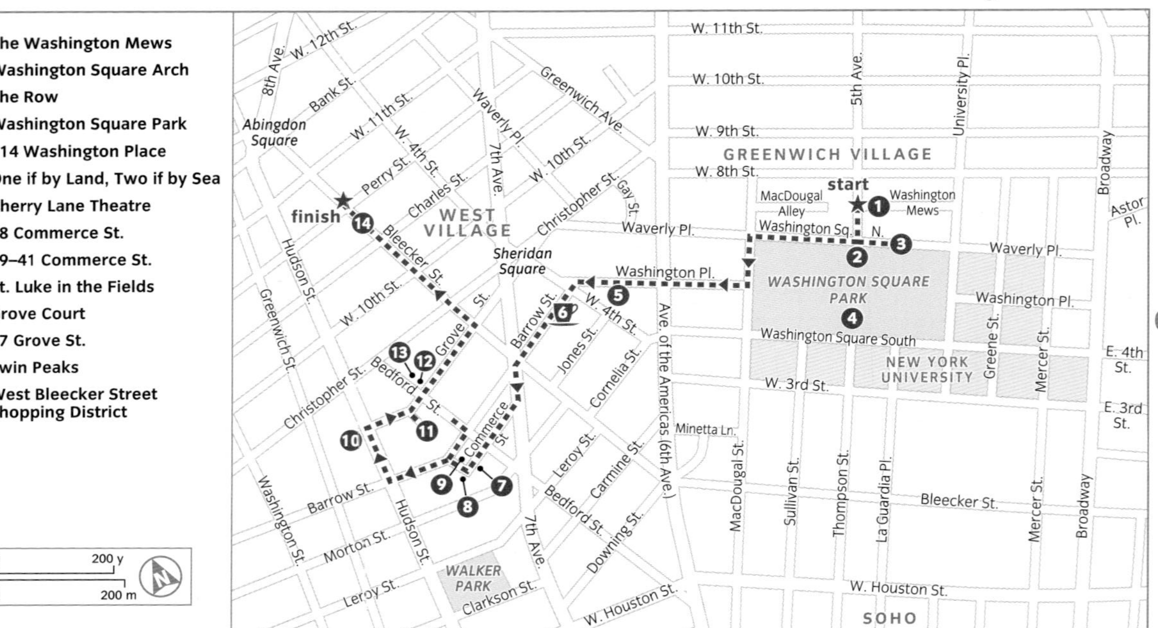

This storied neighborhood has been home to writers, painters, and entertainers for decades. It's also one of Manhattan's most picturesque and historic districts; its small scale, maze-like street plan, and dearth of skyscrapers and industrial space lend it a cozy neighborhood feel. START: **Subway N or R to 8th Street**

1 ★ The Washington Mews. Visitors who stumble upon this cobbled alleyway discover a living slice of old New York. The north side of the mews consists of original 19th-century stables that were converted into stuccoed houses painted in pastels and whimsically decorated—even the stable doors are integrated into the designs. The south side was built in 1939 to mirror the north, but lacks the offbeat grace notes of the original. ***Enter either at University Place or Fifth Ave. btwn. 8th St. & Waverly Place.***

2 ★ Washington Square Arch. This impressive Roman-style arch, designed by Stanford White, was first built of wood in 1889 to commemorate the centennial anniversary of George Washington's inauguration; the current version was completed in 1891 in white marble. The arch is one of the most important landmarks in lower New York. Over the years it has come to be a symbol of the neighborhood's spirit of freedom and individuality. The ivory arch was restored in 2004; now the park itself is undergoing a complete renovation, set to be finished in 2010. ***Fifth Ave. & Waverly Place.***

3 ★★ The Row. These are some of Manhattan's most celebrated town houses, built in elegant Greek Revival style for society's blue bloods from 1832 to 1833 and looking much as they did in the days of early-19th-century New York. Henry James' heroine in *Washington Square* lived here, as did many memorable characters in Edith Wharton's novels. Head west, and you can see more survivors from that era at 19–26 Washington Square North. ***1–13 Washington Sq. N. (btwn. Fifth Ave. & University Place).***

Lion sculptures guard buildings on Washington Square North.

4 Washington Square Park. This relatively small park gets plenty of use (some say overuse) from local residents, New York University students, long-in-the-tooth guitarists, dog-walkers, and assorted riffraff. The land on which it was built in the 1820s was once a cemetery for victims of yellow fever. A centuries-old elm that still stands in the northwest corner of the park was the site of public hangings. These days, a roguish quality persists, with hucksters performing comedy and magic acts

A private entrance at Grove Court.

on a regular basis. ***Note:*** A multi-million-dollar renovation is in the works, and much of the park is currently under construction and off-limits to visitors. *Bordered by University & Waverly places & W. 4th & Macdougal sts.*

5 114 Washington Place. Note the fancy boot scrapers on the wrought-iron stair railings from the days when transportation was largely on horseback and the streets were filled with horse manure. As you stroll, you'll spot boot scrapers of varying design all over the Village.

6 ★ One if by Land, Two if by Sea. The setting couldn't be more romantic—an 18th-century carriage house with candles, tinkling piano music, and great clouds of flowering bouquets. Now, with a heralded new chef, the food is living up to the setting. *17 Barrow St. ☎ 212/255-8649. www.oneifbyland.com. $$$.*

7 Cherry Lane Theatre. Writer/poet Edna St. Vincent Millay and her artist peers converted an 1817 box factory into the Cherry Lane Playhouse in 1924. In 1929, legendary acting teacher Lee Strasberg directed F. Scott Fitzgerald's only published full-length play, *The Vegetable,* here. (It closed after 13 performances.) It's still a working theater; call to see what's playing during your visit. *38 Commerce St. (at Bedford St.). ☎ 212/989-2020. www.cherrylanetheatre.com.*

8 48 Commerce St. Note the working gas lamp in front of the 1844 home of a wealthy merchant. The New York Gas Light Company began laying gas pipes in 1823, and gas lamps—many with an ornamental post design—continued to shine into the 20th century.

9 ★★ 39–41 Commerce St. These three-story twin houses are among the most striking examples of early 19th-century architecture in the Village. The fact that they neatly mirror one another heightens the visual appeal. Topped with elegant mansard roofs and linked by a courtyard, nos. 39 and 41 were built in 1831 and 1832, respectively.

10 ★ St. Luke in the Fields. This charming little church is a reconstruction of the original, which was built in 1822 and badly damaged by fire in 1981. The site on Hudson Street was donated by Trinity Church, and, from 1891 to 1876, St. Luke's was part of Trinity Parish. One of the church's founding wardens was Clement Clarke Moore, a gentleman scholar who is perhaps best known as the author of *'Twas the Night Before Christmas.* You're welcome to stroll about the interior and linger in the pretty church gardens (open Tues–Sun 8:30am–dusk). Sunday services at 8, 9:15, and 11:15am. *487 Hudson St. (at Grove St.).*

11 ★ Grove Court. This lovely gated mews set back from the

Bohemian Ghosts

Nineteenth-century writers such as Mark Twain, Edgar Allan Poe, Henry James, and the painter Winslow Homer first gave the Village its reputation for embracing the unconventional. Groundbreaking artists such as Edward Hopper and Jackson Pollock were drawn in later, as were writers such as Eugene O'Neill, e e cummings, and Dylan Thomas. Radical thinkers from John Reed to Upton Sinclair basked in the neighborhood's liberal ethos, and beatniks Allen Ginsberg, Jack Kerouac, and William Burroughs dug the free-swinging atmosphere. Now, like so many neighborhoods, gentrification and escalating real-estate values conspire to push out the creative element, but culture and counterculture still rub shoulders in cafes, jazz clubs, neighborhood bars, Off- and Off-Off- Broadway theaters, and an endless variety of tiny shops and restaurants.

street was once considered a slum; it was built for workingmen around 1853, when it was known as "Mixed Ale Alley." Today, the genteel Greek Revival structures share a large open courtyard—a rarity in a city where space is at a premium. *10–12 Grove St. (btwn. Hudson & Bedford sts.).*

⓬ **17 Grove St.** This 1822 house is one of the last remaining wood-framed houses in the Village. Note the little 1823 cottage in back (behind the slatted fence), at 100 Bedford St., which was the workshop of the former owner, a sash maker.

⓭ **Twin Peaks.** This 1830 house was given a fanciful Tudoresque renovation in 1925. It stands out among the straightforward 19th-century architecture that dominates the neighborhood. *102 Bedford St. (at Grove St.).*

⓮ ★ **West Bleecker Street Shopping District.** West Bleecker Street, from Christopher Street to Bank Street, became a trendy boutique alley almost overnight. Small-scale and pleasant to stroll, it's now home to **Intermix** *(no. 365; ☎ 212/929-7180)*, **Ralph Lauren** *(nos. 380–381; ☎ 212/645-5513)*, **Marc Jacobs** *(nos. 385 and 403–405; ☎ 212/924-6126)*, **Lulu Guinness** *(no. 394; ☎ 212/367-2120)*, and more. *West Bleecker St. (btwn. Christopher & Bank sts.).*

One if by Land, Two if by Sea is known for its romantic setting.

Prospect Park & **Park Slope**

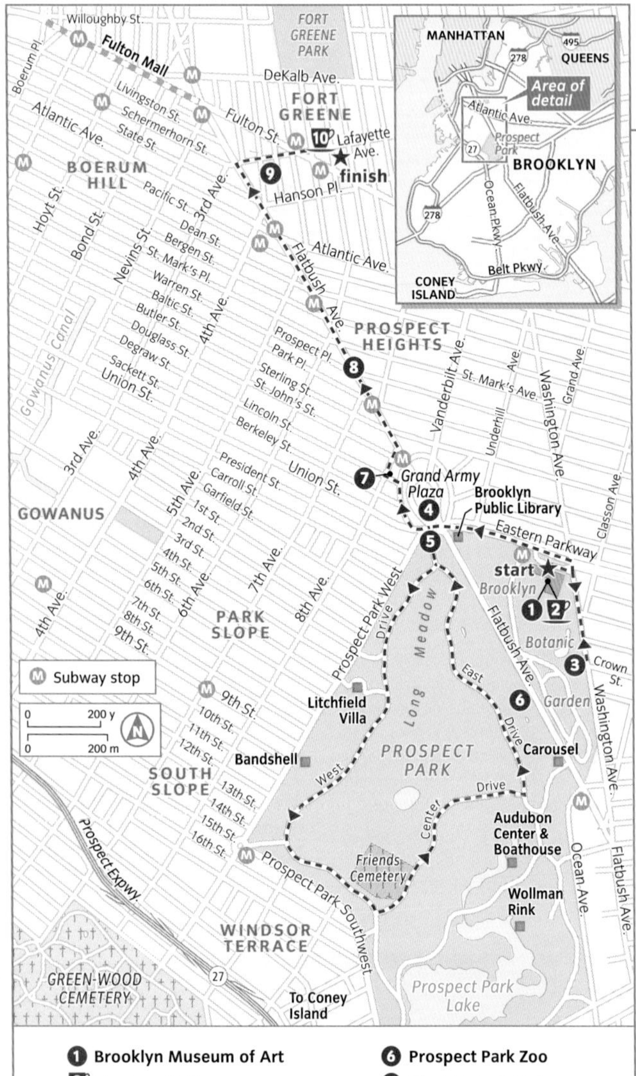

1 Brooklyn Museum of Art
2 Museum Café
3 Brooklyn Botanic Garden
4 Grand Army Plaza
5 Prospect Park
6 Prospect Park Zoo
7 The Montauk Club
8 Flatbush Avenue
9 BAM Rose Cinemas
10 Stonehome Wine Bar

The attractions in and around Prospect Park are well worth the 25-minute subway ride from midtown. Expect gorgeous parkland designed by Frederick Law Olmsted and Calvert Vaux, the city's second largest art museum, plus lovely 19th-century brownstones and hip clothing boutiques. START: **Subway 2 or 3 to Eastern Parkway**

❶ ★★★ kids **Brooklyn Museum of Art.** In any other city, this spectacular museum would be a star attraction, but in New York it's often overlooked because of its location outside Manhattan. The collection in New York's second-largest museum is well worth a trip, however. Highlights include the **Ancient Egyptian collection,** the **Asian art collection** (which specializes in both classic and contemporary works from Japan), and the **Luce Center for American Art** (an "open storage" annex holding 9,000 works, from Tiffany lamps to 19th-century furniture by local artisans). Designed by architects McKim, Mead & White in 1897, the museum received a new front entrance and a dramatic plaza complete with fountains in 2004. *2–3 hr. 200 Eastern Pkwy. (at Washington Ave.). ☎ 718/638-5000. www.brooklynmuseum.org. Admission $8 adults, $4 seniors & students, free for children under 12. Wed–Fri 10am–5pm; Sat–Sun 11am–6pm. Subway: 2/3 to Eastern Pkwy.*

❷ The ground-floor **Museum Café** ($) at the Brooklyn Museum of Art is a good place to refuel before you continue. But if the weather's nice, wait until you get to the Botanic Garden (bullet 3) and eat at the casual outdoor **cafe** ($).

❸ ★★★ **Brooklyn Botanic Garden.** This tranquil, elegant retreat is my favorite garden in the city. It encompasses the **Cranford Rose Garden,** a **Children's Garden,** the **Osborne Garden** (3 acres/1.2 hectares of formal gardens), the **Fragrance Garden** (designed for the visually impaired but appreciated by all), and the **Japanese Hill-and-Pond Garden.** In colder weather you can investigate one of the world's largest collections of bonsai in the **C. V. Starr Bonsai**

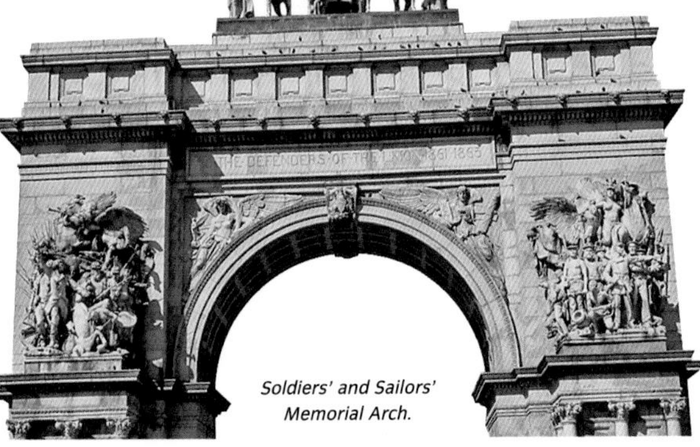

Soldiers' and Sailors' Memorial Arch.

Prospect Park's Boathouse.

Museum, and indoor plants (everything from cacti to orchids) in the **Steinhardt Conservatory.** If you come in April or May, seek out the lush carpet of bluebells and check the website for the timing of the **Cherry Blossom Festival.** ⏱ *1–2 hr. 1000 Washington Ave. (at Eastern Pkwy.). ☎ 718/623-7200. www.bbg.org. Admission $8 adults, $4 seniors & students, free for children under 12. Mar 9–Oct 31 Tues–Fri 8am–6pm, Sat–Sun 10am–6pm; Nov 1–Mar 8 Tues–Fri 8am–4:30pm, Sat–Sun 10am–4:30pm.*

4 Grand Army Plaza. This multilane traffic circle and the tremendous **Soldiers' and Sailors' Memorial Arch** presiding over it are reminiscent of Paris' Place Charles de Gaulle and the Arc de Triomphe. The arch was built in 1892 to honor Union soldiers who died in the Civil War. *Within Plaza St. at the intersection of Flatbush Ave., Prospect Park W., Eastern Pkwy., and Vanderbilt Ave.*

5 ★★★ kids Prospect Park. Central Park designers Frederick Law Olmsted and Calvert Vaux considered Prospect Park to be their masterpiece. The park has 562 acres (225 hectares) of woodland, including Brooklyn's last remaining virgin forest, plus meadows, bluffs, and ponds. For the best views, enter at Grand Army Plaza and walk to your right either on the park's ring road (called West Dr. here) or on the parallel pedestrian path to Meadowport Arch, and proceed to **Long Meadow.** Overlooking Long Meadow is **Litchfield Villa,** an 1857 mansion that became the headquarters for the New York Parks system. Eventually West Drive turns into Center Drive, which will take you past the **Friends' Cemetery** Quaker burial ground. Center Drive leads to East Drive, which on its way back to Grand Army Plaza, passes the 1906 Beaux Arts **boathouse;** the 1912 **carousel;** the zoo; and **Lefferts Homestead Children's Historic House Museum** (☎ 718/789-2822), a 1783 Dutch farmhouse with a museum of period furniture and exhibits. *Bounded by Prospect Park W., Parkside Ave. & Flatbush Ave. ☎ 718/965-8951. www.prospectpark.org.*

6 ★ kids Prospect Park Zoo. Families won't want to miss the zoo at the eastern end of the park. Children in particular take delight in encountering the animals up close, including wallabies and prairie dogs. ⏱ *1 hr. ☎ 718/399-7339. http://ny*

A detail from the Montauk Club.

Park Slope's brownstones

zoosandaquarium.com/ppz. Admission $8 adults, $4 seniors, $3 children 3–12. Mon–Fri 10am–5pm; Sat–Sun 10am–5:30pm (till 4:30 in fall/winter).

7 ★ **The Montauk Club.** The northwestern side of Prospect Park is home to the upscale neighborhood of Park Slope, and its tree-lined streets are a great place to spend an afternoon. Many of the late-19th-century brownstones have been lovingly restored (walk along Montgomery Place between Eighth Ave. and Prospect Park W. to see what I mean). If there were an award for most stunning building, it would go to the **Montauk Club,** which was designed in 1891 by architect Francis H. Kimball to resemble a Venetian palace. It's a private club, but hosts many public events throughout the year. *25 Eighth Ave. (at Lincoln Place). ☎ 718/638-0800.*

8 ★ **Flatbush Avenue.** Shops on Flatbush range from fast-food dives to high-fashion boutiques with prices significantly lower than in Manhattan. **Hooti Couture** at no. 321 *(corner of Seventh Ave.; ☎ 718/857-1977)* sells high-quality vintage clothing and accessories, and is one of my favorite places to shop. **Nouveau Décor** at no. 333 *(btwn. Sterling Ave. & Park Place; ☎ 718/230-0310)* sells elegant furnishings with an exotic twist; most of the pieces are American-made. Both international and local clothing designers are on show at **Redberi** at no. 339 *(btwn. Sterling Ave. & Park Place; ☎ 718/622-1964),* making it a great source for unique pieces.

9 **BAM Rose Cinemas.** When this movie theater opened in the Brooklyn Academy of Music (BAM) in 1998 near Fort Green, its art-house movies brought a much-needed cultural boost to the neighborhood. And it couldn't be more accessible: You can catch the 2/3/4/5/B/D/N/R/Q subway lines back to Manhattan at the Atlantic Avenue station, a couple blocks south of BAM on Flatbush Avenue. *Peter Jay Sharp Bldg., 30 Lafayette Ave. (btwn. Ashland Place & St. Felix St.). ☎ 718/636-4100. $$.*

10 **Stonehome Wine Bar** (*87 Lafayette Ave.; ☎ 718/624-9443; http://stonehomewinebar.com; $$–$$$*) is a great place to stop in for drinks or dinner before or after a show at BAM; an outdoor patio is pleasant on a summer night. The seasonal menu may feature butternut squash ravioli, braised Berkshire pork shank, or seared sea scallops.

Chinatown & Lower East Side

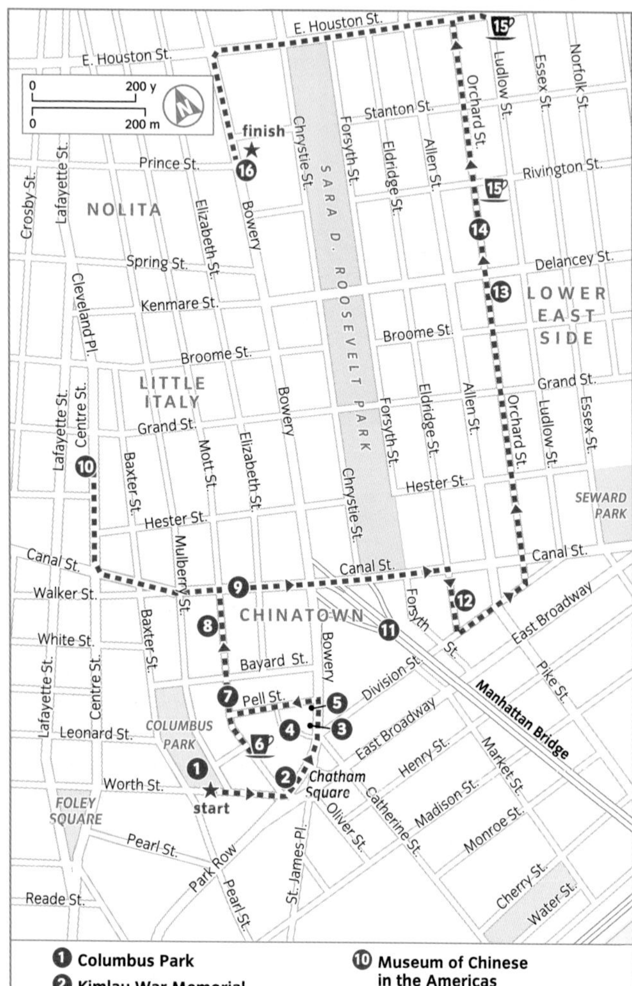

1 Columbus Park
2 Kimlau War Memorial
3 Lin Sister Herb Shop
4 Doyers Street
5 Edward Mooney House
6 Dim sum
7 Mott Street
8 Ten Ren Tea & Ginseng Co.
9 Canal Street
10 Museum of Chinese in the Americas
11 Manhattan Bridge
12 Eldridge Street Synagogue
13 Lower East Side Tenement Museum
14 Orchard Street
15 Katz's Delicatessen
15 Teany Café
16 New Museum

Long known for its vibrant street life, the Lower East Side was also home to notorious slums (including Five Points) where Irish, Italian, Jewish, and Chinese immigrants crowded into tenements. Although much survives from that era—including a number of tenement buildings—today the neighborhood buzzes with the energy of new restaurants, bars, and live-music clubs. START: **Subway 4, 5, or 6 to Brooklyn Bridge/City Hall**

❶ ★ **Columbus Park.** This park lies where New York's worst slum, known as Mulberry Bend, once stood surrounded by tenements with names such as Bone Alley, Kerosene Row, and Bandits' Roost. Most of the houses were torn down in the early 20th century. The exception was the Chinatown section, which was left alone out of racist fears that the Chinese would move into other neighborhoods. *Bounded by Mosco, Mulberry, Bayard, and Baxter sts. Subway: 4/5/6 to Brooklyn Bridge/City Hall.*

❷ **Kimlau War Memorial.** This memorial arch in Chatham Square was erected in 1962 to honor the Chinese Americans who gave their lives fighting in World War II. The square also contains an imposing statue of Lin Ze Xu, a 19th-century anti-drug hero in China. *Chatham Sq.*

❸ ★ **Lin Sister Herb Shop.** This three-story apothecary is a marvel. A wall of wooden drawers, each containing medicinal herbs, dominates the first floor. On the upper levels, reflexology massage and acupuncture treatments are offered, and a homeopathic doctor is available for consultations. *4 Bowery. (at Division St.). ☎ 212/962-5417. www.linsisterherb.com.*

❹ **Doyers Street.** As you walk along Bowery, keep an eye out for Doyers Street, a small alleyway. This area was once notorious for activity by gangs known as ***tongs*** (the "activity" was mainly of the violent sort and often involved hatchets, which gave rise to the term "hatchet man"). Doyers Street has a sharp bend in it—locals call it an elbow—which made it impossible to see who was around the corner.

❺ **Edward Mooney House.** This Georgian brick structure, painted red, is the oldest row house in the city, dating from George Washington's New York days. Wealthy merchant Edward Mooney had the house built in 1785 on property abandoned by a Tory during the American Revolution. *18 Bowery (at Pell St.).*

❻ ★★ **Dim sum.** Chinatown is famous for its dim sum palaces, where servers offer choice little delicacies from carts they wheel around the restaurant floor. Great for sharing (and a smart economical choice), these morsels often include *har gow* (shrimp dumplings), pork buns, even chicken feet. Among my favorites: **Ping's** (*22 Mott St.; ☎ 212/602-9988; $*), which has exceptionally fresh seafood, and **Oriental Garden** (*14 Elizabeth St.; ☎ 212/619-0085; $*), a smaller, quieter place with delicious food.

❼ ★ **Mott Street.** This is the heart of old Chinatown, and the epicenter of the boisterous Chinese New Year celebrations that begin with the first full moon after January 21st. But at any time of year it's a great place to wander and shop. Some addresses to note: **Sinotique** at no. 19A for handsome Chinese antiques and decorative home

A Chinatown restaurant window.

furnishings; **Golden Fung Wong Bakery** at no. 41 for fresh-baked egg tarts or a big bag of fortune cookies to take home; and **Madame Design** at no. 38 will make you a traditional Chinese cheongsam out of colorful Chinese silk for a little more than $400.

8 ★ Ten Ren Tea & Ginseng Co. The famous Taiwanese tea maker Ten Ren has a particularly charming outpost on Mott Street. Some of the teapots on display are museum-worthy, and the selection of teas is hard to beat. *75 Mott St. (btwn. Canal & Bayard sts.). ☎ 212/349-2286. www.tenrenusa.com.*

The Museum of Chinese in the Americas.

9 Canal Street. From West Broadway to the Manhattan Bridge, this is one of the city's liveliest and most congested thoroughfares. Stalls hawk everything from "designer" handbags to electronics. **Kam Man,** at no. 200, has a supermarket upstairs (great for candy made in Japan) and a massive collection of ceramics downstairs. Other good bets are **Pearl Paint** (see p. 100), and **195 Dragon Jewelry** at no. 195 for beautifully carved jade.

10 ★★ kids Museum of Chinese in the Americas. It is difficult to comprehend the cruel hardships that the first generations of Chinese suffered in New York. Moving into a brand-new space on Centre Street in fall 2008, this museum documents the history and culture of the Chinese in America from the early 1800s to the present. *⌚ 45 min. 211–215 Centre St. (btwn. Howard & Grand sts.). ☎ 212/619-4785. www.mocanyc.org. Adults $2, seniors & students $1, under 12 free; free Fri. Subway: N/R/Q/W/J/M/Z/6 to Canal St.*

11 ★ Manhattan Bridge. This 1905 suspension bridge may not be as artistically inspired as the Brooklyn Bridge, but the monumental Beaux Arts colonnade and arch at its entrance are quite arresting. *Canal St. & Bowery.*

⑫ ★★ **Eldridge Street Synagogue.** When it was built by Eastern European Jews in 1887, it was the most magnificent synagogue on the Lower East Side. Its congregation included such luminaries as Eddie Cantor, Jonas Salk, and Edward G. Robinson. Over the years, however, membership declined and the structure fell into disrepair. The rickety interior sanctuary was cordoned off in the 1950s, where it remained empty for more than 25 years, suffering termite infestation, staircase collapses, and near-total deterioration of the roof, among other indignities. A $20-million renovation project to restore the synagogue to its former glory celebrated its completion in December 2007. Designed by the Herter Brothers, specialists in tenements, the landmark structure is largely enveloped in the daily hustle and bustle of Chinatown life, but its terra-cotta-and-brick Moorish facade still boldly stands out, and the interior decor includes delicate stained-glass rose windows. *20 min. 12 Eldridge St. (btwn. Canal & Division sts.). ☎ 212/219-0888. www.eldridgestreet.org. Guided tours available Sun–Thurs 10am–4pm. Tour tickets $10 adults, $8 seniors & students; $6 children 5–18, free children under 5. Subway: B/D to Grand St.; 6/N/R to Canal St.*

Eldridge Street Synagogue.

Ten Ren Tea on Mott St.

⑬ ★★★ kids **Lower East Side Tenement Museum.** Conceived as a monument to the experience of "urban pioneers" in America, this don't-miss museum documents the lives of immigrant residents in a six-story tenement built in 1863 at 97 Orchard St. (accessible only via the highly recommended guided tours). The tenement rooms are eerily authentic, and for good reason: 97 Orchard was essentially boarded up from 1935 to 1987; when it was finally opened, everything was exactly as it had been left in 1935, a virtual time capsule of tenement life. Artifacts found range from the mundane (medicine tins and Russian cigarettes) to the personal (a 1922 Ouija board and an infant's button-up shoe). Among several tours to choose from, "Getting By" is an account of the backbreaking, hard-scrabble life that many immigrants faced in the late 19th and early 20th centuries. Another, "Piecing It Together," explains how crucial the garment trade was to many new arrivals. Book your visit online at least a week in advance—this is one of New York's most popular museums. *1–1½ hr. Visitors' Center at 90 Orchard St. (Delancey St.). ☎ 212/431-0233. www.tenement.org. Tours $17 adults, $13 seniors & students. Tues–Fri 1–5pm; Sat–Sun 11am–4:45pm. Subway: B/D to Grand St.; F to Delancey.*

14 Orchard Street. In the 19th century, this street was a vast outdoor marketplace lined with rows of pushcarts. Today, stores have replaced the pushcarts, but in the spirit of tradition, many shop owners are willing to haggle over prices. You can also discover the stylish little boutiques and cafes that have sprung up in the neighborhood. It's a brand-new melting pot. On Sundays the street is closed to vehicular traffic between Delancey and Houston streets. Keep in mind that many of the shops are closed Friday afternoon and Saturday for the Jewish Sabbath. Check out stores between Rivington and Grand streets such as: **Harry Zarin** *(318 Grand; ☎ 212/925-6112; www.harryzarin. com)*, for great fabrics and trims; **Frock** *(148 Orchard St.; ☎ 212/594-5380)*, for vintage designer clothing; **Altman Luggage** *(135 Orchard St.; ☎ 212/254-7275)*, which has been selling quality luggage at great prices since 1920; and **Guss' Pickles** *(85 Orchard St.; ☎ 800/252-GUSS)*, which moved to this site 6 years ago after spending 25 years on Essex Street. Guss' Pickles has been a fixture on the Lower East Side since 1920, when Izzy Guss peddled his wares with a pushcart. Can't decide which pickle to purchase? "Full sour" is the most popular pickle by far.

15 Meat eaters should make a beeline for the Dagwood-style pastrami sandwiches at **Katz's Delicatessen** *(205 E. Houston St., at Ludlow St.; ☎ 212/254-2246)*. Vegetarians can make their way to musician Moby's **Teany Cafe** *(90 Rivington St., btwn. Ludlow & Orchard sts.; ☎ 212/475-9190; $)* for soups, salads, sandwiches, and teas.

16 The New Museum. This 30 year-old showcase for contemporary art lives up to its name in these spanking new digs—an off-kilter stack of aluminum mesh cubes, designed by Kazuyo Sejima and Ryue Nishizawa, teetering over the Bowery's brick tenements since 2007. Don't miss the view of the neighborhood from the 7th-floor observation deck, open to the public on weekends. *1½ hrs. 235 Bowery (at Prince btw. Stanton and Rivington sts.). ☎ 212/219-1222. www.newmuseum.org. Open Wed, Sat, Sun noon–6pm, Thurs–Fri noon–10pm. Admission $12, $8 seniors, $6 students; under 18 free; free to all Thurs 7–10pm. Metro: 6 to Spring, N/R to Prince.*

Orchard Street is usually jammed with shoppers every day but Saturday.

5 The Best **Shopping**

Shopping **Best Bets**

Best **Designer Clothing Discounts**
★★★ Century 21 *22 Cortlandt St.* *(p 95)*

Best **Food Store**
★★ Dean & DeLuca *560 Broadway* *(p 98)*

Best **Place to Deck Out Your Dream House**
★★★ ABC Carpet & Home *881 & 888 Broadway* *(p 98)*

Best **Footwear**
★★ Jeffrey New York *449 W. 14th St.* *(p 96)*

Best **All-Around Department Store**
★★ Barneys *660 Madison Ave.* *(p 95)*

Best **Browsing**
★★ Takashimaya *693 Fifth Ave.* *(p 96)*

Best **for Kids**
★★ FAO Schwarz *767 Fifth Ave.* *(p 100)*; and Kid O *123 W. 10th St.* *(p 100)*

Best **Men's Designer Clothes**
★★ Bergdorf Goodman for Men *645 Fifth Ave.* *(p 95)*

Best **Women's Designer Clothes**
★ Searle *156 Fifth Ave.* *(p 97)*

Best **Vintage Jewelry**
★ Pippin *72 Orchard St.* *(p 99)*

Best **Wine & Liquor**
★ Sherry-Lehmann *679 Madison Ave.* *(p 98)*

Best **Deals on Electronics**
J&R Music & Computer World *23 Park Row* *(p 96)*

Best **Stationery**
Kate's Paperie *561 Broadway* *(p 100)*

Best **Art Supplies**
★ Pearl Paint *308 Canal St.* *(p 100)*

Best **Beauty Products**
★★ C.O. Bigelow's *414 Sixth Ave.* *(p 94)*

Tip

New York City sales tax is 8.375%, but it is not added to clothing and footwear items under $110. If you're visiting from out of state, consider having your purchases shipped directly home to avoid paying sales tax. As with any shipped purchase, be sure to get proper documentation of the sale and keep those receipts handy until the merchandise arrives at your door.

Previous page: A window display at Bergdorf Goodman.

Downtown Shopping

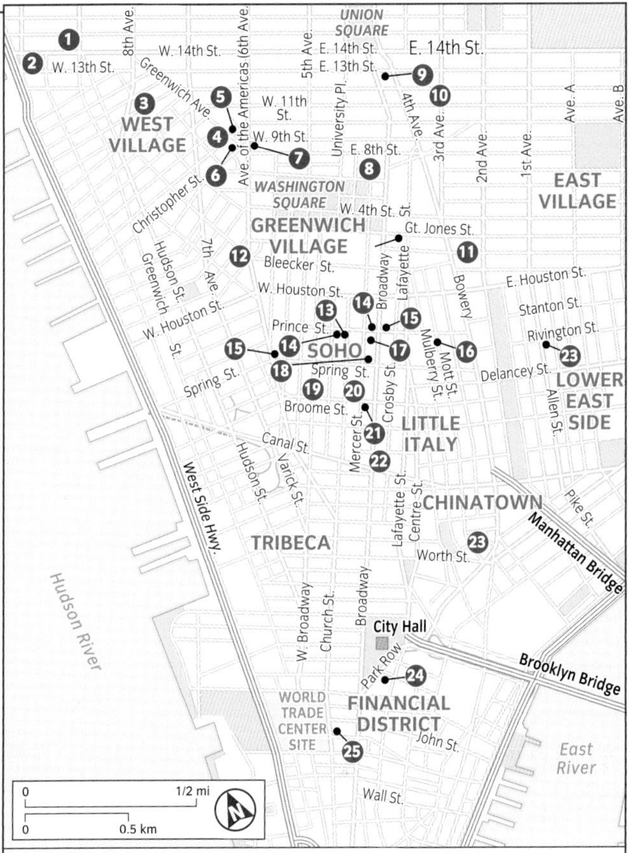

Aedes De Venustas 6
Agent Provocateur 20
Anthropologie 19
Bleecker St. Records 12
Broadway Panhandler 8
C. O. Bigelow 7
Century 21 25
Dean & DeLuca 15
Fragments 13
J&R Music & Computer World 24
Jeffrey New York 1
John Derian Company 11
Kate's Paperie 18
Kid O 5
Kiehl's 10
Le Fanion 3
Pearl Paint 22
Pearl River 21
Prada 14
Scoop 2
Sigerson Morrison 16
Sinotique 23
Space NK 17
The Strand 9
Three Lives & Co. 4

Midtown & Uptown Shopping

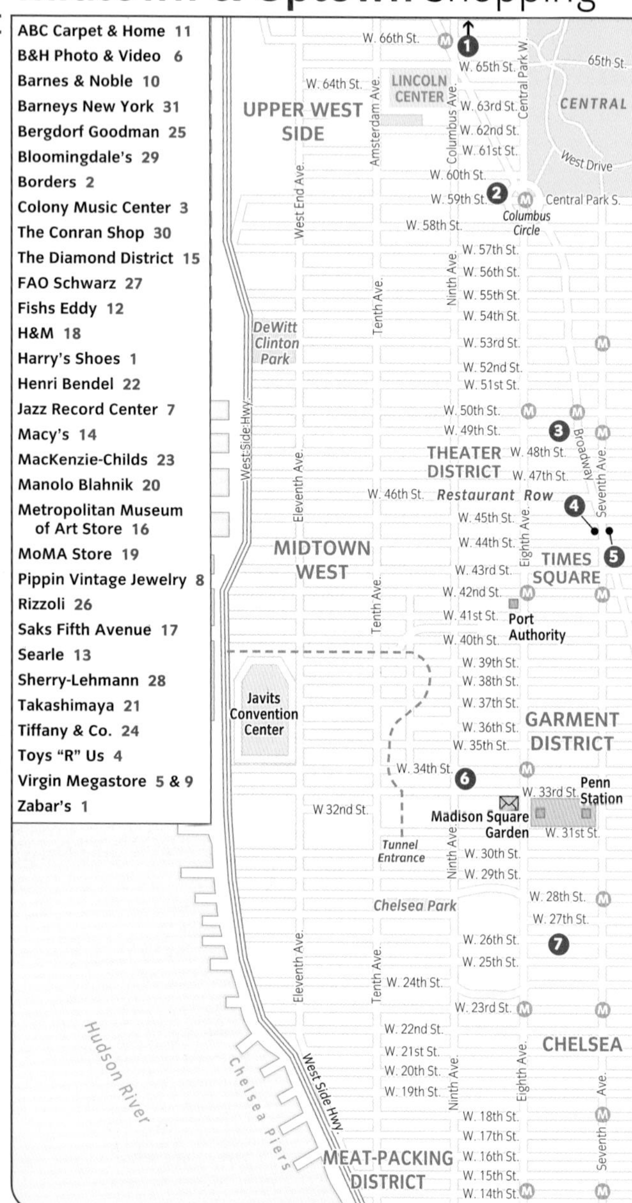
ABC Carpet & Home 11
B&H Photo & Video 6
Barnes & Noble 10
Barneys New York 31
Bergdorf Goodman 25
Bloomingdale's 29
Borders 2
Colony Music Center 3
The Conran Shop 30
The Diamond District 15
FAO Schwarz 27
Fishs Eddy 12
H&M 18
Harry's Shoes 1
Henri Bendel 22
Jazz Record Center 7
Macy's 14
MacKenzie-Childs 23
Manolo Blahnik 20
Metropolitan Museum of Art Store 16
MoMA Store 19
Pippin Vintage Jewelry 8
Rizzoli 26
Saks Fifth Avenue 17
Searle 13
Sherry-Lehmann 28
Takashimaya 21
Tiffany & Co. 24
Toys "R" Us 4
Virgin Megastore 5 & 9
Zabar's 1
UPPER WEST SIDE
LINCOLN CENTER
CENTRAL
West Drive
Columbus Circle
Central Park S.
DeWitt Clinton Park
THEATER DISTRICT
Restaurant Row
MIDTOWN WEST
TIMES SQUARE
Port Authority
Javits Convention Center
GARMENT DISTRICT
Penn Station
Madison Square Garden
Tunnel Entrance
Chelsea Park
CHELSEA
MEAT-PACKING DISTRICT
Hudson River
Chelsea Piers
West Side Hwy.
West End Ave.
Amsterdam Ave.
Columbus Ave.
Central Park W.
Eleventh Ave.
Tenth Ave.
Ninth Ave.
Eighth Ave.
Broadway
Seventh Ave.
W. 66th St.
W. 65th St.
65th St.
W. 64th St.
W. 63rd St.
W. 62nd St.
W. 61st St.
W. 60th St.
W. 59th St.
W. 58th St.
W. 57th St.
W. 56th St.
W. 55th St.
W. 54th St.
W. 53rd St.
W. 52nd St.
W. 51st St.
W. 50th St.
W. 49th St.
W. 48th St.
W. 47th St.
W. 46th St.
W. 45th St.
W. 44th St.
W. 43rd St.
W. 42nd St.
W. 41st St.
W. 40th St.
W. 39th St.
W. 38th St.
W. 37th St.
W. 36th St.
W. 35th St.
W. 34th St.
W. 33rd St.
W 32nd St.
W. 31st St.
W. 30th St.
W. 29th St.
W. 28th St.
W. 27th St.
W. 26th St.
W. 25th St.
W. 24th St.
W. 23rd St.
W. 22nd St.
W. 21st St.
W. 20th St.
W. 19th St.
W. 18th St.
W. 17th St.
W. 16th St.
W. 15th St.
W. 14th St.

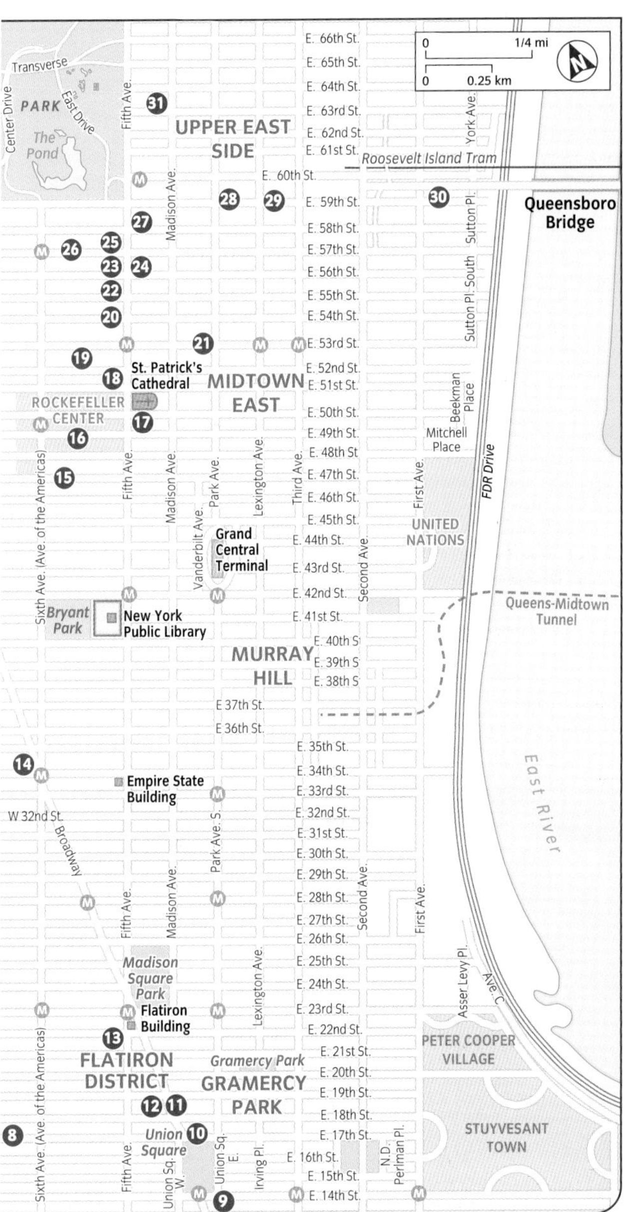

0 1/4 mi
0 0.25 km
PARK
Transverse
East Drive
Center Drive
The Pond
UPPER EAST SIDE
MIDTOWN EAST
MURRAY HILL
FLATIRON DISTRICT
GRAMERCY PARK
Gramercy Park
ROCKEFELLER CENTER
St. Patrick's Cathedral
Grand Central Terminal
New York Public Library
Bryant Park
Empire State Building
Madison Square Park
Flatiron Building
Union Square
UNITED NATIONS
PETER COOPER VILLAGE
STUYVESANT TOWN
Queensboro Bridge
Roosevelt Island Tram
Queens-Midtown Tunnel
FDR Drive
East River
Mitchell Place
Beekman Place
Sutton Pl.
Sutton Pl. South
York Ave.
First Ave.
Second Ave.
Third Ave.
Lexington Ave.
Park Ave.
Park Ave. S.
Vanderbilt Ave.
Madison Ave.
Fifth Ave.
Sixth Ave. (Ave. of the Americas)
Broadway
W 32nd St.
Irving Pl.
Union Sq. E.
Union Sq. W.
N.D. Perlman Pl.
Asser Levy Pl.
Ave. C
E. 66th St.
E. 65th St.
E. 64th St.
E. 63rd St.
E. 62nd St.
E. 61st St.
E. 60th St.
E. 59th St.
E. 58th St.
E. 57th St.
E. 56th St.
E. 55th St.
E. 54th St.
E. 53rd St.
E. 52nd St.
E. 51st St.
E. 50th St.
E. 49th St.
E. 48th St
E. 47th St.
E. 46th St.
E. 45th St.
E. 44th St.
E. 43rd St.
E. 42nd St.
E. 41st St.
E. 40th St
E. 39th St
E. 38th St
E 37th St.
E 36th St.
E. 35th St.
E. 34th St.
E. 33rd St.
E. 32nd St.
E. 31st St.
E. 30th St.
E. 29th St.
E. 28th St.
E. 27th St.
E. 26th St.
E. 25th St.
E. 24th St.
E. 23rd St.
E. 22nd St.
E. 21st St.
E. 20th St.
E. 19th St.
E. 18th St.
E. 17th St.
E. 16th St.
E. 15th St.
E. 14th St.
8
9
10
11
12
13
14
15
16
17
18
19
20
21
22
23
24
25
26
27
28
29
30
31

New York **Shopping A to Z**

Beauty/Apothecary

★★ **C. O. Bigelow** GREENWICH VILLAGE This 162-year-old apothecary carries an eclectic but solid collection of personal care products, including its own excellent house label (the quality is high but prices are reasonable). Its motto, "If you can't get it anywhere else, try Bigelow's," is right on the money. *414 Sixth Ave. (btwn. 8th & 9th sts.). ☎ 212/533-2700. www.bigelowchemists.com. AE, DISC, MC, V. Subway: A/C/E/F/V to W. 4th St. Map p 91.*

★ **Kiehl's** EAST VILLAGE This 150-year-old family-run apothecary developed its own line of beauty products over the years and drew a cultish following among the fashion crowd. The free product samples added to its quirky charm. And yes, it's now owned by L'Oreal, and the samples have shrunk. *109 Third Ave. (btwn. 13th & 14th sts). ☎ 212/677-3171. www.kiehls.com. AE, DC, MC, V. Subway: 4/5/6 to Union Sq. Map p 91.*

★★ **Space NK** SOHO This new British-based shop has culled the best of the best product lines and put them all in a soothing environment. *99 Greene St. (btwn. Prince & Spring sts.). ☎ 212/941-4200. www.spacenk.com. AE, DISC, MC, V. Subway: N/R to Prince St or 6 to Spring St. Map p 91.*

Books

★★ **Barnes & Noble** UNION SQUARE This is one of the chain's biggest and best stores for browsing. *33 E. 17th St. (Broadway). ☎ 212/253-0810. www.bn.com. AE, DC, DISC, MC, V. Subway: 4/5/6 to Union Sq. Map p 92.*

★★ **Borders** COLUMBUS CIRCLE This well-organized shop is a joy to spend time in. *10 Columbus Circle (at W. 59th St. and Central Park West). ☎ 212/823-9775. www.bordersstores.com. AE, DC, DISC, MC, V. Subway: 1/2/3/9/A/B/C/D to 59 St./Columbus Circle. Map p 92.*

Tableware at Fishs Eddy.

★★ **Rizzoli** MIDTOWN WEST This clubby Italian bookstore is the place to browse for visual art and design books, plus quality fiction and gourmet cookbooks. *31 W. 57th St. (btwn. Fifth & Sixth aves.). ☎ 212/759-2424. www.rizzoliusa.com. AE, MC, V. Subway: N/R to Fifth Ave. Map p 92.*

★★ **The Strand** UNION SQUARE AREA This local legend is worth a visit for the staggering "18 miles of books" and bargain titles at up to 85% off list price. *828 Broadway (at 12th St.). ☎ 212/473-1452. www.strandbooks.com. AE, DC, DISC, MC, V. Subway: L/N/R/4/5/6 to Union Sq. Map p 91.*

★★ **Three Lives & Co.** GREENWICH VILLAGE This cozy, independent store has good stock and a knowledgeable staff. *154 W. 10th St. (near Seventh ave.). ☎ 212/741-2069. http://threelives.com. AE, DC, MC, V. Subway: 1 to Christopher St. Map p 91.*

Collectibles

Fishs Eddy UNION SQUARE AREA Come here for vintage and reproduction dishes, flatware, and glasses. *889 Broadway (at 19th St.). ☎ 212/420-9020. www.fishseddy.com. AE, MC, V. Subway: L/N/R/4/5/6 to 14th St./Union Sq. Map p 92.*

★ **Sinotique** CHINATOWN Handsome exotic furniture, wall coverings, carvings, and statues—all imported from Asia, and all antique originals. *19A Mott St. (btwn. Mosco St. & Bowery). ☎ 212/587-2393. www.sinotique.com. MC, V. Subway: J/M/Z/6 to Canal St. Map p 91.*

Department Stores

★ **Barneys New York** MIDTOWN EAST This smart-looking store is always on the cutting edge of fashion; check out the Co-op for less pricey designers and solid house brands. *660 Madison Ave. (at 61st St.). ☎ 212/826-8900. www.barneys.com. Subway: N/R to Fifth Ave. Map p 92.*

★★ **Bergdorf Goodman** MIDTOWN The place for ladies who lunch and anyone who reveres couture and clothes built to last. It's pricey, but the sales are terrific. The men's store across the street (745 Fifth Ave.) has a great selection. *754 Fifth Ave. (at 57th St.). ☎ 212/753-7300. www.bergdorfgoodman.com. AE, DC, MC, V. Subway: E/F to Fifth Ave. Map p 92.*

★★ **Bloomingdale's** MIDTOWN EAST Packed to the gills with goods, Bloomie's is more accessible and affordable than Barneys, Bergdorf, or Saks. *1000 Third Ave. (Lexington Ave. at 59th St.). ☎ 212/705-2000. www. bloomingdales.com. AE, MC, V. Subway: 4/5/6 to 59th St. Map p 92.*

★ **Century 21** FINANCIAL DISTRICT It's easy to become addicted to the seriously discounted designer clothes, but expect crowds—and don't expect to be pampered with service or flattering lighting. *22 Cortlandt St. (btwn. Broadway & Church St.). ☎ 212/227-9092. www.c21stores.com. AE, MC, V. Subway: 1/2/3/4/5/M to Fulton St.; A/C to Broadway/Nassau St.; E to Chambers St. Map p 91.*

★ **Henri Bendel** MIDTOWN Set inside a gorgeous landmark building, this is the place for grown-up girls who love the funky and the frilly. The makeup section is one of the best in the city. *712 Fifth Ave. (btwn. 55th & 56th sts.). ☎ 212/247-1100. www.henribendel.com. AE, DC, DISC, MC, V. Subway: N/R to Fifth Ave. Map p 92.*

Macy's HERALD SQUARE The size is unmanageable and the service is clueless, but they do sell *everything*.

And *everything* goes on sale. This is where to come to get a seriously stylish—and seriously marked-down—winter coat in the January sales. *At Herald Sq., W. 34th St. & Broadway. ☎ 212/695-4400. www.macys.com. AE, MC, V. Subway: B/D/F/N/Q/R/1/2/3/9 to 34th St. Map p 92.*

★ Saks Fifth Avenue MIDTOWN This legendary flagship store is a classic. It stocks big-name designers in fashion, accessories, and cosmetics, all with price tags to match. Look for smartly priced house brands on the 4th and 5th floors. *611 Fifth Ave. (btwn. 49th & 50th sts.). ☎ 212/753-4000. www.saksfifthavenue.com. AE, DC, DISC, MC, V. Subway: B/D/F/Q to 47th-50th sts./Rockefeller Center; E/F to Fifth Ave. Map p 92.*

★★ Takashimaya MIDTOWN This serene, elegant outpost of Japan's most famous department store chain is a charmer, with serendipitous finds on every floor. *693 Fifth Ave. (btwn. 54th & 55th sts.). ☎ 212/350-0100. www.ny-takashimaya.com. AE, DC, MC, V. Subway: E/F to Fifth Ave. Map p 92.*

Electronics

★ B&H Photo & Video GARMENT DISTRICT This camera superstore has everything from lenses to darkroom equipment. ***Note:*** It's closed on Saturdays. *420 Ninth Ave. (at 34th St.). ☎ 800/606-6969. www.bhphotovideo.com. AE, DISC, MC, V. Subway: A/C/E to 34th St. Map p 92.*

★ J&R Music & Computer World FINANCIAL DISTRICT This is the city's top computer, electronics, small appliance, and office equipment retailer. *23 Park Row (at Ann St., opposite City Hall Park). ☎ 800/806-1115 or 212/238-9000. www.jr.com. AE, DISC, MC, V. Subway: 2/3 to Park Place; 4/5/6 to Brooklyn Bridge/City Hall. Map p 91.*

Fashion (Men & Women)

★ H&M MIDTOWN The Swedish super-discounter has *très* chic men's and women's clothing, and the prices are low, low, low. *640 Fifth Ave. (at 51st St.). ☎ 212/489-0390. www.hm.com. AE, MC, V. Subway: E/F to Fifth Ave. Map p 92.*

★★ Jeffrey New York MEAT-PACKING DISTRICT This outpost of the famed Atlanta megaboutique may be pricey as hell, but it's very accessible and the staff is warm and friendly. The fantastic shoe selection makes it a worthy schlep for style hounds. *449 W. 14th St. (10th Ave.). ☎ 212/206-1272. www.jeffrey*

Bergdorf Goodman's holiday window displays are legendarily creative.

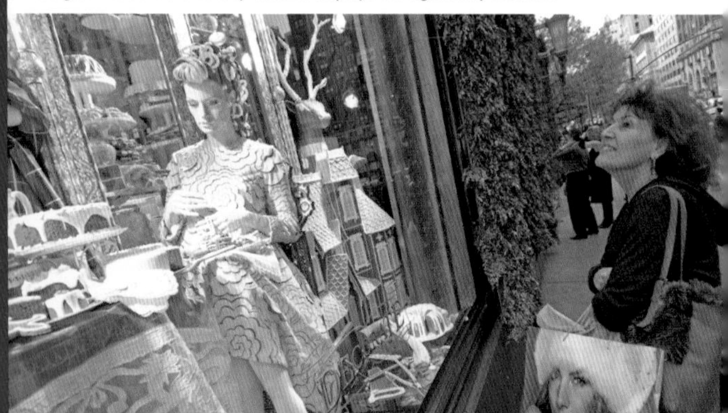

newyork.com. AE, MC, V. Subway: A/C/E/L to 14th St. Map p 91.

★ **Prada** SOHO The sleek, chic Italian trendsetter occupies a spectacular space designed by architect Rem Koolhaas. *575 Broadway (Prince St.). ☎ 212/334-8888. AE, DISC, MC, V. Subway: N/R to Prince St. Map p 91.*

★ **Scoop** MEAT-PACKING DISTRICT Ever wonder what a fashion editor's closet looks like? This small chain is it: a collection of pieces from a variety of designers whose work is fashion-forward but not so cutting edge as to be unwearable. *873 Washington St. (btwn. 13th & 14th sts.). ☎ 212/929-1244. www.scoopnyc.com. Check website for other store locations. AE, DC, DISC, MC, V. Subway: A/C/E to 14th St. Map p 91.*

Fashion (Women)

★ **Agent Provocateur** SOHO This outpost of the British fantasy lingerie emporium is a must-see. The line runs the gamut from the PVC-and-steel "Dita" playsuit to the sophisticated and romantic "Yasmine" undies. *133 Mercer St. (btwn. Prince & Spring sts.). ☎ 212/965-0229. www.agentprovocateur.com. AE, MC, V. Subway: R/W to Prince St. Map p 91.*

Anthropologie SOHO This chain sells funky, slightly exotic, and affordable clothing and accessories—not to mention some original and very stylish housewares and gifts. *375 W. Broadway (btwn. Spring & Broome sts.). ☎ 212/343-7070. www.anthropologie.com. AE, MC, V. Subway: C/E to Spring St. Map p 91.*

★★ **Searle** FLATIRON DISTRICT This small chain always has an impeccable collection of beautiful clothes, with very good end-of-season sales. *156 Fifth Ave. (at 21st sts.). ☎ 212/924-4330. www.searlenyc.com. AE, DISC, MC, V. Check website for other locations. Subway: N/R to 23rd St. Map p 92.*

A window display at Henri Bendel.

Gifts

★★ **John Derian Company** EAST VILLAGE Fabulous decoupage items, colorful candleholders handmade in Paris, and terracotta pottery are but a few of the delicious treats here. *6 E 2nd St. (btwn. Second Ave. & the Bowery). ☎ 212/677-3917. www.johnderian.com. AE, MC, V. Subway: 6 to Bleecker St., F/V to Second Ave. Map p 91.*

★★ **Le Fanion** GREENWICH VILLAGE Beautiful French Country pottery in a charming Village shop. *299 W. Fourth St. (at Bank St.) ☎ 212/463-8760. www.lefanion.com. AE, MC, V. Subway: 1/9/2/3 at 14th St. Map p 91.*

★ **MacKenzie-Childs** MIDTOWN Whimsy in a teacup. Colorful, artisanal dinnerware, hand-painted furniture, and home furnishings in a delightful store. *14 W. 57th St. (at Fifth Ave.) ☎ 212/570-5070. www.mackenzie-childs.com. AE, MC, V. Subway: N/R to Fifth Ave. Map p 92.*

Jeffrey in Chelsea.

★★ Metropolitan Museum of Art Store UPPER EAST SIDE Great for reproduction jewelry, china, books, toys, textiles, and objets d'art from the Met's collection. *Rockefeller Center, 15 W. 49th St. ☎ 212/332-1360. www.metmuseum.org/store. AE, DISC, MC, V. Subway: B/D/F/V to 47th-50th sts./Rockefeller Center. Map p 92.*

★★ MOMA Store MIDTOWN Fabulous, unique gifts, from silk scarves with Frank Lloyd Wright designs to Eames chairs. The Christmas ornaments are gorgeous. *44 W. 53rd St. ☎ 212/767-1050. www.momastore.org. AE, DISC, MC, V. Subway: E/V to Fifth Ave/53rd St. Map p 92.*

★ Pearl River SOHO I love browsing this store, stocked with Asian clothing, housewares, foods, and gifts. *477 Broadway (Grand St.). ☎ 212/431-4770. www.pearlriver.com. AE, DISC, MC, V. Subway: N/R to Canal St. Map p 91.*

Home Design & Housewares

★★★ ABC Carpet & Home UNION SQUARE AREA This magical two-building emporium is legendary, and it deserves to be: It's the ultimate home fashions and furnishings store, with everything from zillion-thread-count sheets to magical children's furniture. *881 & 888 Broadway (at 19th St.). ☎ 212/473-3000. www.abchome.com. AE, DISC, MC, V. Subway: L/N/R/4/5/6 to 14th St./Union Sq. Map p 92.*

★ Broadway Panhandler GREENWICH VILLAGE Cooks will love browsing for professional-quality cookware in this longtime favorite, now in its new location. *65 E. Eighth St. (btwn. Broadway and University Ave.). ☎ 866/266-5927. www.broadwaypanhandler.com. AE, MC, V. Subway: N/R to 8th St. Map p 91.*

★ The Conran Shop MIDTOWN EAST Goods here have sleek, contemporary lines, lightweight materials (chrome, blond woods, colorful plastic), and delicious twists on standard household goods. *407 E. 59th St. (at First Ave. under the 59th St. Bridge). ☎ 212/755-9079. www.conranusa.com. AE, DC, MC, V. Subway: 4/5/6 to 59th St. Map p 92.*

Gourmet Food & Wine

★★ Dean & DeLuca SOHO This place has everything—from excellent cheese, meat, fish, and dessert counters to fresh sushi and luscious prepared foods. *560 Broadway (at Prince St.). ☎ 212/226-6800. www.deandeluca.com. AE, DISC, MC, V. Subway: N/R to Prince St. Map p 91.*

★ Sherry-Lehmann UPPER EAST SIDE One of the city's best selections of wine has moved to a new three-story store on Park Avenue after 60 years on Madison Avenue—but it still has the same savvy staff. *505 Park Ave. (btwn. 59th and 60th sts.). ☎ 212/838-7500. www.sherry-lehmann.com. AE, MC, V. Subway: N/R to Lexington Ave.; 4/5/6 to 59th St. Map p 92.*

★★ Zabar's UPPER WEST SIDE The one-and-only Zabar's is the place to go for great smoked salmon and all the works—not to mention terrific prepared foods, gourmet edibles, coffees, cheeses, you name it. *2245 Broadway (at 80th St.). ☎ 212-496-1234. www.zabars.com. AE, DC, MC, V. Subway: 1/9 to 79th St. Map p 92.*

Jewelry & Precious Stones

The Diamond District MIDTOWN This is the heart of the city's diamond trade, though many of the merchants deal in semi-precious stones, too. If you know your four C's, it's a great place to get a deal on diamonds; if you don't, stick with window-shopping. Most shops are open Monday to Friday only. *47th St. (btwn. Fifth & Sixth aves.). Subway: B/D/F/V to Rockefeller Center. Map p 92.*

★ **Fragments** SOHO Looking for original pieces? Fragments sells jewelry by more than 100 artists working in various mediums. Prices vary dramatically, starting at $50 and spiking above $20,000. *116 Prince St. (btwn. Greene & Wooster sts.). ☎ 212/334-9588. www.zabars.com. AE, DC, DISC, MC, V. Subway: C/E to Spring St. Map p 91.*

★ **Pippin Vintage Jewelry** CHELSEA From stately pearls to funky Bakelite, this gem of a shop carries it all. The news is that Pippin has moved from the Lower East Side to Chelsea and opened **Pippin Home,** a small shop selling antiques and home furnishings, behind the jewelry store. *112 W. 17th St. (btwn. Sixth & Seventh aves.). ☎ 212/505-5159. AE, MC, V. Subway: A/E to 14th St. Map p 92.*

★★ **Tiffany & Co.** MIDTOWN Deservedly famous, this iconic multi-level store carries jewelry, watches, tableware and stemware, and a variety of gift items. Love the silver yo-yo! *727 Fifth Ave. (57th St.). ☎ 212/755-8000. www.tiffany.com. AE, DC, DISC, MC, V. Subway: N/R to Fifth Ave. Map p 92.*

Music & Video

★ **Bleecker St. Records** GREENWICH VILLAGE The well-organized CD and LP collections include rock, jazz, folk, blues, and punk. *239 Bleecker St. (Carmine St.). ☎ 212/255-7899. AE, MC, V. Subway: A/C/E/F/V to W. 4th St. Map p 91.*

Colony Music Center TIMES SQUARE This nostalgia emporium is filled with a pricey but excellent collection of vintage vinyl and new CDs (sheet music and theater posters, too). *1619 Broadway (49th St.). ☎ 212/265-2050. www.colonymusic.com. AE, DISC, MC, V. Subway: N/R to 49th St.; 1/9 to 50th St. Map p 92.*

★ **Jazz Record Center** CHELSEA This is the place to find rare and out-of-print jazz records. *236 W. 26th St. (btwn. Seventh & Eighth aves., 8th floor). ☎ 212/675-4480. www.jazzrecordcenter.com. AE, MC, V. Subway: 1/9 to 28th St. Map p 92.*

Virgin Megastore MIDTOWN Always busy, this complex has an extensive singles department, countless listening posts, and a huge video section. *1540 Broadway (at 45th St.). ☎ 212/921-1020. www.virginmega.com. AE, DC, DISC, MC, V. Subway: N/R/1/2/3/7/9 to Times Sq./42nd St. Also at 52 E. 14th St. (at Broadway). ☎ 212/598-4666. AE, DC, DISC, MC, V. Subway: 4/5/6/N/R/L to 14th St./Union Sq. Map p 92.*

Perfumes/Scents

★★ **Aedes De Venustas** GREENWICH VILLAGE Evoking a romantic boudoir out of the Victorian era, this whimsical spot offers exotic and hard-to-find scents. *9 Christopher St. (at Gay St.). ☎ 212/206-86747. www.aedes.com. AE, MC, V. Subway: 1/9 to Christopher St. Map p 91.*

Shoes

★ **Harry's Shoes** UPPER WEST SIDE This old-school shoe store doesn't sell sex (à la Manolo); it sells shoes. Great selection of comfortable styles. **Harry's Shoes for Kids** is a half-block away, at 2315 Broadway. *2299 Broadway. (at 83rd St.). ☎ 866/489-0984. http://harrysshoes.reachlocal.net. AE, DISC, MC, V. Subway: 1/9 to 79th St. or 86th St. Map p 92.*

★★ **Manolo Blahnik** MIDTOWN WEST These wildly sexy women's shoes could turn anyone into a foot fetishist. *31 W. 54th St. (btwn. Fifth & Sixth aves.). ☎ 212/582-3007. AE, MC, V. Subway: E/F to Fifth Ave. Map p 92.*

★ **Sigerson Morrison** NOLITA Very modern shoes with clever retro detailing. *28 Prince St. (btwn. Mott & Elizabeth sts.). ☎ 212/219-3893. www.sigersonmorrison.com. AE, MC, V. Subway: B/D/F/Q to Broadway/Lafayette St.; N/R to Prince St.; 6 to Spring St. Map p 91.*

Rem Koolhaas's SoHo Prada.

Stationery & Art Supplies

★ **Kate's Paperie** SOHO It's fun just to browse the exquisite and high-priced paper products at Kate's. It also has branches in the West Village, Upper East Side, and Midtown (check website for locations). *72 Spring St. (btwn. Crosby & Lafayette sts.). ☎ 212/941-9816. www.katespaperie.com. AE, DISC, MC, V. Subway: N/R to Prince St. Map p 91.*

★ **Pearl Paint** CHINATOWN All the cool art school students shop at this vintage Canal Street store. It's hands-down New York's best discount art-supply store. *308 Canal St. (btwn. Broadway & Mercer sts.). ☎ 212/431-7932. www.pearlpaint.com. AE, DISC, MC, V. Subway: N/R to Canal St. Map p 91.*

Toys

★★ kids **FAO Schwarz** MIDTOWN It gets crowded and the music can drive you nuts. But it's the mother lode of toys in New York. *767 Fifth Ave. (at 59th St.). ☎ 212/644-9400. www.fao.com. Subway: N/R/W to Fifth Ave. & 59th St. Map p 92.*

★★ kids **Kid O** WEST VILLAGE I recently went to a toddler's birthday party, and every gift had the same telltale Kid-O wrapping. A great selection of hip and original creative preschool toys and books chosen with an eco-friendly sensibility. *123 W. 10th St. (btwn. Sixth & Greenwich aves.). ☎ 212/366-KIDO. www.kidonyc.com. AE, MC, V. Subway: 1/9/2/3 to 14th St. Map p 91.*

kids **Toys "R" Us** TIMES SQUARE Check out the T-Rex on the second floor and take a spin on the Ferris wheel if you can tear your kids away from the lavish toy displays. *1514 Broadway (44th St.). ☎ 800/869-7787. AE, DISC, MC, V. Subway: 1/2/3/7/9/A/C/E/N/Q/R/S to 42nd St. Map p 92.* ●

6 The Great Outdoors

Central Park

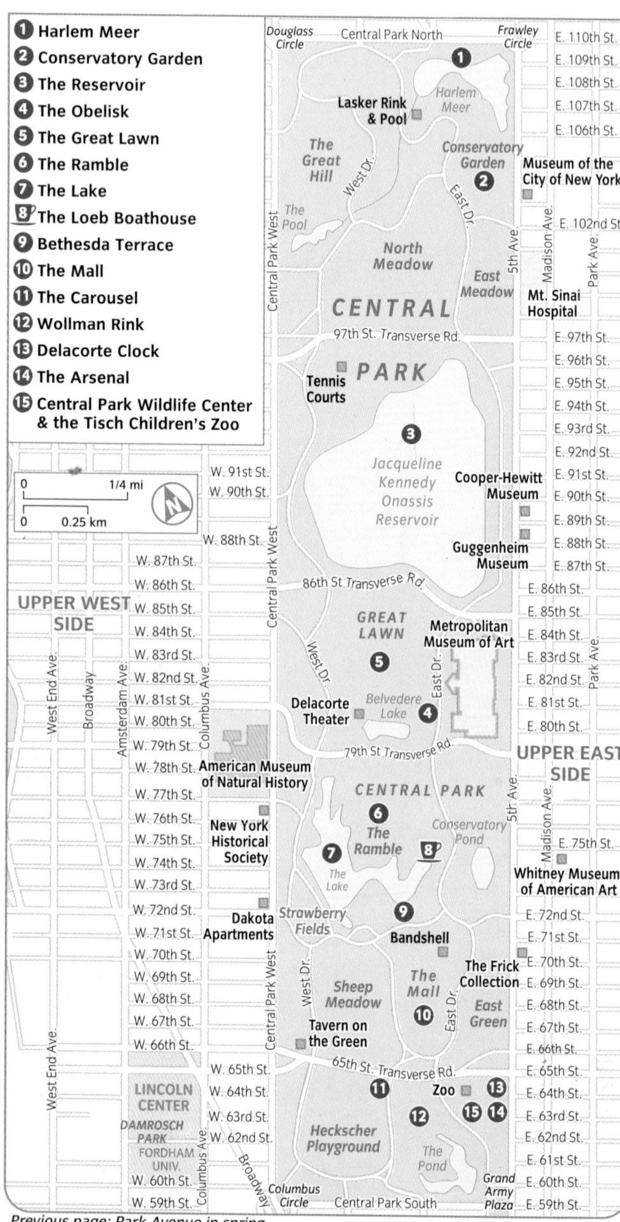

Previous page: Park Avenue in spring.

Often called Manhattan's backyard, Central Park is all that and far more. It's a vibrant 843-acre (337-hectare) masterpiece that was carved from a muddy swamp and squatters' camp in the 1850s by landscape architects Frederick Law Olmstead and Calvert Vaux. Today thousands of city residents and visitors flock here to stroll, run, bike, row boats, ride horseback, picnic, and play. START: **Subway 2 or 3 to Central Park North**

❶ **Harlem Meer.** This 11-acre (4.4-hectare) *meer* (the Dutch word for lake) wasn't part of the original Central Park. Added in 1863, it has a natural, rugged shoreline and community of swans. The **Charles A. Dana Discovery Center** (☎ *212/860-1370),* on the northern shore, contains a year-round visitor center and hosts Central Park Conservancy seasonal exhibitions, community programs, and holiday celebrations in its Great Hall. *East side from 106th to 110th sts.*

The Conservatory Garden's Burnett Fountain, inspired by The Secret Garden.

❷ ★★ **Conservatory Garden.** This formal garden was commissioned by the WPA (Work Projects Administration) in 1936. Its showpieces are many: an elegant Italian garden built around a classical fountain, a lovely mazelike English garden, a bronze statue of the children from the novel *The Secret Garden* standing in a reflecting pool. In summer, water lilies float in the pool, and flowering plants and shrubs fill the garden. From here walk south through the park, or, to save a mile of walking, take any bus down Fifth Avenue and get off at 86th Street, reentering the park at this point. *Fifth Ave. & 105th St.*

❸ **The Reservoir.** Created in 1862 as part of the Croton Water System, the reservoir was in use until 1994. Occupying 106 acres (42 hectares) and extending the width of the park, it is surrounded by bridle and running paths. Many a celebrity (Jackie O, Madonna) has jogged along the 1.6-mile (2.6km) upper track, which overlooks the reservoir and affords great skyline views. The reservoir holds a billion gallons of water, is 40 feet (12m) at its greatest depth, and now serves only as an emergency backup water supply. Walk along the path behind the Metropolitan Museum of Art to reach the Obelisk. *85th to 96th sts.*

❹ ★★ **The Obelisk.** This 71-foot (21m) artifact from Ancient Egypt was an 1881 gift to the U.S. from the khedive of Egypt. *See p 12, bullet* ❹.

❺ ★ **The Great Lawn.** Expansive enough for simultaneous games of softball, volleyball, or soccer, the Great Lawn is also a plum spot for a picnic—especially on those warm summer nights when the New York Philharmonic or Metropolitan Opera performs for free. Find the schedule at **www.centralparknyc.org** or http://nyphil.org, and bring along picnic fare from nearby gourmet grocery **Zabar's** (Broadway and 80th St.). At the southern end, ★ **Belvedere Castle** (*see p 12, bullet* ❺) and its surrounding duck pond are particularly picturesque. *Midpark from 79th to 85th sts.*

❻ ★ **The Ramble.** It looks wild—especially in comparison with the rest of the park—but it was actually designed that way to mirror untamed nature. Olmstead called it his "wild garden," and it takes up 38 acres (15 hectares) of the park. The Ramble has a bad reputation after dark (I wouldn't set foot in it after sunset), but during the day it's wonderful to explore. The curving paths that lead through the wooded area are inviting and offer some of the best scouting ground for birdwatchers in the city—some 230 species have been spotted here so far. A statue of a panther overlooks the east drive between 77th and 76th streets. *Midpark from 73rd to 79th sts.*

❼ ★★ **The Lake.** It's not quite as large as the Reservoir, but it's by far the most beautiful body of water in the park. Who would guess this idyllic lake was once a swamp? Everyone appreciates the serenity of this part of the park, but I love the fact that you can actually see skyscrapers reflected in the water. Rent a rowboat or kayak at the Loeb Boathouse (see below) and take your sweetie for a turn around the lake—the views from the water are superb ($12/first hour). *Midpark from 71st to 78th sts.*

Bethesda Terrace is a great people-watching spot in summer.

❽ **The Loeb Boathouse.** At the eastern end of the Lake is the Loeb Boathouse, where you can rent boats and bikes, as well as dine—and dine well. The **Boathouse at Central Park** restaurant, open for lunch and dinner from April 15 through November, is a lovely fine-dining space with alfresco lakeside seating on a wooden deck under a white canopy. The menu is contemporary American. An **outdoor grill/bar** is very popular in the warm months (Apr–Nov 11am–11pm daily) and an **express cafe** serves breakfast and light fare (year-round 8am–6pm daily; to 4:30 in winter). *East side btwn. 74th and 75th sts. ☎ 212/517-2233. $–$$$.*

❾ ★★ **Bethesda Terrace.** Meet *Bethesda, the Angel of the Waters,* the only sculpture commissioned as part of the park's original design. Olmstead and Vaux were both determined to put nature first, second, and third (as Vaux was once quoted saying), but they acknowledged the need for a central meeting place in the park. The surrounding two-tiered terrace was part of the original design. *Midpark at 72nd St.*

❿ ★★ **The Mall.** This lovely promenade is shaded by a canopy of American elms—a favorite tree of the park's designers. At the south end of the Mall is the **Literary Walk,** flanked by statues of Shakespeare, Robert Burns, Sir Walter Scott, and other historic and literary figures. *Midpark from 66th to 72nd sts.*

⓫ kids **The Carousel.** It's hard to believe that this beautiful vintage carousel was ever relegated to a dusty warehouse. The Central Park

Carousel's 58 colorful steeds are among the largest carousel ponies in the world and were hand-carved by Russian immigrants Solomon Stein and Harry Goldstein in 1908. The original carousel was built in 1871; fires destroyed it and a successor. Park officials searched high and low for a replacement, only to discover this treasure abandoned in an old trolley building on Coney Island. *Central Park (64th St.). $2 ride. Apr–Oct Mon–Fri 10am–5/6pm, Sat–Sun 10am–7pm. http://centralparkcarousel.com.*

⓬ kids **Wollman Rink.** This relative newcomer was built into the northern bay of The Pond in 1951. In winter it's for ice skates, and for the rest of the year it's home to a series of special attractions, such as the Victoria Gardens Amusement Park, which has great rides for young children. *Central Park (east side btwn. 62nd & 63rd sts.). ☎ 212/439-6900. www.wollmanskatingrink.com. Mon–Tues 10am–2:30pm; Wed–Thurs 10am–10pm; Fri–Sat 10am–11pm; Sun 10am–9pm. Admission $9.50–$12 adults, $4.75–$8.25 seniors, $4.75–$5 children. Subway: A/B/C/D/1/9 to 59th St. or N/R to Fifth Ave.*

The Central Park carousel.

⓭ kids **Delacorte Clock.** With six dancing animals designed by Italian sculptor Andrea Spadini, this clock has been captivating park visitors since the '60s. The tunes played on the hour are the best; the half-hour ones are shorter but still sweet. *East side & 65th St. (in the zoo).*

⓮ **The Arsenal.** This Gothic Revival building actually predates the park. It looks like the fortress it briefly was when it housed troops during the Civil War. It later served as the original home of the American Museum of Natural History. It was even home to some of P. T. Barnum's circus animals, from a black bear to white swans. Today it houses the park headquarters and a third-floor art gallery. *64th St. & Fifth Ave. ☎ 311 in New York City or 212/NEW-YORK. www.nycgovparks.org. Mon–Fri 9am–5pm.*

⓯ ★★ kids **Central Park Wildlife Center & the Tisch Children's Zoo.** Better known as the Central Park Zoo, the Wildlife Center was built in 1988 to replace a 1934 WPA-built structure that had become cramped and outdated. Today the zoo's 5½ acres (2.2 hectares) house more than 400 animals. Watch the sea lions playing in the Central Garden pool and the polar bears splashing around in their watery den. In the small Tisch Children's Zoo, kids can feed and pet tame farm animals, including pot-bellied pigs. 🕘 *75 min. Central Park (east side btwn. 63rd & 66th sts). ☎ 212/861-6030. http://nyzoosandaquarium.com/cpz. Admission $8 adults, $4 seniors, $3 children 3–12, under 3 free. Daily 10am–4:30pm (extended hours for weekends, holidays & spring/summer).*

Green-Wood Cemetery

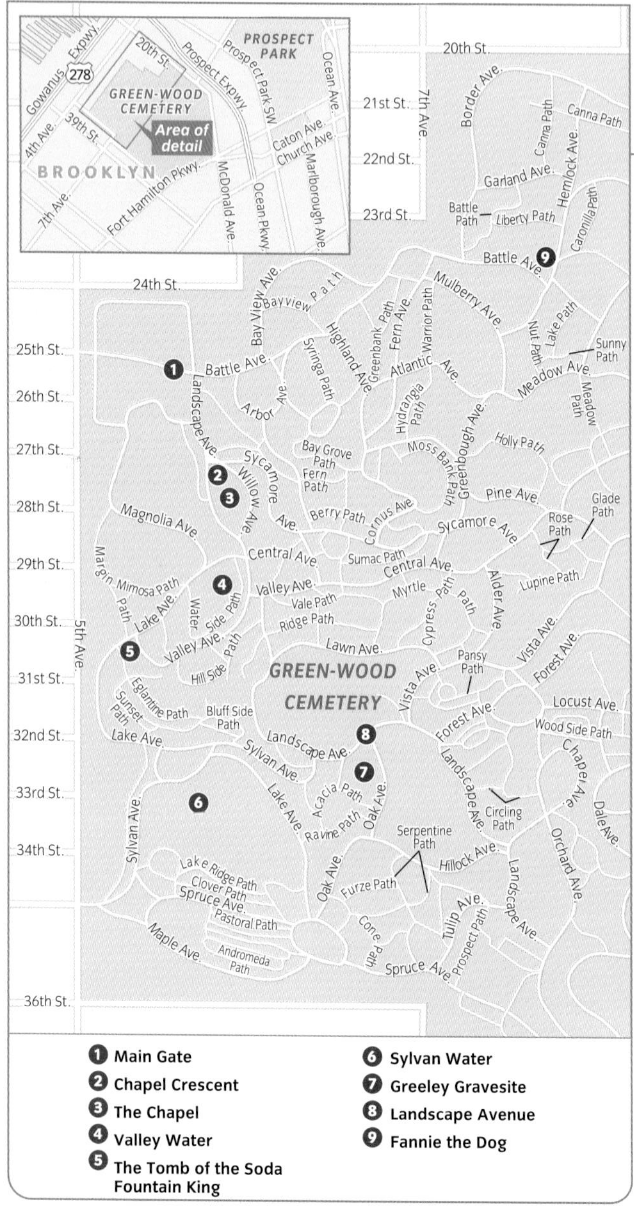

"It is the ambition of the New Yorker to live upon Fifth Avenue, to take his airings in the Park, and to sleep with his fathers in Green-Wood." So declared the *New York Times* in 1866. Today Brooklyn's Green-Wood Cemetery is a great place to revel in the outdoors. This 1838 necropolis has stunning scenery, a breathtaking chapel, and ornate mausoleums. START: **Subway N or R to 25th Street in Brooklyn**

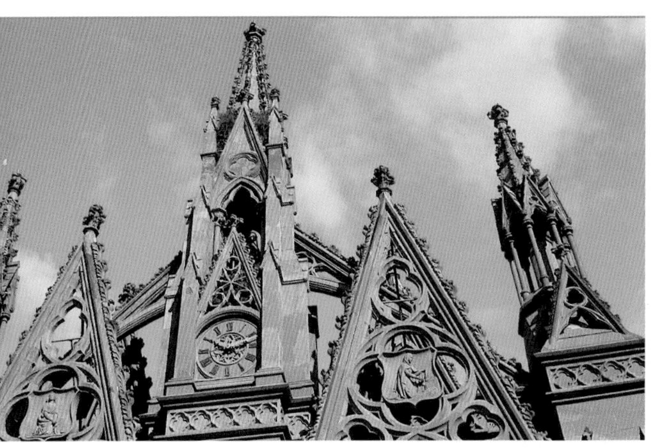

Green-Wood's elaborate main gate.

1 ★★ Main Gate. Green-Wood has five entrances, but this Gothic gate with spires that stretch churchlike into the sky is by far the most spectacular. A New York City Historic Landmark, it was built from 1861 to 1865 by architect Richard M. Upjohn. At the information booth inside you can pick up a free map of the grounds. It lists the many famous (and infamous) residents—some 600,000 in all. These include Samuel Morse, Henry Ward Beecher, Leonard Bernstein, Boss Tweed, Nathaniel Currier and James Ives, and hundreds of Civil War soldiers. Self-guided walking tour booklets are also available for a fee. You will see NO PHOTOGRAPHY signs, but that rule isn't generally enforced unless you try to take pictures of mourners. *2 hr. 500 25th St. (Fifth Ave.), Brooklyn. ☎ 718/768-7300. www.green-wood.com. Daily 8am–5pm (extended hours in summer). Subway: N/R to 25th St. in Brooklyn.*

2 ★ Chapel Crescent. Green-Wood's grand chapel (bullet 3) is surrounded by stunning tombs. The B. Stephens tomb is shaped like a small Egyptian pyramid. The Chambettaz tomb has an angel statue overlooking the crescent as well as symbols from the secret society of the Freemasons.

3 ★★★ The Chapel. A few minutes' walk from the main gates is Green-Wood's crowning glory. The 1911 chapel is a relatively recent arrival, its design inspired by Tom Tower at Oxford's Christ Church college, which was designed by Christopher Wren in the 17th century. The multidomed structure is built entirely of Indiana limestone. The small interior frequently hosts readings and special exhibits that explore funerary art. Check the

Green-Wood's chapel is a popular wedding venue.

website for a schedule. ☎ *718/768-7300. www.green-wood.com.*

❹ **Valley Water.** Some of Green-Wood's ponds have been filled in to create new burial plots, but this one is surrounded by evergreens. The avenue that curves around Valley Water is a treasure trove of 19th-century sculpture. Many of the monuments are partially draped by a carved "cloth." This popular Victorian Resurrectionist style reflected a belief that the body in the grave would rise on Judgment Day, when the cloth would fall away as if pulled back by the hand of God.

❺ ★ **The Tomb of the Soda Fountain King.** This towering work of sculpture is really just one giant tombstone: In 1870, it won the Mortuary Monument of the Year award (didn't know there was such a thing, did you?). This is the resting place of John Matthews, the man who invented the soda fountain—and that information is about the only thing not carved into it. Gargoyles, members of the Matthews family, and Matthews himself are all here.

❻ **Sylvan Water.** This is the largest body of water in Green-Wood. It's surrounded by a series of tombs, some of which look large enough to house a (living) family.

❼ ★ **Greeley Gravesite.** Horace Greeley was an anti-slavery advocate who founded the *New York Tribune* and was a national figure ("Go West, young man" is one of his famous aphorisms). The views from his family plot are lovely.

❽ **Landscape Avenue.** This winding, twisting avenue offers memorable vistas and some great statuary.

❾ **Fannie the Dog.** Anyone who has ever loved a pet will find the engraving on Fannie's headstone moving. "Frosts of winter nor heat of summer / Could make her fail if my footsteps led / And memory holds in its treasure casket / The name of my darling who lies dead." ●

Valley Water pond is ringed by evergreens and monuments.

7 The Best **Dining**

Dining Best Bets

Best for a Red Meat Fix
★★★ Keens $$$ *72 W. 36th St. (p 117)*; and ★★★ Peter Luger $$$ *178 Broadway (Brooklyn; p 121)*

Best Vegetarian
★★★ Pure Food and Wine $$ *54 Irving Place (p 121)*

Best French (Classic or Modern)
★★ Daniel $$$$ *60 E. 65th St. (p 116)*

Best Meal for Under $25
★ Nyonya $ *194 Grand St. (p 119)*

Best Upscale Mexican
★ Rosa Mexicano $$ *61 Columbus Ave. (p 121)*

Best Chinese
★★ Shun Lee West $$$ *43 W. 65th St. See p 13 bullet 13.*

Best Food Court
★★ Chelsea Market $ *75 9th Ave. (p 115)*

Best Vietnamese
★ Nha Trang $ *87 Baxter St. (p 119)*

Best Deli
★ Katz's $ *205 E. Houston St. (p 117)*; and ★★ Barney Greengrass $ *541 Amsterdam Ave. (p 112)*

Best Pizza
★ John's Pizza $ *278 Bleecker St. (p 117)*

Best Seafood
★★★ Aquavit $$$ *65 E. 55th St. (p 114)*; and ★★★ Le Bernardin $$$$ *55 W. 51st St. (p 118)*

Previous page: Fresh oysters at Aquagrill.

Best Brunch
★★★ Aquavit $$$ *65 E. 55th St. (p 114)*

Best Splurge
★★★ Blue Hill $$$$ *75 Washington Place (p 115)*; ★★★ Jean-Georges $$$$ *1 Central Park West (p 117)*; and ★★★ Le Bernardin $$$$ *55 W. 51st St. (p 118)*

Best Sushi
★★★ Nobu/Next Door Nobu $$$ *105 Hudson St. (p 119)*

Best Indian
★★ Tabla $$ *11 E. Madison Ave. (p 122)*

Best for Families
★★ Carmine's $$ *2450 Broadway (p 115)*

Best Burger
★ Shake Shack $ *105 Thompson St. (p 122)*

Best Thai
★ Pam Real Thai $ *404 W. 49th St. (p 120)*

Best Italian
★★ Babbo $$$ *110 Waverly Place (p 114)*; and ★★ Dominick's $$ *2335 Arthur Ave. (Bronx; p 116)*

Best New Restaurant
★★ Olana $$$ *72 Madison Ave. (p 120)*; and ★★ Perilla $$$ *9 Jones St. (p 121)*

Downtown Dining

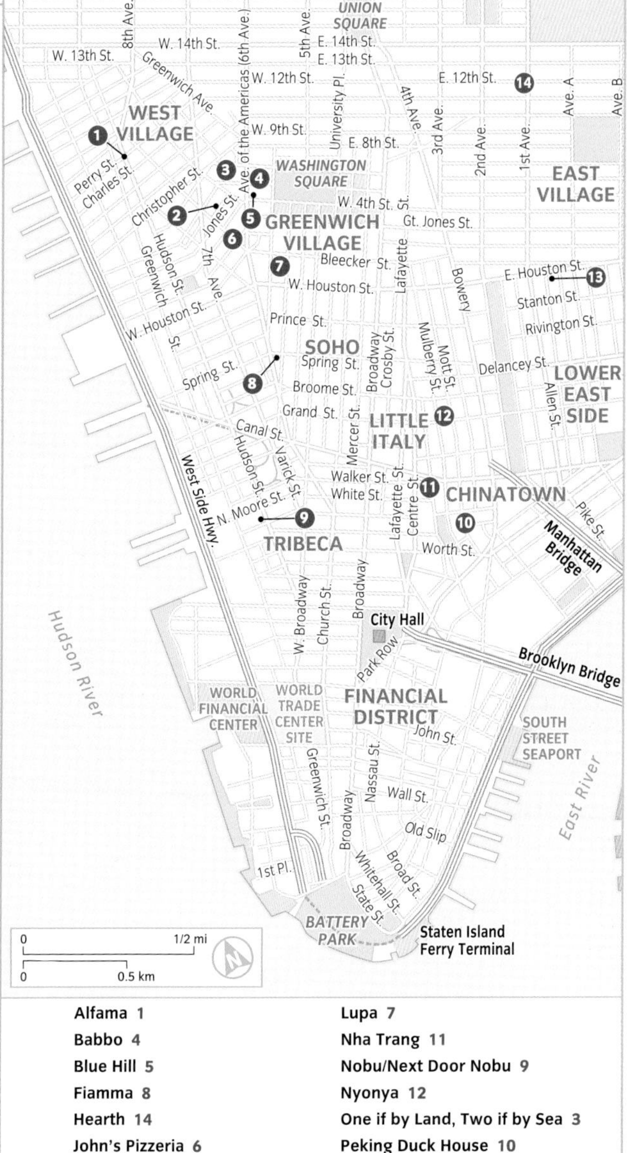

Alfama 1	**Lupa** 7
Babbo 4	**Nha Trang** 11
Blue Hill 5	**Nobu/Next Door Nobu** 9
Fiamma 8	**Nyonya** 12
Hearth 14	**One if by Land, Two if by Sea** 3
John's Pizzeria 6	**Peking Duck House** 10
Katz's Delicatessen 13	**Perilla** 7

Midtown & Uptown Dining

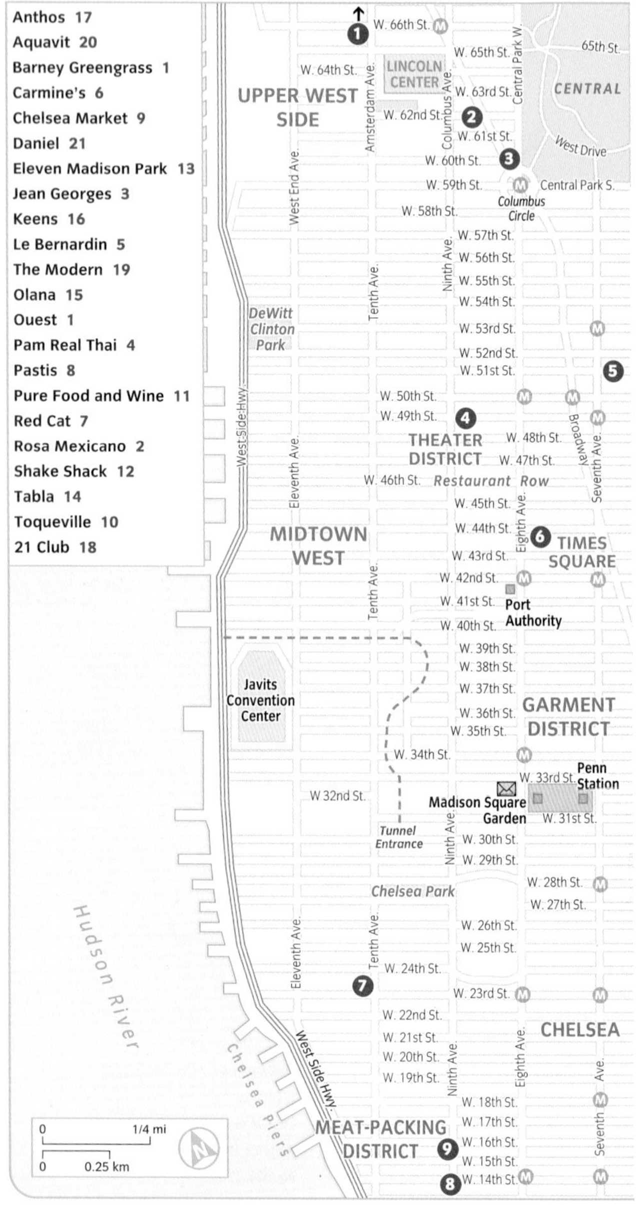

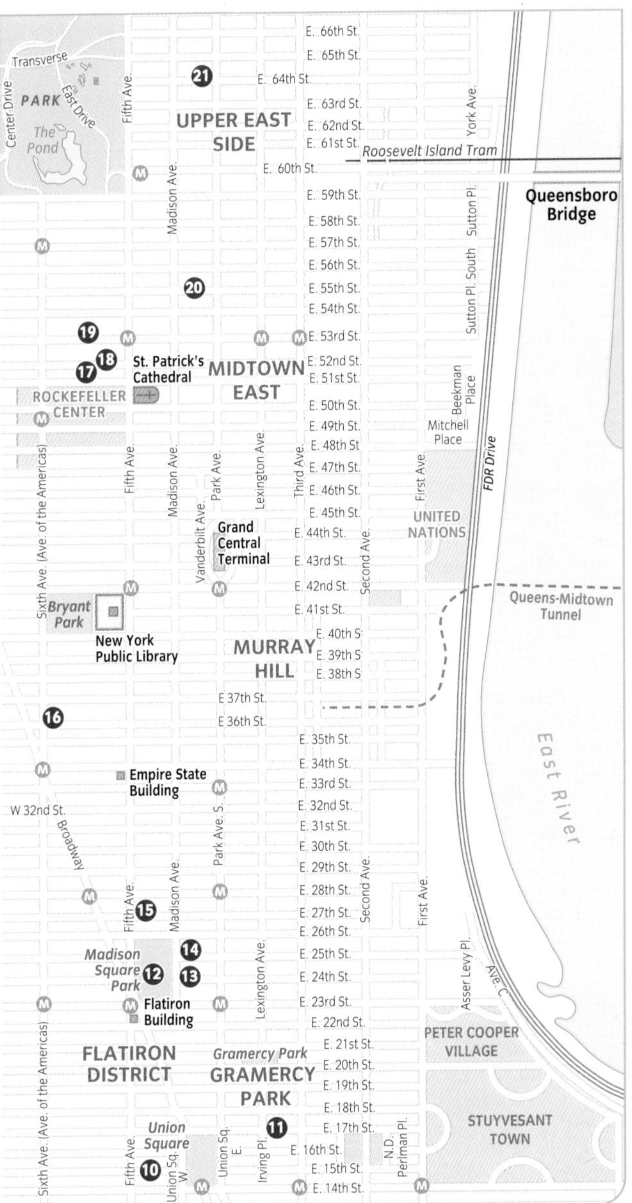

UPPER EAST SIDE
MIDTOWN EAST
MURRAY HILL
FLATIRON DISTRICT
GRAMERCY PARK
PARK
The Pond
Transverse
Center Drive
East Drive
Fifth Ave.
Madison Ave.
Park Ave.
Vanderbilt Ave.
Lexington Ave.
Third Ave.
Second Ave.
First Ave.
York Ave.
Sutton Pl.
Sutton Pl. South
Beekman Place
Mitchell Place
FDR Drive
Sixth Ave. (Ave. of the Americas)
Broadway
Park Ave. S.
Union Sq. W.
Union Sq. E.
Irving Pl.
N.D. Perlman Pl.
Asser Levy Pl.
Ave. C
W 32nd St.
E. 66th St.
E. 65th St.
E. 64th St.
E. 63rd St.
E. 62nd St.
E. 61st St.
E. 60th St.
E. 59th St.
E. 58th St.
E. 57th St.
E. 56th St.
E. 55th St.
E. 54th St.
E. 53rd St.
E. 52nd St.
E. 51st St.
E. 50th St.
E. 49th St.
E. 48th St
E. 47th St.
E. 46th St.
E. 45th St.
E. 44th St.
E. 43rd St.
E. 42nd St.
E. 41st St.
E. 40th St
E. 39th St
E. 38th St
E 37th St.
E 36th St.
E. 35th St.
E. 34th St.
E. 33rd St.
E. 32nd St.
E. 31st St.
E. 30th St.
E. 29th St.
E. 28th St.
E. 27th St.
E. 26th St.
E. 25th St.
E. 24th St.
E. 23rd St.
E. 22nd St.
E. 21st St.
E. 20th St.
E. 19th St.
E. 18th St.
E. 17th St.
E. 16th St.
E. 15th St.
E. 14th St.
Roosevelt Island Tram
Queensboro Bridge
St. Patrick's Cathedral
ROCKEFELLER CENTER
Grand Central Terminal
UNITED NATIONS
Queens-Midtown Tunnel
Bryant Park
New York Public Library
Empire State Building
East River
Madison Square Park
Flatiron Building
Gramercy Park
PETER COOPER VILLAGE
STUYVESANT TOWN
Union Square
10
11
12
13
14
15
16
17
18
19
20
21

New York Restaurants A to Z

★ **Alfama** WEST VILLAGE *PORTUGUESE* Everything from the warm welcome to the homey cooking makes this spot feel like a little corner of Portugal. The *Pasteis de Belem* cream pastries are the closest to the real thing I've had outside of Lisbon. ***551 Hudson St. (Perry St.). ☎ 212/645-2500. www.alfamarestaurant.com. Main courses $21–$32. AE, MC, V. Dinner daily; Sun brunch. Subway: 1/9 to Christopher St. Map p 111.***

★★ **Anthos** MIDTOWN *GREEK* Recent James Beard award nominee for Best New Restaurant in the U.S., Anthos is under the direction of Michael Psilakis, the chef *New York* magazine has called "the Mario Batali of New Aegean cuisine." The food? Dazzling and inventive takes on Greek standards. ***36 W. 52nd St. (Fifth Ave.) ☎ 212/582-6900. Main courses $28–$44. AE, DC, DISC, MC, V. Lunch & dinner daily. Subway: E/V to Fifth Ave/53rd St. Map p 112.***

★★★ **Aquavit** MIDTOWN WEST *SCANDINAVIAN* The interior won't impress anyone familiar with the indoor waterfall at the original location, but the food is as spectacular as ever. The herring, salmon, and gravlax are simply irresistible. ***65 E. 55th St. (btwn. Madison & Park aves.). ☎ 212/307-7311. www.aquavit.org. Three-course prix-fixe dinner $84; tasting menus $90–$115; Sun Swedish buffet brunch $48. AE, DC, MC, V. Lunch Sun–Fri, dinner Mon–Sat. Subway: 4/5/6/N/R/W to 59th St. Map p 112.***

Pasta at Fiamma Osteria.

Chef Daniel Boulud at work.

★★ **Babbo** WASHINGTON SQUARE AREA *ITALIAN* This is the centerpiece of celebrity chef "Molto" Mario Batali's edible empire—and boy, does he love his *guanciale* and *lardo*. The pasta tasting menu is a good choice. ***110 Waverly Place (Sixth Ave.). ☎ 212/777-0303. www.babbonyc.com. Main courses $19–$29; 7-course tasting menus $69–$75. AE, MC, V. Dinner daily. Subway: A/C/E/F/B/D to 4th St. Map p 111.***

★★ **Barney Greengrass** UPPER WEST SIDE *DELI* The Sturgeon King has been selling lox and bagels for a century at this favorite weekend brunch spot for Upper West Siders. The vintage counters and dairy case are beautiful. *541 Amsterdam Ave. (btwn. 86th and 87th sts.). ☎ 212/724-4707. www.barneygreengrass.com. Main courses $6.75–$19; smoked fish platters $26–$45. AE, MC, V. Tues–Fri 8:30am–4pm, Sat–Sun 8:30am–5pm. Subway: 1/9 to 86th St. Map p 112.*

★★★ **Blue Hill** GREENWICH VILLAGE *AMERICAN* This soothing, understated Village townhouse space quietly goes about its business serving some of the most delicious food in town, with an admirable sustainable-foods philosophy that travels beautifully from purveyor to plate. Chef and James Beard award nominee Dan Barber coaxes the best out of the best ingredients—no flashy alchemy here. Even lowly Brussels sprouts become irresistible. *75 Washington Place (btwn. 6th Ave, and Washington Sq. W.). ☎ 212/539-1776. www.bluehillnyc.com. Main courses $26–$32. AE, DC, MC, V. Dinner daily. Subway: B/D/F/V/A/C/E to W. 4th St. Map p 111.*

★ **kids** **Carmine's** MIDTOWN WEST *ITALIAN* A place this big and this busy doesn't have to have stellar food—but Carmine's does a lot of things very well. The vast dining room manages to feel both warm and festive, and the family-style portions of hearty pastas and Southern Italian favorites more than satisfy. *200 W. 44th St. (btwn. Seventh & Eighth aves.). ☎ 212/221-3800. www.carminesnyc.com. Main courses $21–$49. AE, DC, DISC, MC, V. Lunch & dinner daily. Subway: 1/2/3/7/9/A/C/E/S to 42th St./Times Sq. Map p 112.*

Caviar in an eggshell at Jean-Georges.

★★ **Chelsea Market** WEST CHELSEA/MEAT-PACKING DISTRIC *FOOD COURT* You won't find a better place to eat takeout food in the city than in this wholesale/retail food market in a cleverly restored old biscuit factory. You've never seen a "food court" like this one, with massive exposed pipes, a gushing "waterfall," and a million square feet of market space. It's got seriously good food, too: Thai, Italian, seafood,

The counter line is long but moves fast at Katz's.

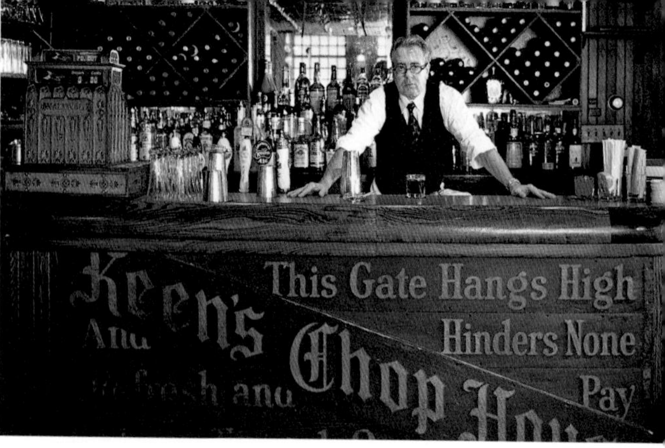

Carnivores have flocked to Keens for more than a century.

soup, deli, desserts, even lovingly made comfort food from sustainable sources (the Cleaver Co.). *75 9th Ave. (btwn. 15th and 16th sts.). www.chelseamarket.com. Mon–Sat 7am–9m; Sun 10am–8pm. Subway: A/C/E to 14th St. Map p 112.*

★★ **Daniel** UPPER EAST SIDE *FRENCH COUNTRY* The eye-popping neoclassical setting pairs well with Daniel Boulud's refined cooking. The menu changes frequently but highlights have included venison with a chestnut crust and sweet-potato puree. *60 E. 65th St. (btwn. Madison & Park aves.). ☎ 212/288-0033. www.danielnyc.com. Main courses $34–$38; 3-course prix-fixe menu $98. AE, DC, MC, V. Dinner Mon–Sat. Subway: 6 to 68th St. Map p 112.*

★★ **Dominick's** THE BRONX *ITALIAN* It doesn't look like much. It's small and slightly cramped. On weekends it's crazy, with long waits upstairs in the bar. But hang in and you will be well taken care of by the taciturn but topnotch waitstaff at this legendary spot, which has no menus and no checks. You want some clams to start? A salad or a stuffed artichoke maybe? Yes, yes, and yes. Follow with a sampling of perfect seafood pastas, buttery shrimp *franchese*, and a sizzling steak. It's killer. *2335 Arthur Ave. (btwn. 187th St. & Crescent Ave.). ☎ 718/733-2807. Main courses $10–$25. Cash only. Lunch & dinner Wed–Mon. Subway: B/D to 183rd St.*

★★ **Eleven Madison Park** FLATIRON DISTRICT *FRENCH COUNTRY/ AMERICAN* This gem from restaurateur Danny Meyer is set in a soaring Art Deco space. The two-story windows have spectacular views of the park at night. *11 Madison Ave. (at 24th St.). ☎ 212/889-0905. www.elevenmadisonpark.com. 3- and 4-course prix-fixe menus $82/$102; 13-course tasting menu $145. AE, DC, DISC, MC, V. Lunch Mon–Sat, dinner daily. Subway: N/R/6 to 23rd St. Map p 112.*

★★ **Fiamma** SOHO *ITALIAN* The stunning decor is surpassed only by the sumptuous, modern Italian food cooked by James Beard award–winning chef Fabio Trabocchi. Don't expect quiet conversation; dinner can be raucous. *206 Spring St. (btwn. Sixth Ave. & Sullivan St.). ☎ 212/653-0100. www.brguestrestaurants.com. Prix-fixe menus $85–$125; 5-course tasting menu $105. AE, DISC, MC, V. Dinner Tues–Sat. Subway: C/E to Spring St. Map p 111.*

★★ Hearth EAST VILLAGE *MEDITERRANEAN/ITALIAN* This warm East Villager is a favorite of diners and critics alike. It's all about fresh, seasonal Greenmarket food cooked with tender loving care. *403 E. 12th St. (at First Ave.). ☎ 646/602-1300. www.restauranthearth.com. Main courses $26–$34; 5-course tasting menu $85. AE, DISC, MC, V. Dinner daily. Subway: N/R/4/5/6 to Union Square. Map p 111.*

★★★ Jean Georges COLUMBUS CIRCLE *FRENCH* A meal here underscores why chef/owner Jean-Georges Vongerichten is universally loved by foodies. Asian flavors heat up the French menu. *In the Trump International Hotel & Tower, 1 Central Park West (at 60th St./Columbus Circle). ☎ 212/299-3900. www.jean-georges.com. Main courses $26–$42; 3- and 7-course tasting menus $98–$148. AE, DC, MC, V. Lunch Mon–Fri, dinner Mon–Sat. Subway: A/B/C/D/1/9 to 59th St./Columbus Circle. Map p 112.*

★ John's Pizzeria of Bleecker Street kids GREENWICH VILLAGE *PIZZA* The decor in this longtime Bleecker Street favorite, founded in 1929, hasn't changed much over the years; its wooden booths, old Italy mural, and tin ceiling are still intact.

Frog leg at One if by Land, Two if by Sea.

Chef Nobuyuki Matsuhisa opened Nobu in partnership with Robert De Niro.

The pizza hasn't changed, either—and hallelujah for that. Pizza pies cooked up in the brick oven are thin, crispy, and delicious. There's also a branch in Times Square (260 W. 44th St.; ☎ 212/391-7560). *278 Bleecker St. (btwn. 6th and 7th aves.). ☎ 212/243-1680. www.johnsbrickovenpizza.com. Pizzas $12–$14, toppings $2. No credit cards. Lunch & dinner daily. Subway: A/C/E/B/D/F/V at W 4th St. Map p 111.*

★ Katz's Delicatessen LOWER EAST SIDE *DELI* Founded in 1888, this homely, cacophonous space is one of the city's last great delis. No one has better pastrami or brisket sandwiches. *205 E. Houston St. (Ludlow St.). ☎ 212/254-2246. Sandwiches $2.15–$10; other items $5–$18. AE, MC, V. Breakfast, lunch & dinner daily. Subway: F to Second Ave. Map p 111.*

★★★ Keens MIDTOWN WEST *STEAK/MUTTON* If you're searching for old New York, look no further than this 1885 survivor tucked away on a side street near Madison Square Garden. The space has always been wonderful; now the food is its equal. I had one of the best steaks I've ever eaten in the city here. *72 W. 36th St. (at Sixth Ave.) ☎ 212/947-3636.*

Revolution on Smith Street

It started as it usually does: The rents were cheap, and enterprising young chefs saw potential in the modest mom-and-pop storefronts. Today Smith Street, in the Cobble Hill section of Brooklyn, is a celebrated restaurant scene where some of the most heralded chefs in the city prepare delicious food with an emphasis on the local, the seasonal, and the artisanal—bringing the nabe full circle with a hands-on mom-and-pop sensibility. Among the best: **Saul** (140 Smith St.; ☎ 718/935-9844), the Michelin-starred husband-and-wife labor of love; the **Grocery** (288 Smith St.; ☎ 718/596-3335), which shocked the Manhattan restaurant world in 2003 when it shot to the top spot in the Zagat restaurant survey; **Chestnut** (271 Smith St.; ☎ 718/243-0049), a charming brunch spot; and **Robin des Bois** (195 Smith St.; ☎ 718/596-1609), a funky antiques-filled spot with a fireplace and a garden. All can be reached by taking the F subway train to Bergen St.

www.keens.com. Main courses $31–$54. AE, DC, DISC, MC, V. Lunch & dinner Mon–Fri; dinner Sat & Sun. Subway: 1/2/3/9 to 34th St./Penn Station. Map p 112.

★★★ **Le Bernardin** MIDTOWN WEST *FRENCH/SEAFOOD* Seafood doesn't get better than this. The formal service is impeccable, as is the pricey wine list. *55 W. 51st St. (btwn. Sixth & Seventh aves.). ☎ 212/489-1515. www.le-bernardin.com. Fixed-price dinner $87; tasting menus $135–$180. AE, DC, DISC, MC, V. Lunch Mon–Fri, dinner Mon–Sat. Subway: N/R to 49th St.; 1/9 to 50th St. Map p 112.*

★ **Lupa** GREENWICH VILLAGE *ITALIAN* This handsome homage to a Roman trattoria has been filled to

The fresh guacamole at Rosa Mexicano.

Breakfast includes grits at Sylvia's in Harlem.

capacity since it opened. And why not? The food is impeccable and often inventive, and the prices won't bankrupt you. It's part of the Batali/Bastianich empire. *170 Thompson St. (btwn. Houston and Bleecker sts.) ☎ 212/982-5089. www.luparestaurant.com. Main courses $11–$20. AE, MC, V. Lunch & dinner daily. Subway: B/D/F/V/A/C/E to W. 4th St. Map p 111.*

★★ **The Modern** MIDTOWN WEST *AMERICAN* Dining in this glorious space makes you feel as if you're at the center of a very sophisticated urban universe—and you are. The food lives up to the setting, and the cross-section of New Yorkers crisply doing business makes this a great spot to see the local tribe in action. *The Museum of Modern Art. 9 W. 53rd St. (btwn. Fifth and Sixth aves.). ☎ 212/333-1220. www.themodernnyc.com. 3-course prix-fixe $85; 7-course tasting menu $125. AE, DC, DISC, MC, V. Lunch & dinner Mon–Fri; dinner Sat. Subway: E/V to Fifth Ave./53rd St. Map p 112.*

★ **Nha Trang** CHINATOWN *VIETNAMESE* This is one of best of the Baxter Street Vietnamese restaurants—a friendly, bustling place with delicious and reasonably priced food. *87 Baxter St. (btwn. Canal & Bayard sts.). ☎ 212/233-5948. Main courses $5–$16. AE, MC, V. Brunch & dinner daily. Subway: N/R/6 to Canal St. Map p 111.*

★★★ **Nobu/Next Door Nobu** TRIBECA *JAPANESE* Renowned chef Nobuyuki Matsuhisa's cooking bursts with creative spirit. Can't get a reservation at Nobu? Take heart. **Next Door Nobu,** a slightly more casual alternative, has a no-reservations policy. *105 Hudson St. (at Franklin St.). ☎ 212/219-0500 for Nobu; ☎ 212/334-4445 for Next Door Nobu. www.myriadrestaurantgroup.com. Small plates and main courses $8.50–$42; sushi $4–$8 per piece. AE, DC, MC, V. Nobu lunch & dinner Mon–Fri; dinner Sat–Sun. Next Door Nobu dinner daily. Subway: 1/9 to Franklin St. Map p 111.*

★ **Nyonya** LITTLE ITALY *MALAYSIAN* Spacious and bustling, this restaurant looks like a South Asian tiki hut. Try the Malaysian national dish, *roti canai* (an Indian pancake with a curry chicken dipping sauce). *194 Grand St.*

Restaurant Week: Prix-Fixe Dining

Everyone loves a deal, and Restaurant Week is one of New York's best. It started more than a decade ago, when some of the city's best dining spots began to offer three courses for a fixed low price at lunch ($24) and dinner ($35). Now it's an institution—and lasts for several weeks in January and July. Some restaurants offer prix-fixe menus year-round or have discounted menus on certain days or times. For example, the 21 Club (21 W. 52nd St., btwn. Fifth & Sixth aves; (☎ 212/582-7200) has a $35 prix-fixe lunch menu. Check out www.opentable.com or www.nycvisit.com for more information on Restaurant Week and participating restaurants.

(btwn. Mulberry & Mott sts.). ☎ 212/334-3669. Main courses $5.95–$22. No credit cards. Lunch & dinner daily. Subway: 6 to Spring St. Map p 111.

★★ **Olana** MURRAY HILL *NEW AMERICAN* This beautiful new restaurant was inspired by the owners' love for the eponymous Hudson River estate of artist Frederick Church. The impeccably sourced seasonal food includes sweet pea soup with Applewood smoked bacon and a monkfish *osso buco*. *72 Madison Ave. (btwn. 27th & 28th sts.). ☎ 212/725-0957. Main courses $24–$38. www.olananyc.com. Lunch & dinner Mon–Fri; dinner Sat. Subway: 6 to 28rd St. Map p 112.*

★ **One if by Land, Two if by Sea** GREENWICH VILLAGE *AMERICAN* This candlelit, flower-filled 18th-century carriage house is a perennial favorite among romantics. And now the food actually lives up to the setting. You can still order the traditional favorite, beef Wellington. *17 Barrow St. (btwn. W. 4th St. & Seventh Ave. S.). ☎ 212/255-8649. www.oneifbyland.com. 3-course prix fixe $75; 6-course tasting menu $95. AE, DC, DISC, MC, V. Dinner daily; Sun brunch ($20). Subway: 1/9 to Christopher St.; A/E/C/F/B/D to 4th St. Map p 111.*

★★ **Ouest** UPPER WEST SIDE *NEW AMERICAN* Living well is the best revenge, and you'll feel comfortable and cosseted while dining on Tom Valenti's wonderful American-bistro food in this festive spot. *2315 Broadway (84th St.). ☎ 212/580-8700. www.ouestny. Dinner daily; Sun brunch. Main courses $26–$42. AE, DC, DISC, MC, V. 1/9 to 86th St. Map p 112.*

★ **kids** **Pam Real Thai** MIDTOWN WEST *THAI* Good Thai food is scarce in New York, making this place a terrific find. The crispy duck yum is deliciously spicy. *404 W. 49th St. (Ninth Ave.). ☎ 212/333-7500. www.pamrealthai.com. Main courses $6.50–$9.95. AE, MC, V. Lunch & dinner daily. Subway: C/E to 50th St./Eighth Ave. Map p 112.*

★ **Pastis** MEAT-PACKING DISTRICT *FRENCH BISTRO* Yes, Keith McNally's cool Balthazar looks just like an authentic Parisian brasserie, but its sister restaurant Pastis feels like the Provençal bistro it's designed to emulate. Plus, it has a much more desirable setting, and you can sit outside overlooking a wide cobblestone plaza in the Meatpacking District. It's kid- and dog-friendly and the bistro fare is terrific: steak frites, croques, and salad Niçoise. *9 Ninth Ave. (btwn. Little W. 12th & 13th sts.) ☎ 212/929-4844. http://pastisny.com. Main courses $19–$34. AE, MC, V. Breakfast, lunch (or brunch) & dinner daily. Subway: A/C/E to 14th St. Map p 112.*

★ **Peking Duck House** CHINATOWN *CHINESE* Now that my beloved Canton is closed, this is my favorite "upscale" restaurant in Chinatown, with white tablecloths and a minimalist setting. The Peking duck is worth the trip; the "Special House Dinner" ($37 per person) includes half a Peking duck. *28 Mott St. (btwn. Pell & Mosco sts.). ☎ 212/227-1810. www.pekingduckhousenyc.com. Main courses $7.50–$26; Peking duck $40. Lunch & dinner daily. Subway: J/M/Z/N/R/6 to Canal St. Map p 111.*

★★ **Perilla** GREENWICH VILLAGE *SEASONAL AMERICAN* A reality-show TV winner runs this small but exciting new Village restaurant. *Top Chef* 2006 winner Harold Dieterle is a talent; his menu includes pancetta-wrapped pork tenderloin and spicy duck meatballs. *9 Jones St. (btwn. W. 4th and Bleecker sts.) ☎ 212/929-6868. www.perillanyc.com. Main courses $22–$27. Dinner daily; brunch Sat–Sun. Subway: A/C/E/B/D/F/V to W. 4th St. Map p 111.*

★★★ **Peter Luger Steakhouse** BROOKLYN *STEAK* This Brooklyn institution is porterhouse heaven. The meat cuts like butter, and the waiters are properly crusty. *178 Broadway (Driggs Ave.), Williamsburg, Brooklyn. ☎ 718/387-7400. www.peterluger.com. Main courses $20–$35 at dinner. No credit cards. Lunch & dinner daily. Subway: J/M/Z to Marcy Ave. (Or take a cab.)*

★ **Pure Food and Wine** GRAMERCY *VEGETARIAN* Standard-bearer of the Raw Food movement, where nothing is cooked above 118°F (48°C). The dishes are sublime. *54 Irving Place (17th St.). ☎ 212/477-1010. www.purefoodandwine.com. Main courses $23–$29; 5-course tasting menu $59. AE, MC, V. Dinner daily. Subway: L/N/R/4/5/6 to 14th St./Union Sq. Map p 112.*

★ **Red Cat** CHELSEA *AMERICAN BISTRO* Sometimes you don't want to be dazzled; sometimes you don't want to be stampeded by trendoids. Sometimes you just want a good, solid meal in warm, relaxing surroundings. This casual bistro makes it look easy, plus it's got an attractive setting, topnotch service, and reliably good food. *227 10th Ave., btwn. 23rd and 24th sts. ☎ 212/242-1122. www.theredcat.com. Main courses: $20–$32. AE, DC, DISC, MC, V. Dinner daily. Subway: C/E/1/9 to 23rd St. Map p 112.*

★ **Rosa Mexicano** UPPER WEST SIDE *CONTEMPORARY MEXICAN* The 30-foot-high (9m) blue-tile waterfall competes for attention with the guacamole prepared tableside. The frozen pomegranate margarita is a must. *61 Columbus Ave. (62nd St.).*

Rare greens at The Spotted Pig.

☎ 212/977-7700. www.rosamexicano.info. *Main courses $12–$21 at lunch, $18–$26 at dinner. AE, DC, DISC, MC, V. Lunch & dinner daily. Subway: A/B/C/D/1/9 to 59th St. Map p 112.*

★ **Shake Shack** MADISON PARK *BURGERS* Some people swear that the burgers at this food stand in Madison Park are the best in the city. As part of Danny Meyer's restaurant empire, the Shack's pedigree is impeccable—so why shouldn't the food be as well? Order a Shackburger, a Flat-Top Dog (a Viennese all-beef dog butterflied and griddled), and a handspun milkshake, and dine alfresco in one of the city's nicest small parks. *Madison Sq. Park, Madison Ave. and 23rd St.* ☎ *212/889-6600. www.shakeshacknyc.com. Burgers/hot dogs $3.75–$8.75. AE, MC, V. Daily 11am–9pm. Subway: N/R/6 to 23rd St. Map p 112.*

Once a speakeasy, the 21 Club has a Prohibition-era wine cellar.

Sylvia's HARLEM *SOUL FOOD* Sylvia the lady has become an empire (canned food products, fragrances, and such), but the Sunday gospel brunch at her original Harlem restaurant is still a delight. Think fried chicken, smothered chicken, collards, and barbecue ribs. *328 Lenox Ave. (btwn. 126th & 127th sts.).* ☎ *212/996-0660. Main courses $8.95–$19. www.sylviassoulfood.com. AE, DC, DISC, MC, V. Breakfast Mon–Fri, lunch & dinner daily. Subway: 2/3 to 125th St.*

★★ **Tabla** MADISON PARK/FLATIRON *NEW INDIAN* Set in a beautiful space in the old MetLife building, this restaurant is really two in one: the main dining room on the second level, which serves American food with Indian-inspired seasonings; and the street-level Bread Bar, with "home-style" Indian food. Both make meals a special occasion. *11 E. Madison Ave. (at 25 St.).* ☎ *212/889-0667. http://tablany.com. Dining Room tasting menus $79–$89; Bread Bar family-style "wazwan" (tasting menu): $49 per person. AE, DC, DISC, MC, V. Lunch & dinner daily (no lunch in Dining Room on weekends). Subway: N/R/4/5/6 to 23rd St. Map p 112.*

★★ **Tocqueville** UNION SQUARE AREA *AMERICAN/FRENCH* This elegant and very grownup place (in its new location) has food worth whooping it up about—seared sea scallops with foie gras; Berkshire pork tenderloin; and heirloom *tartare*. *1 E. 15th St. (btwn. University & Fifth aves.).* ☎ *212/647-1515. www.tocquevillerestaurant.com. Main courses $28–$46. AE, MC, V. Lunch & dinner Mon–Sat. Subway: L/N/R/4/5/6 to 14th St./Union Sq. Map p 112.*

8 The Best Nightlife

Nightlife Best Bets

Best **Place to Swig a Microbrew**
★★ Blind Tiger *281 Bleecker St. (p 128)*

Best **Wine Bar**
★★ Enoteca i Trulli *122 E. 27th St. (p 129)*

Best **Historic Bar**
★★ King Cole Bar *2 E. 55th St. (p 129)*

Best **Choice of Single-Malt Scotches**
★★ dba *41 First Ave. (p 128)*

Best **Place to Bowl & Sip a Martini**
★★ Bowlmor *110 University Place (p 128)*

Best **Neighborhood Bar**
★ The Ginger Man *11 E. 36th St. (p 129)*

Best **Piano Bar**
★★ Brandy's Piano Bar *235 E. 84th St. (p 132)*

Best **Hotel Bar**
★★ Rose Bar *2 Lexington Ave. (p 130)*

Best **Museum Bar**
★★★ Great Hall Balcony Bar and ★★★ Roof Garden, Metropolitan Museum of Art *1000 Fifth Ave. (p 129)*

Best **Vodka Selection**
★ Pravda *281 Lafayette St. (p 130)*

Best **Irish Pub**
★★ Tír Na Nóg *5 Penn Plaza (p 131)*

Best **Views**
★ Rainbow Room *30 Rockefeller Plaza (p 130)*

Best **Drag Queens**
★★★ Splash *50 W. 17th St. (p 132)*

Best **Sangria & Tapas**
★★ Ñ *33 Crosby St. (p 129)*

Take the L Train: Billyburg Bars

Just over the bridge in Brooklyn, Williamsburg mushroomed when artists, young professionals, and expats from the Lower East Side poured in to escape soaring Manhattan rents. It's a happening neighborhood, with a multicultural mix, big living lofts and railroad apartments, and a lively nightlife. Take the short ride from Manhattan on the L train, at 14th St., and check out some of the city's most interesting bars and clubs. **Union Pool** (☎ 718/609-0484) is a bright, attractive bar with a large outdoor space, velvet lounges, and a post-hipster crowd. A refugee from Ludlow Street, **Luna Lounge** (www.lunalounge.com) serves booze and live rock. The bar/bistro/concert hall **Warsaw** (http://warsawconcerts.com) is a charmer set in the Polish National Home. **Pete's Candy Store** (www.petescandystore.com) is a wonderful bar with live music, trivia and spelling-bee nights, and a Sunday backyard barbecue. And if you want to see a hot band in a top-notch setting, the **Music Hall of Williamsburg** (www.musichallofwilliamsburg.com)—a sister club to the Mercury Lounge in Manhattan—is a good bet.

Previous page: Bowlmor Lanes near Union Square.

Downtown Nightlife

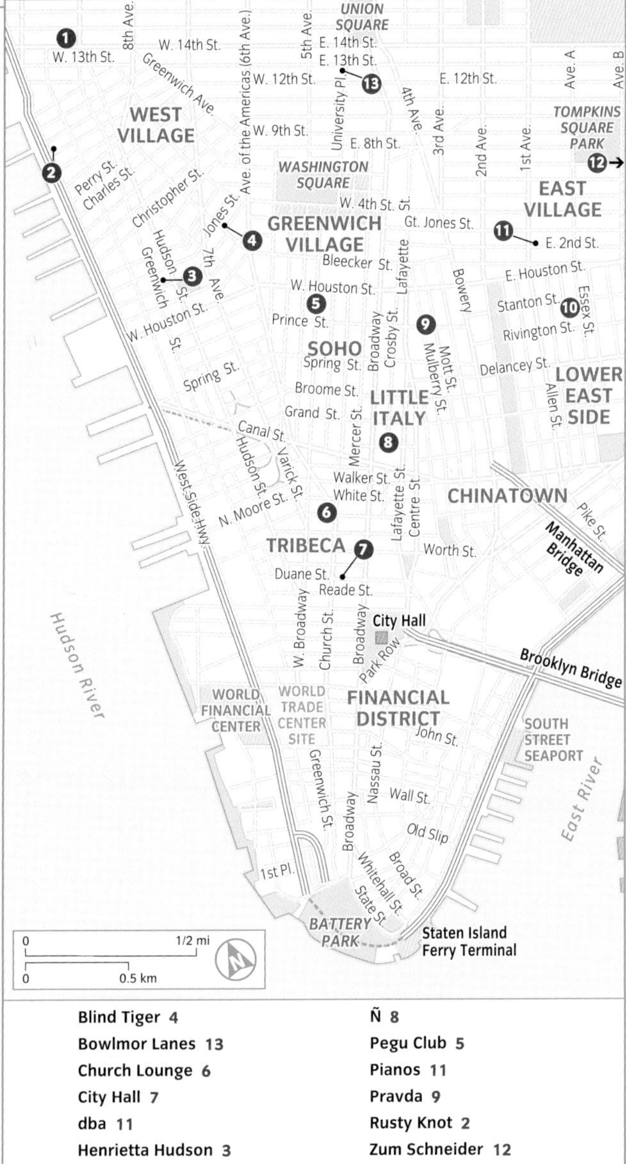

Blind Tiger 4	**Ñ 8**
Bowlmor Lanes 13	**Pegu Club 5**
Church Lounge 6	**Pianos 11**
City Hall 7	**Pravda 9**
dba 11	**Rusty Knot 2**
Henrietta Hudson 3	**Zum Schneider 12**
Lotus 1	

Midtown & Uptown Nightlife

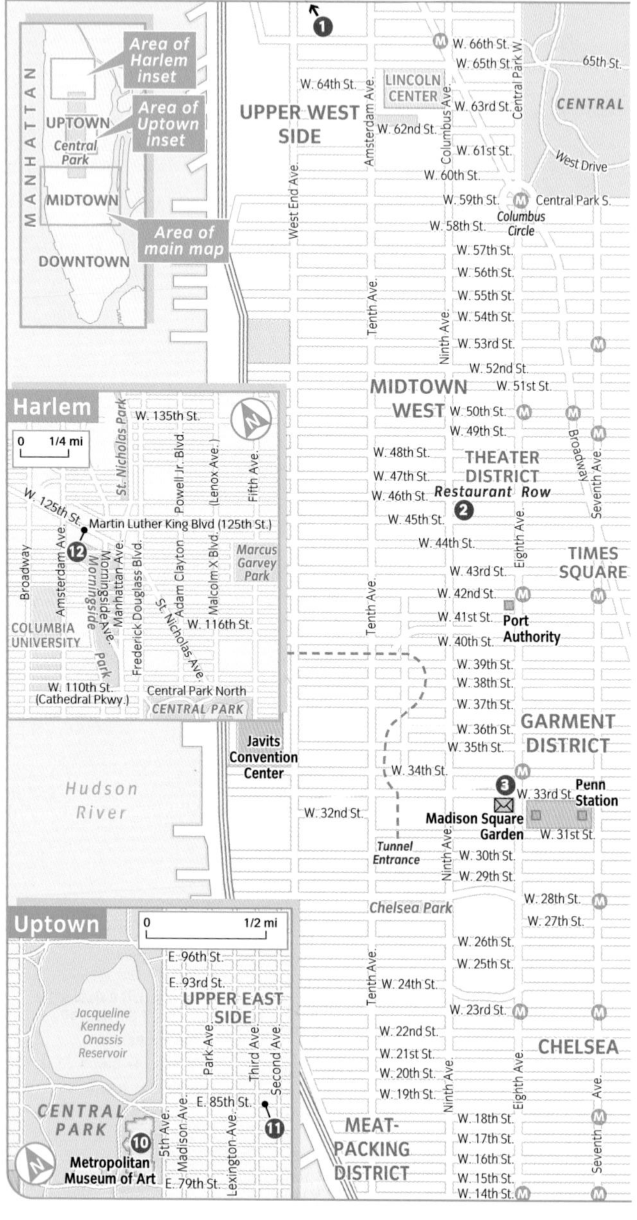

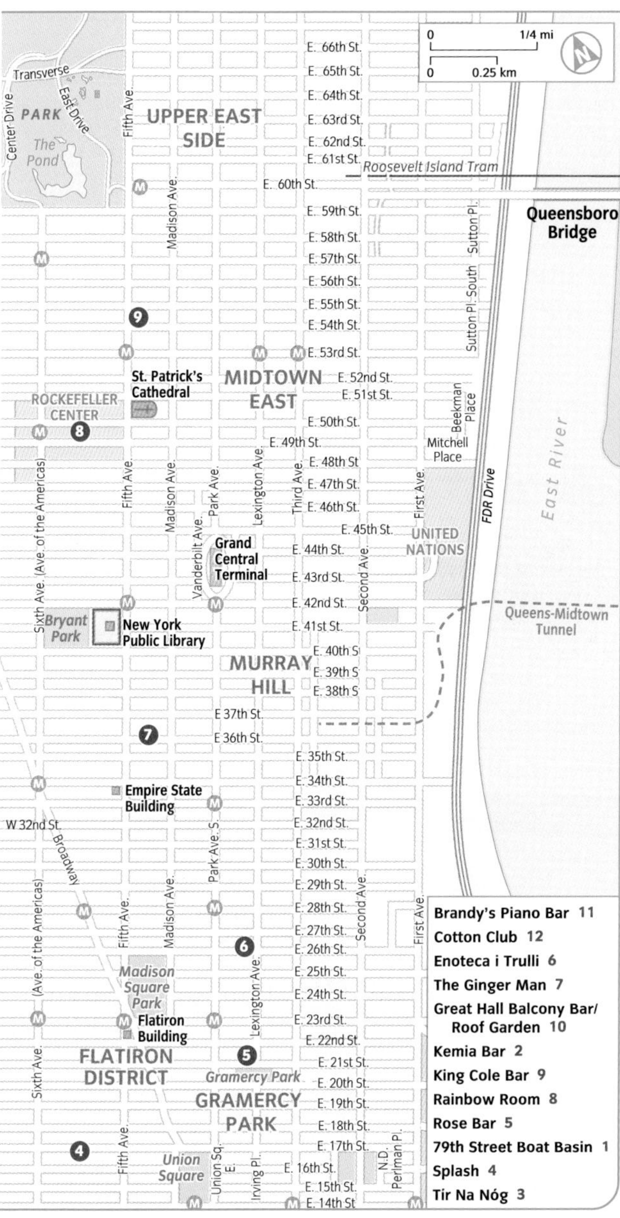
0 1/4 mi
0 0.25 km
N
Transverse
PARK
East Drive
Center Drive
The Pond
Fifth Ave.
UPPER EAST SIDE
E. 66th St.
E. 65th St.
E. 64th St.
E. 63rd St.
E. 62nd St.
E. 61st St.
Roosevelt Island Tram
E. 60th St.
Madison Ave.
E. 59th St.
Queensboro Bridge
Sutton Pl.
E. 58th St.
E. 57th St.
E. 56th St.
E. 55th St.
E. 54th St.
Sutton Pl. South
E. 53rd St.
St. Patrick's Cathedral
MIDTOWN EAST
E. 52nd St.
E. 51st St.
ROCKEFELLER CENTER
Beekman Place
E. 50th St.
E. 49th St.
Mitchell Place
East River
E. 48th St
E. 47th St.
E. 46th St.
Sixth Ave. (Ave. of the Americas)
Fifth Ave.
Madison Ave.
Park Ave.
Lexington Ave.
Third Ave.
First Ave.
FDR Drive
E. 45th St.
Vanderbilt Ave.
Grand Central Terminal
E. 44th St.
UNITED NATIONS
E. 43rd St.
Second Ave.
E. 42nd St.
Bryant Park
New York Public Library
E. 41st St.
Queens-Midtown Tunnel
MURRAY HILL
E. 40th St
E. 39th St
E. 38th St
E 37th St.
E 36th St.
E. 35th St.
E. 34th St.
Empire State Building
E. 33rd St.
W 32nd St.
Broadway
E. 32nd St.
E. 31st St.
E. 30th St.
Park Ave. S.
E. 29th St.
E. 28th St.
Sixth Ave. (Ave. of the Americas)
Fifth Ave.
Madison Ave.
E. 27th St.
Second Ave.
First Ave.
E. 26th St.
Lexington Ave.
Madison Square Park
E. 25th St.
E. 24th St.
Flatiron Building
E. 23rd St.
E. 22nd St.
FLATIRON DISTRICT
E. 21st St.
Gramercy Park
E. 20th St.
GRAMERCY PARK
E. 19th St.
E. 18th St.
E. 17th St.
Fifth Ave.
Union Square
Union Sq. E.
Irving Pl.
E. 16th St.
N.D. Perlman Pl.
E. 15th St.
E. 14th St
Brandy's Piano Bar 11
Cotton Club 12
Enoteca i Trulli 6
The Ginger Man 7
Great Hall Balcony Bar/ Roof Garden 10
Kemia Bar 2
King Cole Bar 9
Rainbow Room 8
Rose Bar 5
79th Street Boat Basin 1
Splash 4
Tír Na Nóg 3

New York Nightlife A to Z

Bars & Cocktail Lounges

★★ **Blind Tiger** WEST VILLAGE This homey, classic pub, with wood-beam ceilings, a working fireplace, and a chummy vibe, is the place to sip a beer. Among the options are 30-odd crafted drafts. *281 Bleecker St. (at Jones St.). ☎ 212/462-4682. http://blindtigeralehouse.com. Subway: 1/9 to Christopher St. Map p 125.*

★★ **Bowlmor Lanes** UNION SQUARE This 1938 bowling alley has gone mod, with candy-colored lanes, martinis, and even a VIP room. Monday "Night Strikes" feature glow-in-the-dark bowling to DJ house and techno music ($24). Upstairs is **Pressure** (www.pressurenyc.com), a huge billiards lounge that Austin Powers would feel right at home in. *110 University Place (btwn. 12th & 13th sts.). ☎ 212/255-8188. www.bowlmor.com. Subway: 4/5/6/L/N/R to 14th St./Union Sq. Map p 125.*

★ **Church Lounge** TRIBECA Want to rub elbows with Hollywood types? Or people who just look like Hollywood types? Drop by the handsome lobby bar at the Tribeca Grand Hotel (p 157). *2 Sixth Ave. (at White & Church sts.). ☎ 212/519-6600. Subway: 1/9 to Franklin St.; A/C/E to Canal St. Map p 125.*

★★ **City Hall** DOWNTOWN Debate all you like over a bottle of this bar's more than 800 wines. Set in a landmark 1863 building, the towering columns, cavernous ceiling, and elegant banquettes create a sense of grandeur. Another plus is the service, which is helpful, knowledgeable, and warm. *131 Duane St. (Church St.). ☎ 212/227-7777. Subway: A/C/1/2/3/9 to Chambers St. Map p 125.*

★★ **dba** EAST VILLAGE Lounges dominate the city, but dba is a refreshing change of pace. It's an unpretentious neighborhood bar—a beer- or whiskey-lover's dream. The collection of single-malt scotches is phenomenal. *41 First Ave. (btwn. 2nd & 3rd sts.). ☎ 212/475-5097. www.drinkgoodstuff.com. Subway: F to Second Ave. Map p 125.*

Pressure, the pool hall at Bowlmor Lanes.

Lotus in full swing.

★★ **Enoteca i Trulli** MURRAY HILL This handsome Italian-style *enoteca* (wine bar) next door to the main restaurant (i Trulli) is a great date spot. You can taste flights of Italian vino and sample cheeses, meats, or olives or such heartier fare as veal stew with potatoes and mushrooms. *122 E. 27th St. (btwn. Park & Lexington aves.). ☎ 212/481-7372. www.itrulli.com. Subway: 6 to 28th St. Map p 127.*

★ **The Ginger Man** MURRAY HILL This is a favorite neighborhood pub among the midtown business crowd. See if you can snag a seat in the back room, which has velvety couches. Expect a huge after-work crowd, a welcoming feel, and 66 ales on tap. *11 E. 36th St. (btwn. Fifth & Madison aves.). ☎ 212/532-3740. Subway: 6 to 33rd St. Map p 127.*

★★★ **Great Hall Balcony Bar/ Roof Garden** UPPER EAST SIDE Every Friday and Saturday night from 4 to 8:30pm, the lobby's mezzanine level transforms into a lounge with live classical music. When the weather warms, take the elevator up to the **Roof Garden,** for drinks with sumptuous views of the park. *Metropolitan Museum of Art, 1000 Fifth Ave. (82nd St.). ☎ 212/535-7710. www.metmuseum.org. Subway: 4/5/6 to 86th St. Map p 127.*

★★ **Kemia Bar** MIDTOWN WEST This bar looks sexy and exotic, with a Moroccan-themed setting, but it's comfy and welcoming. Vanilla- and sugarcane-infused martinis and a friendly waitstaff make it practically irresistible. Kemia's proximity to the Theater District makes it an ideal stop after a show. *630 Ninth Ave. (btwn. 44th & 45th sts.). ☎ 212/582-3200. Subway: A/C/E to 42nd St. Map p 127.*

★★ **King Cole Bar** MIDTOWN EAST The Bloody Mary was born here, in the tony St. Regis Hotel. The Maxfield Parrish mural alone is worth the price of a classic cocktail (but egads, what a price!). It's a small but memorable spot. *2 E. 55th St. (Fifth Ave.). ☎ 212/744-4300. Subway: E to Fifth Ave./53rd St. Map p 127.*

★★ **Ñ** SOHO This dark, narrow, candlelit tapas bar is a gem. **Ñ** (pronounced like the Spanish letter, *eh-nyeh*) is a great place to savor some very good tapas and fruity sangria. On Wednesday nights, arrive early to claim a seat for the weekly flamenco performance, which begins around 8pm. *33 Crosby St. (btwn. Grand & Broome sts.). ☎ 212/219-8856. Subway: N/R to Prince St.; 6 to Spring St. Map p 125.*

★★ **Pegu Club** SOHO Self-described "gatekeepers of classic cocktail culture," the Pegu Club brings uptown to downtown in this sleek and polished venue. *77 W. Houston St., 2nd Floor (at W. Broadway). ☎ 212/473-PEGU. www.peguclub.com. Subway: 6/V/F to Bleecker St./Lafayette St. Map p 125.*

★★ **Pianos** LOWER EAST SIDE This multilevel former piano store gets high marks both as a bar and as a music venue. On any given night, three or four different performances

dba's drink offerings are written on blackboards.

may be going on. *158 Ludlow St. ☎ 212/505-3733. www.pianosnyc.com. Subway: F/V to Second Ave. Map p 125.*

★ **Pravda** SOHO This glam underground caviar lounge is no longer the "it" place in town, but consider that good news: It means you won't be surrounded by preening trendsters. This Keith McNally concoction still entertains with a great atmosphere (sexy red banquettes) and some 70 types of vodka from 18 countries. The only street-level sign reads "281"; follow the stairwell down. *281 Lafayette St. (btwn. Houston & Prince sts.). ☎ 212/226-4944. www.pravdany.com. Subway: N to Prince St. Map p 125.*

★ **Rainbow Room** MIDTOWN WEST Cocktails are priced sky-high, but the view is incomparable. Combine that view with Art Deco elegance and live piano music, and you've got one great, romantic date. *30 Rockefeller Plaza (49th St.). ☎ 212/632-5000. www.rainbowroom.com. Subway: B/D/F/V to 47th–50th sts./Rockefeller Center. Map p 127.*

★★ **Rose Bar** GRAMERCY PARK Ian Schrager's 2006 head-to-toe renovation of the old Gramercy Park Hotel included the sumptuous and original redesign of the bar by artist Julian Schnabel; it's now like the great room in the country estate of some slightly nutty 21st-century Venetian prince. Even so, it's

The mural at the King Cole Bar.

Dancing at the Rainbow Room.

demoted one star for the pricey drinks and, some say, uncool attitude. *2 Lexington Ave. (at Gramercy Park). ☎ 212/920-3300. www.gramercyparkhotel.com. Subway: 6 to 23rd St. Map p 127.*

★ **Rusty Knot** WEST VILLAGE/HUDSON RIVER This determinedly downscale, nautically themed bar/restaurant is packing 'em in on West Street across from the Hudson River. Of course it is: Among its siblings is the ever-cool Spotted Pig. It's a comfortable, agreeable spot to drink beer, play pool, and watch the river sunsets. *425 West St. (at 11th St.). ☎ 212/645-5668. Subway: 1 to Christopher St.-Sheridan Sq. Map p 125.*

★★ **79th Street Boat Basin** UPPER WEST SIDE When spring finally arrives, nature-starved New Yorkers flock here to sip beer on the outdoor patio, mingle under the limestone arches, and gaze out at the Hudson River. This is as much a casual restaurant as it is a bar, with hamburgers, hot dogs, and "garden burgers" sizzling on an outdoor grill. *79th Street Boat Basin, 79th St. & the Hudson River. ☎ 212/496-5542. www.boatbasincafe.com. Subway: 1/9 to 79th St. Map p 127.*

★ **Tír Na Nóg** MIDTOWN WEST New York is packed with Irish bars, but this standout makes you feel as if you're on a patch of the Emerald Isle. The friendly bartenders, Murphy's on tap, and lively music make for an authentic Celtic pub experience. *5 Penn Plaza (Eighth Ave., btwn. 33rd & 34th sts.). ☎ 212/630-0249. www.tirnanognyc.com. Subway: A/C/E to 34th St./Penn Station. Map p 127.*

Zum Schneider EAST VILLAGE Just what Alphabet City needed: a genuine indoor Bavarian beer garden. With its long tables and bench seating, this is a *sehr gut* place to go with a group. *107 Ave. C (7th St.). ☎ 212/598-1098. www.zumschneider.com. Subway: F to Second Ave.; L to First Ave. Map p 125.*

Dance Clubs

★ **Cotton Club** HARLEM Although the legendary 1920s Harlem hot spot closed for good in 1940, the current incarnation of the club, set in an Art Deco structure 20 blocks away from the original, has good bones and swinging music. The house band—the 13-piece Cotton Club All-Stars—will have you kicking your heels in no time to swing and jazz tunes. A gospel show/buffet brunch is held on weekends. *656 W. 125th St. (Martin Luther King Blvd.). ☎ 888/640-7980 or 212/663-7980. www.cottonclub-newyork.com. $15–$32 cover. Subway: 1/9 to 125th St. Map p 127.*

The Cotton Club was New York's most famous nightclub in the 1920s and 1930s.

★ **Lotus** MEAT-PACKING DISTRICT This triple-decker space is a restaurant in the early evening (no cover charge) and a nightclub from 10pm till 4am. It's a beauty, with "Urban Asian street food" and divine watermelon martinis. Guest DJs have included Mark Ronson, Grandmaster Flash, and Jazzy Jeff. *409 W. 14th St. (Ninth Ave.). ☎ 212/243-4420. www.lotusnewyork.com. $10–$20 cover. Subway: A/C/E to 14th St. Map p 125.*

The Gay & Lesbian Scene

★★ **Brandy's Piano Bar** UPPER EAST SIDE The crowd is a mix of gay and straight, men and women, at this intimate piano bar. It's friendly and relaxed—so much so that the talented waitstaff who do most of the singing don't mind when patrons join in. *235 E. 84th St. (btwn. Second & Third aves.). ☎ 212/650-1944. www.brandysnyc.com. Subway: 4/5/6 to 86th St. Map p 127.*

Henrietta Hudson has a sidewalk cafe and a pool table.

★ **Henrietta Hudson** WEST VILLAGE This popular ladies' lounge has been calling out to lipstick lesbians since 1991. The theme nights pack the house: Discothèque Fridays feature classic disco, and Mas Flow Wednesdays are devoted to reggae and hip-hop. *438 Hudson St. (Morton St.). ☎ 212/924-3347. www.henriettahudsons.com. Subway: 1/9 to Houston St. Map p 125.*

★★ **Splash** CHELSEA Welcome to gay heaven: This is a world of beautiful bartenders, mirrors everywhere the eye can see, and New York's best drag queens. Few theme nights anywhere are more successful than Musical Mondays: These singalongs draw a devoted mixed gay/straight crowd. *50 W. 17th St. (btwn. Fifth & Sixth aves.). ☎ 212/691-0073. www.splashbar.com. Subway: F/V to 14th St.; 4/5/6/N/R/L/Q/W to 14th St./Union Sq. Map p 127.*

9 The Best Arts & Entertainment

A&E Best Bets

Most **Unusual Venue**
★ Bargemusic, Fulton Ferry Landing *Brooklyn (p 139)*

Best **Free Music**
★★★ Juilliard School, Lincoln Center *Broadway at 65th St. (p 139)*

Best **World Music**
★★ S.O.B.'s *204 Varick St. (p 144)*

Best **Historic Venue**
★★★ Apollo Theater *253 W. 125th St. (p 139)*

Best **Food at a Club**
★★ Jazz Standard *116 E. 27th St. (p 143)*

Best **Classical Dance Troupe**
★★★ New York City Ballet, Lincoln Center *Broadway and 64th St. (p 139)*

Best **Modern Dance Troupe**
★★ Alvin Ailey American Dance Theater, Joan Weill Center for Dance *405 W. 55th St. (p 139)*

Best **Author Readings**
★ 92nd Street, Tisch Center for the Arts *1395 Lexington Ave. (p 141)*

Best **Repertory Theater Group**
★ New York Gilbert and Sullivan Players, City Center *130 W. 56th St. (p 144)*

Best **New Comedians**
★ Gotham Comedy Club *34 W. 22nd St. (p 145)*

Best **Rock-'n'-Roll Bar**
★★ Mercury Lounge *217 E. Houston St. (p 143)*

Most **Unforgettable Visual Spectacle**
★★★ Metropolitan Opera, Lincoln Center *Broadway and 64th St. (p 144)*

Best **Jazz Club**
★★ Birdland *315 W. 44th St. (p 142)*; and ★★ Lenox Lounge *288 Malcolm X Blvd. (p 143)*

Most **Avant-Garde Offerings**
★ The Knitting Factory *74 Leonard St. (p 143)*

Best **Find**
★ Amato Opera Theatre *319 Bowery (p 144)*; and ★★ St. Nick's Pub *773 St. Nicholas Ave. (p 144)*

Most **Cutting-Edge Major Venue**
★★★ Brooklyn Academy of Music *30 Lafayette Ave., Brooklyn (p 140)*

Best **Place to See Shakespeare**
★★ Public Theater *425 Lafayette St. (p 141)*

Best **Church Concert Series**
★★ Church of the Transfiguration *1 E. 29th St. (p 140)*

Previous page: The Brooklyn Academy of Music presents Chris Martin of Coldplay. This page: John Legend at the Lenox Lounge.

Downtown A&E

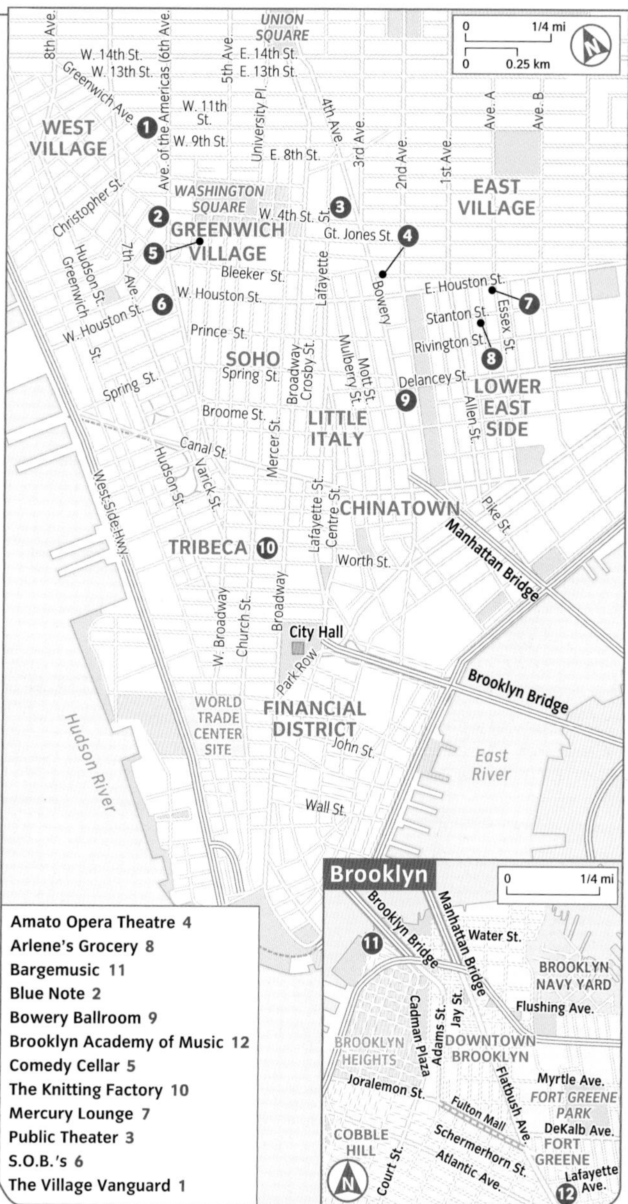
UNION SQUARE
0 1/4 mi
0 0.25 km
N
8th Ave.
W. 14th St.
W. 13th St.
Greenwich Ave.
Ave. of the Americas (6th Ave.)
5th Ave.
E. 14th St.
E. 13th St.
W. 11th St.
W. 9th St.
University Pl.
E. 8th St.
4th Ave.
3rd Ave.
2nd Ave.
1st Ave.
Ave. A
Ave. B
WEST VILLAGE
EAST VILLAGE
Christopher St.
WASHINGTON SQUARE
W. 4th St.
GREENWICH VILLAGE
Gt. Jones St.
Hudson St.
Greenwich St.
7th Ave.
Bleeker St.
Lafayette St.
Bowery
E. Houston St.
W. Houston St.
Stanton St.
Essex St.
Prince St.
Rivington St.
SOHO
Spring St.
Broadway
Crosby St.
Mulberry St.
Mott St.
Delancey St.
LOWER EAST SIDE
Allen St.
Broome St.
LITTLE ITALY
Mercer St.
Canal St.
Varick St.
Pike St.
CHINATOWN
Centre St.
Manhattan Bridge
West Side Hwy.
TRIBECA
Worth St.
W. Broadway
Church St.
City Hall
Park Row
Brooklyn Bridge
WORLD TRADE CENTER SITE
FINANCIAL DISTRICT
John St.
Hudson River
East River
Wall St.
Brooklyn
Water St.
BROOKLYN NAVY YARD
Flushing Ave.
Cadman Plaza
Adams St.
Jay St.
BROOKLYN HEIGHTS
DOWNTOWN BROOKLYN
Joralemon St.
Fulton Mall
Flatbush Ave.
Myrtle Ave.
FORT GREENE PARK
DeKalb Ave.
FORT GREENE
Schermerhorn St.
Atlantic Ave.
COBBLE HILL
Court St.
Lafayette Ave.
Amato Opera Theatre 4
Arlene's Grocery 8
Bargemusic 11
Blue Note 2
Bowery Ballroom 9
Brooklyn Academy of Music 12
Comedy Cellar 5
The Knitting Factory 10
Mercury Lounge 7
Public Theater 3
S.O.B.'s 6
The Village Vanguard 1

Midtown & Uptown A&E

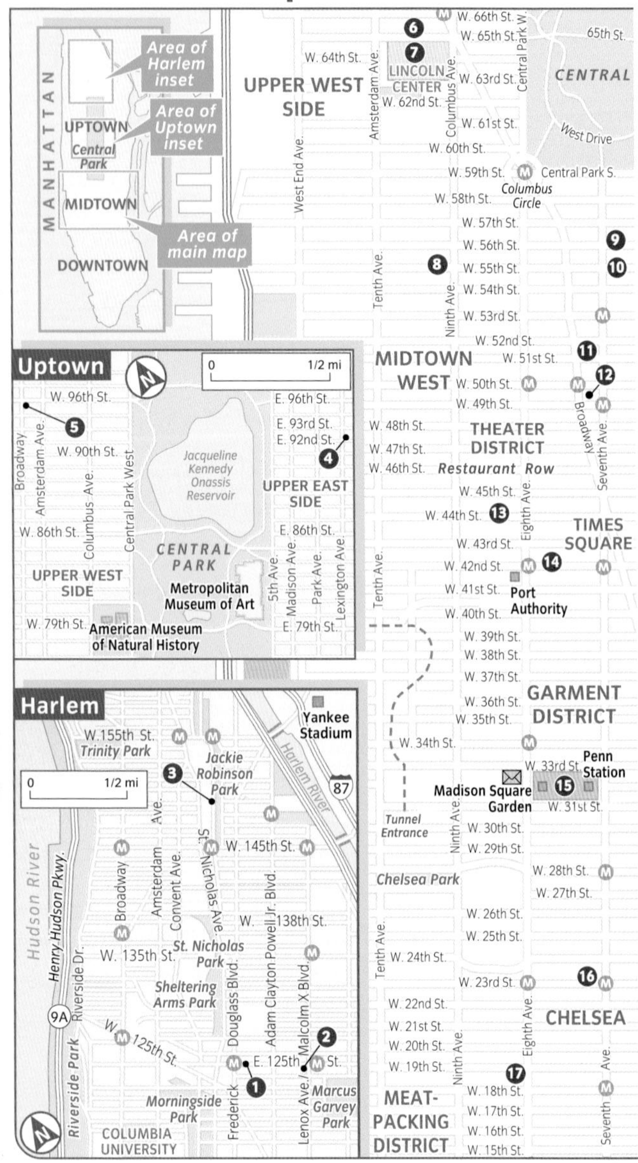

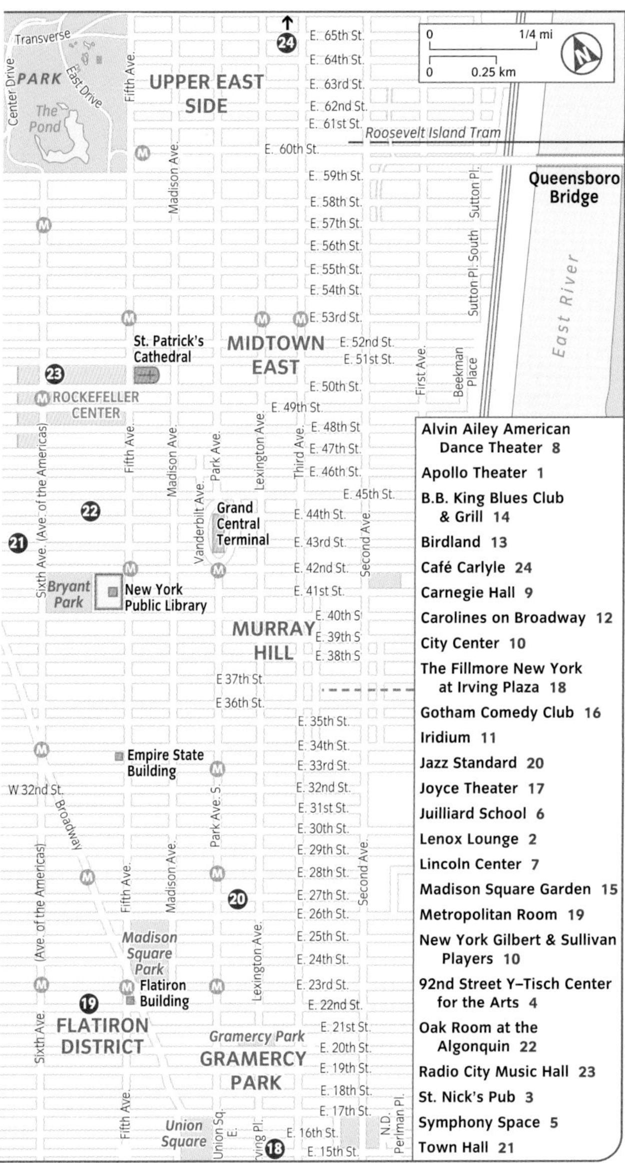

Alvin Ailey American Dance Theater 8
Apollo Theater 1
B.B. King Blues Club & Grill 14
Birdland 13
Café Carlyle 24
Carnegie Hall 9
Carolines on Broadway 12
City Center 10
The Fillmore New York at Irving Plaza 18
Gotham Comedy Club 16
Iridium 11
Jazz Standard 20
Joyce Theater 17
Juilliard School 6
Lenox Lounge 2
Lincoln Center 7
Madison Square Garden 15
Metropolitan Room 19
New York Gilbert & Sullivan Players 10
92nd Street Y–Tisch Center for the Arts 4
Oak Room at the Algonquin 22
Radio City Music Hall 23
St. Nick's Pub 3
Symphony Space 5
Town Hall 21

Broadway Theaters

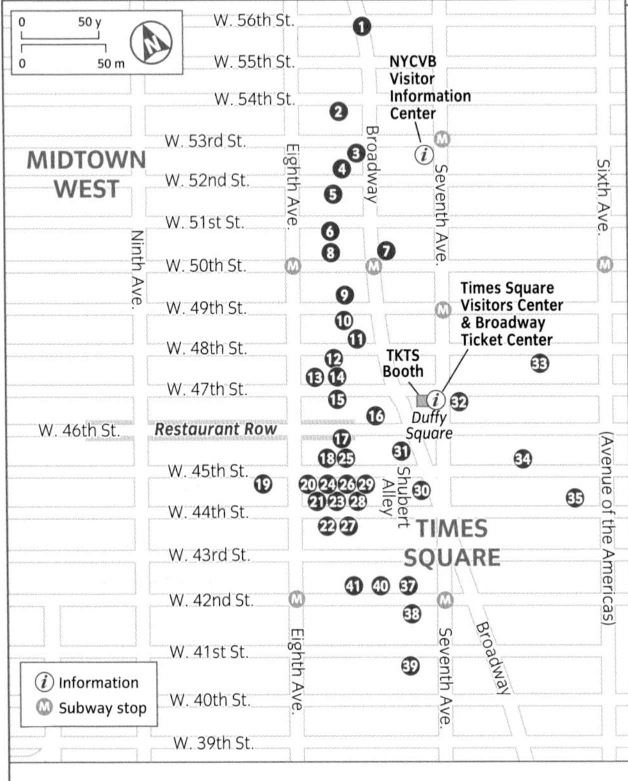

Al Hirschfeld 19
Ambassador 9
American Airlines 41
August Wilson Theater 4
Belasco 35
Biltmore 13
Booth 29
Broadhurst 23
Broadway 3
Brooks Atkinson 15
Circle in the Square 8
Cort 33
Ethel Barrymore 14
Eugene O'Neill 10
Gershwin 6
Helen Hayes 27
Hilton Theatre 40
Imperial 18
John Golden 20
Longacre 12
Lunt-Fontanne 16
Lyceum 34
Majestic 21
Marquis 31
Minskoff 30
Music Box 25
Nederlander 39
Neil Simon 5
New Amsterdam 38
New Victory 37
Palace 32
Plymouth 26
Richard Rogers 17
Royale 24
St. James 22
Shubert 28
Studio 54 2
Vivian Beaumont 1
Walter Kerr 11
Winter Garden 7

New York **A&E A to Z**

Classical Music

★ **Bargemusic** BROOKLYN Talk about original—this permanently docked barge is a primo chamber music concert hall; Thursday nights are jazz nights. *At Fulton Ferry Landing (just south of the Brooklyn Bridge), Brooklyn. ☎ 718/624-2083. www.bargemusic.org. Tickets $20–$35. Subway: 2/3 to Clark St.; A/C to High St. Map p 135.*

★★★ **Juilliard School** LINCOLN CENTER America's premier music school sponsors more than 500 concerts a year, most at no charge. *60 Lincoln Center Plaza (Broadway at 65th St.). ☎ 212/799-5000. www.juilliard.edu. Free admission to most shows; select performances $20. Subway: 1/9 to 66th St. Map p 137.*

★★★ **New York Philharmonic** LINCOLN CENTER Founded in 1842, this is one of the best symphonies on the planet. *At Avery Fisher Hall, Lincoln Center, Broadway & 65th St. ☎ 212/875-5656 for audience services, 212/875-5030 for box office information, or Center Charge 212/721-6500 for tickets. http://nyphil.org. Tickets $34–$119. Subway: 1/9 to 66th St. Map p 136, bullet ❼.*

Dance

★★ **Alvin Ailey American Dance Theater** MIDTOWN WEST This world-renowned modern dance company just celebrated its 50th anniversary. It's located in the eight-floor Joan Weill Center for Dance, the largest facility dedicated to dance in the country. *405 W. 55th St. (at Ninth Ave.). ☎ 212/405-9000. www.alvinailey.org. Tickets $44. Subway: 1/2/3/9/A/C to 59 St./Columbus Circle. Map p 137.*

Alvin Ailey American Dance Theater.

★★ **City Center** MIDTOWN WEST Modern dance doesn't get any better than this, and the sightlines are terrific from all corners. *131 W. 55th St. (btwn. Sixth & Seventh aves.). ☎ 877/247-0430. www.citycenter.org. Tickets $35–$110. Subway: F/N/Q/R/W to 57th St.; B/D/E to Seventh Ave. Map p 137.*

★ **Joyce Theater** CHELSEA Built as a movie house, the Art Deco Joyce has become a great modern dance center. Joyce SoHo hosts experimental works. *175 Eighth Ave. (at 19th St.). ☎ 212/242-0800. www.joyce.org. Tickets $20–$44. Subway: C/E to 23rd St.; 1/9 to 18th St. Joyce SoHo at 155 Mercer St. (btwn. Houston & Prince sts.). ☎ 212/431-9233. Subway: N/R to Prince St. Map p 137.*

★★★ **New York City Ballet** LINCOLN CENTER The legendary George Balanchine founded this stellar company. *At the New York State Theater, Lincoln Center, Broadway & 64th St. ☎ 212/870-5570. www.nycballet.com. Tickets $20–$86. Subway: 1/9 to 66th St. Map p 136, bullet ❼.*

Landmark Venues

★★★ **Apollo Theater** HARLEM A legendary institution. *See p 70, bullet ❿.*

Heavenly Sounds

New York churches may play traditional hymns during their religious services, but many also host afternoon and evening concerts in a variety of secular styles, from classical to opera, from instrumental to thrilling soloists. And the price is right: A few concerts require tickets, but most have a "requested donation" from $2 to $10. Check the websites for schedules. A few of the best: **Church of the Transfiguration** (1 E. 29th St.; www.littlechurch.org), **St. Bartholomew** (www.stbarts.org)(p 117), **St. Paul's Chapel and Trinity Church** (www.saintpaulschapel.org; p 8), **The Cathedral of St. John the Divine** (www.stjohndivine.org; p 67), and **St. Ignatius Loyola** (980 Park Ave.; www.saintignatiusloyola.org).

★★★ **Brooklyn Academy of Music** BROOKLYN Just 25 minutes by subway from midtown, BAM is the place for cutting-edge theater, opera, dance, and music. *30 Lafayette Ave. (off Flatbush Ave.), Brooklyn. ☎ 718/636-4100. www.bam.org. Ticket prices vary. Subway: 2/3/4/5/M/N/Q/R/W to Pacific St./Atlantic Ave. Map p 135.*

★★★ **Carnegie Hall** MIDTOWN WEST One of the world's most respected concert halls. *See p 15, bullet ❷.*

★★★ **Lincoln Center for the Performing Arts** UPPER WEST SIDE A multimillion-dollar modernization project is bringing this world-famous performing-arts complex into the 21st century. It's scheduled for completion in 2009–10, just in time to celebrate Lincoln Center's 50th anniversary. *Map p 137.*

Madison Square Garden GARMENT DISTRICT The most famous names in pop music play this cavernous 20,000-seat arena. *Seventh Ave. & 31st–33rd sts. ☎ 212/465-MSG1. www.thegarden.com. Ticket prices vary. Subway: A/C/E/1/2/3/9 to 34th St. Map p 137.*

The Isaac Stern Auditorium at Carnegie Hall.

★★ 92nd Street Y–Tisch Center for the Arts UPPER EAST SIDE Forget what you know about "the Y"—this Jewish community center offers superb cultural events with the top newsmakers of the day. *1395 Lexington Ave. (at 92nd St.). ☎ 212/415-5500. www.92ndsty.org. Tickets $20–$26. Subway: 4/5/6 to 86th St.; 6 to 96th St. Map p 137.*

★★ Public Theater NOHO Come here for groundbreaking stagings of Shakespeare as well as new plays, classical dramas, and solo performances. *425 Lafayette St. (btwn. Astor Place and E. 4th St.). ☎ 800/276-2392. www.publictheater.org. Ticket prices vary. Subway: 6 to Astor Place. Map p 135.*

★★ Radio City Music Hall MIDTOWN WEST This stunning 6,200-seat Art Deco theater is home to the annual Christmas Spectacular and the Rockettes. *See p 16, bullet ❻.*

★ Symphony Space UPPER WEST SIDE Now in its 30th year, this innovative institution includes the Peter Jay Sharp Theatre and the Leonard Nimoy Thalia Theater and offers a varied program of dance, film, readings, and music. *2537 Broadway (at 95th St.). ☎ 212/864-1414. www.symphonyspace.org. Ticket prices vary. Subway: 1/2/3/9 to 96th St. Map p 137.*

Radio City Music Hall during the holidays.

★ Town Hall MIDTOWN WEST A National Historic Site, this intimate space has outstanding acoustics and performers ranging from Judy Collins to Ornette Coleman, the Klezmatics to flamenco singers. *123 W. 43rd St. (btwn. Sixth & Seventh aves.). ☎ 212/840-2824. www.the-townhall-nyc.org. Ticket prices vary. Subway: N/Q/R/S/W/1/2/3/7/9 to 42nd St./Times Sq.; B/D/F/V to 42nd St. Map p 137.*

Live Music

Arlene's Grocery LOWER EAST SIDE A casual rock music club with

Broadway Theaters

In the Big Apple you'll find a kaleidoscopic mix of big-budget blockbusters and alternative, experimental shows. Broadway is the place to see glorious spectacles such as *The Producers,* classics like *12 Angry Men,* and first-run hits such as *Proof*. Casts often include faces you'll recognize from the big screen: Kevin Spacey, Patrick Stewart, and Glenn Close, to name a few. And these days, even the smaller and alternative shows are frequently lit by star power (Tim Robbins' Actors' Gang are regulars at the Public Theater, above). For information on tickets see "Getting Tickets" (p 145); for a list of theaters, see p 146 or the map on p 138.

a good sound system; great bang for the buck. *95 Stanton St. (btwn. Ludlow & Orchard sts.). ☎ 212/995-1652. www.arlenesgrocery.net. $8–$10 cover. Subway: F to Second Ave. Map p 135.*

B.B. King Blues Club & Grill THEATER DISTRICT This 550-seat venue plays the blues (naturally) as well as pop, funk, and country. *237 W. 42nd St. (btwn. Seventh & Eighth aves.). ☎ 212/997-4144. www.bbkingblues.com. Tickets $26–$100. Subway: A/C/E/Q/W/1/2/3/7/9 to 42nd St. Map p 137.*

★★ **Birdland** MIDTOWN WEST A legendary jazz club and one of the city's favorites. *315 W. 44th St. (btwn. Eighth & Ninth aves.). ☎ 212/581-3080. www.birdlandjazz.com. Tickets $20–$50. Subway: A/C/E to 42nd St. Map p 137.*

Blue Note GREENWICH VILLAGE Soft-jazz fans take note: This Village spot has an excellent sound system and sightlines. *131 W. 3rd St. (at Sixth Ave.). ☎ 212/475-8592. www.bluenote.net. Tickets $5–$40. Subway: A/B/C/D/E/F/V to W. 4th St. Map p 135.*

Bowery Ballroom LOWER EAST SIDE Another Art Deco wonder—this one with a big stage and good sightlines from every corner. Alt-rockers such as Patti Smith perform here, and the Fab Faux, a Beatles tribute band, also makes frequent appearances. *6 Delancey St. (at Bowery). ☎ 212/533-2111. www.boweryballroom.com. Tickets $13–$40. Subway: F/J/M/Z to Delancey St. Map p 135.*

Live bands play throughout the week at Arlene's Grocery.

When the original Birdland opened in 1949, Charlie Parker was the headliner.

★ **Café Carlyle** UPPER EAST SIDE Newly renovated, this classic cabaret lounge was once the domain of the late Bobby Short. Now it's the venue for stars such as Eartha Kitt, Barbara Cook, and Woody Allen and his jazz band. *Carlyle Hotel. 35 E. 76th St. ☎ 212/744-1600. www.thecarlyle.com. Tickets $40–$150. Subway: 6 to 77th St. Map p 137.*

★ **Iridium** THEATER DISTRICT Guitar great Les Paul has played two sets at this glamorous jazz club every Monday for a long time. The Iridium also hosts tributes to the likes of jazz greats Thelonious Monk and Charles Mingus. *1650 Broadway (at 51st St.). ☎ 212/582-2121. www.iridiumjazzclub.com. Tickets $25–$50. Subway: 1/9 to 50th St. Map p 137.*

The Fillmore New York at Irving Plaza GRAMERCY PARK This midsize music hall (formerly Irving Plaza) has a new name but remains a prime stop for rock bands such as Crowded House and the Black Crowes and hot artists like Lily Allen (the first headline performer under the new marquee). *17 Irving Place (1 block west of Third Ave. at 15th St.). ☎ 212/777-1224. www.irvingplaza.com. Tickets $19–$55. Subway: L/N/R/4/5/6 to 14th St./Union Sq. Map p 137.*

★★ **Jazz Standard** GRAMERCY/MURRAY HILL One of the city's largest jazz clubs, Jazz Standard has a retro vibe and the best food of any club (it's part of, and downstairs from, Blue Smoke; see p 117). *116 E. 27th St. (btwn. Park Ave. S. & Lexington Ave.). ☎ 212/576-2232. www.jazzstandard.net. $15–$30 cover. Subway: 6 to 28th St. Map p 137.*

★ **The Knitting Factory** TRIBECA This famed avant-garde music venue has experimental jazz, acoustic folk, poetry readings, and multimedia art. *74 Leonard St. (btwn. Broadway & Church St.). ☎ 212/219-3055. www.knittingfactory.com. $8–$20 cover. Subway: 1/9 to Franklin St. Map p 135.*

★★ **Lenox Lounge** HARLEM This beautifully renovated and historically accurate gem features top jazz vocalists, trios, and quartets. *288 Malcolm X Blvd. (Lenox Ave. btwn. 124th & 125th sts.). ☎ 212/427-0253. www.lenoxlounge.com. $20–$25 cover, $16 drink minimum order. Subway: 2/3 to 125th St. Map p 137.*

Ted Nash & Odeon at the Jazz Standard.

Iridium hosts a jazz brunch buffet on Sundays.

★★ **Mercury Lounge** LOWER EAST SIDE The perfect live-music rock-'n'-roll bar. *217 E. Houston St. (at Essex St./Ave. A). ☎ 212/260-4700. www.mercuryloungenyc.com. $8–$15 cover; some shows require tickets. Subway: F to Second Ave. Map p 135.*

★★ **Metropolitan Room** FLATIRON Just 2 years old, this sexy spot recently won raves from *New York* magazine as the best cabaret in town. *34 W. 22nd St. (btwn. Fifth & Sixth aves.). ☎ 212/206-0440. www.metropolitanroom.com. $20–$35 cover; $15 drink minimum. Subway: N/R to 23rd St. Map p 135.*

★★ **Oak Room at the Algonquin** MIDTOWN For a night on the town, it's a combo that's hard to beat—a topnotch cabaret supper club in a legendary hotel. *The Algonquin Hotel. 59 W. 44th St. (btwn. Fifth & Sixth aves.). ☎ 212/840-6800. www.algonquinhotel.com. $60–$75 cover; $60 prix-fixe supper (optional Tues–Thurs). Subway: B/D/F/V to 42nd St. Map p 137.*

★★ St. Nick's Pub HARLEM Unpretentious St. Nick's in Harlem's Sugar Hill district has great live entertainment every night. It draws the famous (Roy Hargrove, James Carter) and many lesser-knowns, all of whom partake in the late-night jam sessions. *773 St. Nicholas Ave. (at 149th St.). ☎ 212/283-9728. Under $5 cover. Subway: A/C/D/B to 145th St. Map p 137.*

★★ S.O.B.'s SOHO This top world-music venue features Brazilian, Caribbean, and Latin beats. The music is so hot you won't be able to stay in your seat. *204 Varick St. (at West Houston St.). ☎ 212/243-4940. www.sobs.com. $10–$25 cover. Subway: 1/9 to Houston St. Map p 135.*

The Village Vanguard GREENWICH VILLAGE Since 1935, this club has been showcasing jazz artists. Many of the greats, including Sonny Rollins and John Coltrane, have recorded live jazz albums here. *178 Seventh Ave. S. (just below 11th St.). ☎ 212/255-4037. www.villagevanguard.net. Tickets $30–$35. Subway: 1/2/3/9 to 14th St. Map p 135.*

Opera

★ Amato Opera Theatre EAST VILLAGE This off-the-beaten-track find is a showcase for talented young singers. The theater barely seats 100, so buy tickets well in advance. *319 Bowery (at 2nd St.). ☎ 212/228-8200. www.amato.org. Tickets $35 (seniors $30). Subway: F to Second Ave.; 6 to Bleecker St. Map p 135.*

★★★ Metropolitan Opera LINCOLN CENTER Opera aficionados know that this is one of the most electrifying companies in the world. *At the Metropolitan Opera House, Lincoln Center, Broadway & 64th St. ☎ 212/362-6000. www.metopera.org. Tickets $15–$295. Subway: 1/9 to 66th St. Map p 136, bullet ❼.*

★ New York City Opera LINCOLN CENTER NYC Opera's repertoire includes more modern and experimental works than the Met's, but singers are less well known. *At the New York State Theater, Lincoln Center, Broadway & 64th St. ☎ 212/870-5570. www.nycopera.com. Tickets $16–$130. Subway: 1/9 to 66th St. Map p 136, bullet ❼.*

★ New York Gilbert & Sullivan Players MIDTOWN Lighthearted operetta is the ticket here, and no one does it better. The troupe now performs at the 1923 City Center. *130 W. 56th St. ☎ 212/769-1000. http://nygasp.org. Tickets $40–$65. Subway: 1/2/3/9 to 96th St. Map p 137.*

Relaxing with a beer at the Lenox Lounge in Harlem.

The Metropolitan Opera's first performances took place in 1883.

Stand-up Comedy

★★ Carolines on Broadway

THEATER DISTRICT Hot headliners come to this upscale club (Jerry Seinfeld, Rosie O'Donnell, and Tim Allen have all taken the stage; Colin Quinn is here frequently). *1626 Broadway (btwn. 49th & 50th sts.). ☎ 212/757-4100. www.carolines.com. $15–$49 cover. Subway: N/R to 49th St.; 1/9 to 50th St. Map p 137.*

★ Comedy Cellar

GREENWICH VILLAGE This intimate subterranean club is a favorite among comedy cognoscenti. It gets names you'd expect (Dave Chappelle, Chris Rock) and a few you wouldn't (William Shatner). *117 Macdougal St. (btwn. Minetta Lane & W. 3rd St.). ☎ 212/254-3480. www.comedycellar.com. $10–$15 cover. Subway: A/B/C/D/E/F/V/S to W. 4th St. Map p 135.*

★ Gotham Comedy Club

FLATIRON DISTRICT Big names are frequently on the marquee in this large, 1920s-era space next door to the old Chelsea Hotel. The "New Talent Showcase" is a staple. *208 W. 23rd St. (btwn. Seventh & Eighth aves.). ☎ 212/367-9000. www.gothamcomedyclub.com. $12–$25 cover. Subway: F/N/R to 23rd St. Map p 137.*

Getting Tickets

If your heart is set on seeing a particular show, buy tickets in advance from **TeleCharge** (☎ 212/239-6200; www.telecharge.com) or **Ticketmaster** (☎ 212/307-4100; www.ticketmaster.com).

The free membership programs at **www.broadway.com**, **www.playbill.com**, or **www.theatermania.com** can save you up to 50% on tickets. For the best deals on **same-day tickets,** visit **TKTS Times Square** (47th St. and Broadway; www.tdf.org; open 3–8pm for evening performances, 10am–2pm for Wed and Sat matinees, 11am–8pm on Sun for all performances). Tickets are 25% to 50% off, plus a $3 per ticket service charge. You won't find seats to this season's smash hit, but most other shows are available. Only cash and traveler's checks are accepted. ***Tip:*** The lines are much shorter at **TKTS Lower Manhattan** in South Street Seaport (199 Water St. at the corner of Front and John sts.; open Mon–Fri 11am–6pm, Sat 11am–7pm [matinee only]; tickets sold here the day before matinee performances; subway: 2/3/4/5 to Fulton St.). All the same policies apply. Visit www.tdf.org or call NYC/Onstage at ☎ 212/768-1818 for more information.

Broadway **Theaters**

Al Hirschfeld. 302 W. 45th St. ☎ 212/239-6200.

Ambassador. 219 W. 49th St. ☎ 212/239-6200.

American Airlines. 227 W. 42nd St. ☎ 212/719-1300.

August Wilson. 245 W. 52nd St. ☎ 212/239-6200.

Belasco. 111 W. 44th St. ☎ 212/239-6200.

Biltmore. 261 W. 47th St. ☎ 212/239-6222.

Booth. 222 W. 45th St. ☎ 212/239-6200.

Broadhurst. 235 W. 44th St. ☎ 212/239-6200.

Broadway. 1681 Broadway. ☎ 212/239-6200.

Brooks Atkinson. 256 W. 47th St. ☎ 212/719-4099.

Circle in the Square. 1633 Broadway. ☎ 212/239-6200.

Cort. 138 W. 48th St. ☎ 212/239-6200.

Ethel Barrymore. 243 W. 47th St. ☎ 212/239-6200.

Eugene O'Neill. 230 W. 49th St. ☎ 212/239-6200.

Gershwin. 222 W. 51st St. ☎ 212/586-6510.

Helen Hayes. 240 W. 44th St. ☎ 212/944-9450.

Hilton Theatre. 213 W. 42nd St. ☎ 212/307-4100.

Imperial. 249 W. 45th St. ☎ 212/239-6200.

John Golden. 252 W. 45th St. ☎ 212/239-6200.

Longacre. 220 W. 48th St. ☎ 212/239-6200.

Lunt-Fontanne. 205 W. 46th St. ☎ 212/575-9200.

Lyceum. 149 W. 45th St. ☎ 212/239-6200.

Majestic. 245 W. 44th St. ☎ 212/239-6200.

Marquis. 302 W. 45th St. ☎ 212/239-6200.

Minskoff. 200 W. 45th St. ☎ 212/869-0550.

Music Box. 239 W. 45th St. ☎ 212/239-6200.

Nederlander. 208 W. 41st St. ☎ 212/921-8000.

Neil Simon. 250 W. 52nd St. ☎ 212/757-8646.

New Amsterdam. 214 W. 42nd St. ☎ 212/82-2900.

New Victory. 209 W. 42nd St. ☎ 646/223-3020.

Palace. 1564 Broadway. ☎ 212/730-8200

Plymouth. 236 W. 45th St. ☎ 212/239-6200.

Richard Rodgers. 226 W. 46th St. ☎ 212/221-1211.

Royale. 242 W. 45th St. ☎ 212/239-6200.

St. James. 246 W. 44th St. ☎ 212/239-6200.

Shubert. 225 W. 44th St. ☎ 212/239-6200.

Studio 54. 254 W. 54th St. ☎ 212/719-1300.

Vivian Beaumont. 150 W. 65th St. ☎ 212/239-6200.

Walter Kerr. 219 W. 48th St. ☎ 212/239-6200.

Winter Garden. 1634 Broadway. ☎ 212/239-6200. ●

10 The Best Hotels

Hotel Best Bets

Most Romantic
★★★ Inn at Irving Place $$$ *56 Irving Place (p 154)*

Most Historic
★ The Peninsula—New York $$$$ *700 Fifth Ave. (p 155)*

Best Boutique Hotel
★★ Hotel Giraffe $$$ *365 Park Ave. S. (p 153)*

Best Place to Channel Dorothy Parker
★ The Algonquin $$ *59 W. 44th St. (p 152)*

Most Luxurious Hotel
★★★ Ritz-Carlton New York $$$ *2 West St. (p 156)*

Best Budget Hotel
★★ La Quinta Inn $ *17 W. 32nd St. (p 154)*

Best for Kids
★★ Red Roof Inn $ *6 W. 32nd St. (p 156);* and ★★ The Regency $$$$ *540 Park Ave. (p 156)*

Best Value
★★ Belvedere Hotel $$$ *319 W. 48th St. (p 152)*

Best Themed Hotel
★★ The Library Hotel $$$ *299 Madison Ave. (p 155)*

Most Charming B&B
★★ The Inn on 23rd $$ *131 W. 23rd St. (p 154)*

Best for Hobnobbing with Celebrities
★ The Mercer $$$ *147 Mercer St. (p 155);* and ★ The Greenwich $$$ *377 Greenwich St. (p 153)*

Best European-Style Hotel
★ Fitzpatrick Grand Central Hotel $$ *141 E. 44th St. (p 152)*

Best View
★★★ Ritz-Carlton New York $$$ *2 West St. (p 156)*

Best for Business Travelers
★ Wall Street Inn $$ *9 S. William St. (p 157);* and The Benjamin $$$ *125 E. 50th St. (p 152)*

Most Beautiful New Design
★★ The Mark $$$$ *25 E. 77th St. (p 155)*

Best Old-School Glamour
★★ The Sherry-Netherland $$$$ *781 Fifth Ave. (p 156)*

Best for Serenity Seekers
★★ Sofitel New York $$$ *45 W. 44th St. (p 156)*

Previous page: A guest room in the St. Regis.

Downtown Hotels

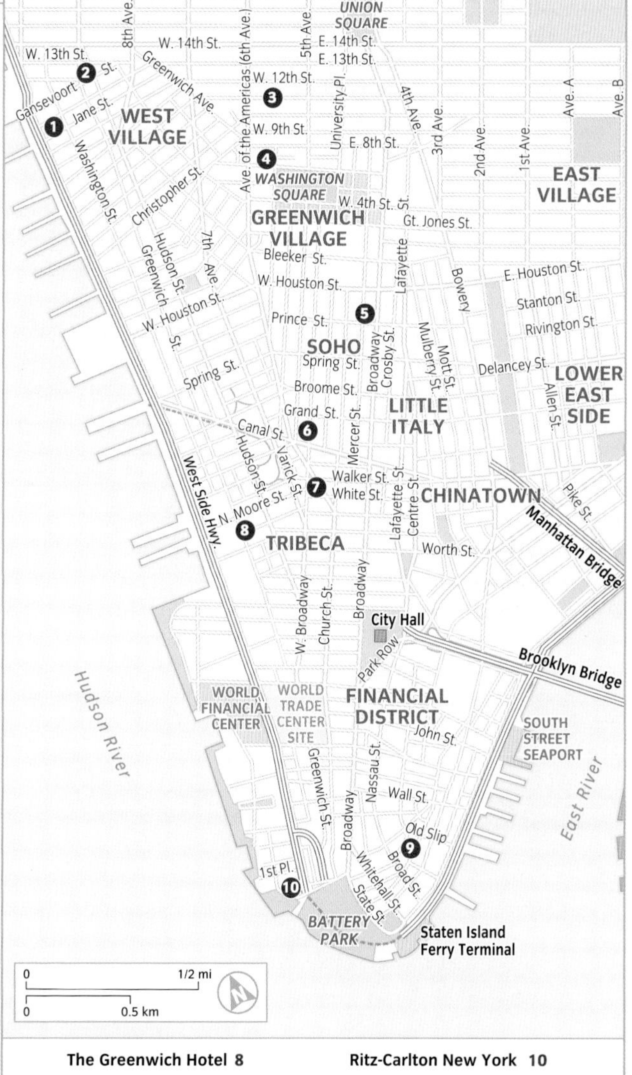

The Greenwich Hotel 8	**Ritz-Carlton New York 10**
The Hotel Gansevoort 2	**Soho Grand Hotel 6**
The Jane 1	**Tribeca Grand Hotel 7**
Larchmont Hotel 3	**The Wall Street Inn 9**
The Mercer 5	**Washington Square Hotel 4**

Midtown & Uptown Hotels

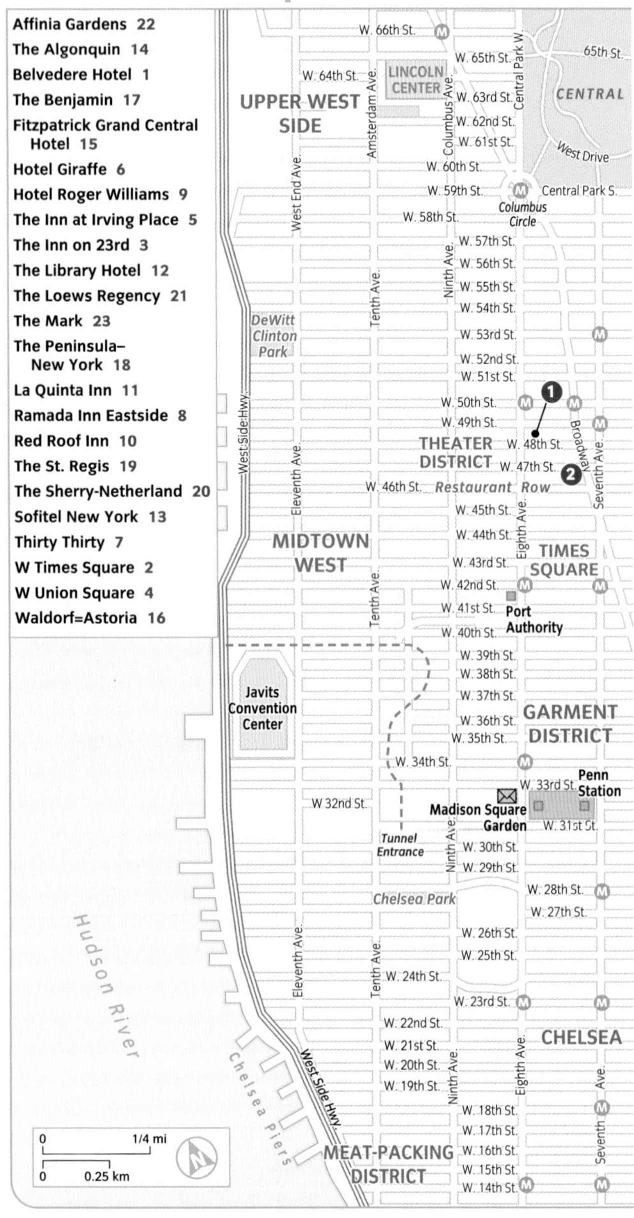

Transverse
Center Drive
PARK
East Drive
The Pond
Fifth Ave.
UPPER EAST SIDE
Madison Ave.
E. 66th St.
E. 65th St.
E. 64th St.
E. 63rd St.
E. 62nd St.
E. 61st St.
E. 60th St.
E. 59th St.
E. 58th St.
E. 57th St.
E. 56th St.
E. 55th St.
E. 54th St.
E. 53rd St.
E. 52nd St.
E. 51st St.
E. 50th St.
E. 49th St.
E. 48th St.
E. 47th St.
E. 46th St.
E. 45th St.
E. 44th St.
E. 43rd St.
E. 42nd St.
E. 41st St.
E. 40th St.
E. 39th St.
E. 38th St.
E 37th St.
E 36th St.
E. 35th St.
E. 34th St.
E. 33rd St.
E. 32nd St.
E. 31st St.
E. 30th St.
E. 29th St.
E. 28th St.
E. 27th St.
E. 26th St.
E. 25th St.
E. 24th St.
E. 23rd St.
E. 22nd St.
E. 21st St.
E. 20th St.
E. 19th St.
E. 18th St.
E. 17th St.
E. 16th St.
E. 15th St.
E. 14th St.
York Ave.
Roosevelt Island Tram
Queensboro Bridge
Sutton Pl.
Sutton Pl. South
Beekman Place
Mitchell Place
St. Patrick's Cathedral
MIDTOWN EAST
ROCKEFELLER CENTER
Sixth Ave. (Ave. of the Americas)
Park Ave.
Lexington Ave.
Third Ave.
Vanderbilt Ave.
First Ave.
FDR Drive
UNITED NATIONS
Grand Central Terminal
Second Ave.
Bryant Park
New York Public Library
MURRAY HILL
Queens-Midtown Tunnel
East River
Empire State Building
W 32nd St.
Broadway
Park Ave. S.
Madison Square Park
Flatiron Building
FLATIRON DISTRICT
Gramercy Park
GRAMERCY PARK
Asser Levy Pl.
Ave. C
PETER COOPER VILLAGE
STUYVESANT TOWN
Union Square
Union Sq. W.
Union Sq. E.
Irving Pl.
N.D. Perlman Pl.

New York Hotels A to Z

The lobby at the Hotel Gansevoort.

★ kids **Affinia Gardens** UPPER EAST SIDE Each suite in this all-suites property (formerly Lyden Gardens) includes a small but fully equipped kitchen so you can save money by preparing some of your own meals. It's pet-friendly, too, with a Jet Set Pets program. ***215 E. 64th St. (btwn. Second & Third aves.). ☎ 212/355-1230. www.affinia.com. 131 units. Suites $379–$999. AE MC, V, Disc. Subway: 4/5/6/N/R/W to 59th St. Map p 150.***

★ **The Algonquin** MIDTOWN WEST This 1902 hotel is a literary landmark (home of the Round Table, frequented by Dorothy Parker and other writers), and renovations have restored its splendor. ***59 W. 44th St. (btwn. Fifth & Sixth aves.). ☎ 888/304-2047. www.algonquinhotel.com. 174 units. Doubles $249–$699. AE, DC, DISC, MC, V. Subway: B/D/F/V to 42nd St. Map p 150.***

★★ kids **Belvedere Hotel** MIDTOWN WEST The design here is sharp, especially in the public spaces, but the real reason to choose the Belvedere is the amenities. Every room has a desk and a kitchenette with minifridge, sink, and microwave. This is ideal for travelers who don't want to eat every meal at a restaurant. ***319 W. 48th St. (at Eighth Ave.). ☎ 888/HOTEL-58. www.belvederehotelnyc.com. 400 units. Double $229–$469. AE, DC, DISC, MC, V. Subway: C/E to 50th St. Map p 150.***

★★ **The Benjamin** MIDTOWN EAST Set in a 1927 landmark building, the Benjamin combines solid old bones with top-flight service and amenities. You will be supremely comfortable here. ***125 E. 50th St. (at Lexington Ave.). ☎ 212/320-8002. www.thebenjamin.com. 209 units. Doubles from $459; suites from $559. AE, DC, DISC, MC, V. Subway: 6 to 51st St. or E/F to Lexington Ave. Map p 150.***

★ **Fitzpatrick Grand Central Hotel** MIDTOWN EAST Attractive and intimate, this Irish-owned property is a terrific choice for those who seek the creature comforts a chain hotel offers but detest the blandness that's usually part of the deal. *141 E. 44th St. (at Lexington Ave.). ☎ 800/367-7701. www.fitzpatrickhotels.com. 155 units. Doubles $229–$399. AE, DC, DISC, MC, V. Subway: 4/5/6/7/S to 42nd St./Grand Central. Map p 150.*

★★ The Hotel Gansevoort

MEAT-PACKING DISTRICT This stylish spot has transcended its annoying initial trendiness and established itself as a very reliable choice for service and comfort. It has spacious rooms, a full-service spa, and a rooftop pool. Plunge, the rooftop bar, has 360-degree views. *18 Ninth Ave. (at 13th St.). ☎ 877/426-7386. www.hotelgansevoort.com. 187 units. Doubles $435–$675 (duplex penthouse $5,000). AE, MC, V. Subway: A/C/E to 14th St. Map p 149.*

★★ Hotel Giraffe

GRAMERCY/MURRAY HILL The stylish guest rooms are graced with high ceilings, velveteen upholstered chairs, and black-and-white photos from the '20s and '30s. The lovely rooftop garden is another draw. *365 Park Ave. S. (at 26th St.). ☎ 877/296-0009. www.hotelgiraffe.com. 73 units. Doubles $329–$579 w/breakfast. AE, DC, MC, V. Subway: 6 to 28th St. Map p 150.*

The Greenwich Hotel.

★★★ The Greenwich Hotel

TRIBECA No detail or expense has been spared at this beautiful small luxury hotel (whose owners include Robert De Niro), where even the bricks are handcrafted. It's meant to feel like an 88-room home—and if you live in a rustically elegant country manor filled with antiques, you'll feel right at home. It's everything a hip, edgy downtown hotel isn't—and that makes it the hippest place in town. *377 Greenwich St. (at N. Moore St.). ☎ 212/941-8900. www.greenwichhotelny.com. 88 units. Doubles $625–$825; suites $1,350–$2,250. AE, DC, DISC, MC, V. Subway: 1/9 to Franklin St. Map p 149.*

Inn at Irving Place.

Larchmont Hotel.

★★ The Hotel Roger Williams MURRAY HILL This boutique hotel on Madison Avenue manages to be both hip (rooms with flatscreen plasma TVs) and comfy (quilts on the beds), with a mezzanine lounge. *131 Madison Ave. (at 31st St.). ☎ 888/241-3333. www.hotelrogerwilliams.com. 193 units. Doubles $250–$350. AE, DC, DISC, MC, V. Subway: 6 to 28th St. Map p 150.*

★★★ Inn at Irving Place GRAMERCY This 170-year-old town house is all about 19th-century elegance. Spacious rooms have antiques and art, nonworking fireplaces, and big bathrooms. *56 Irving Place (btwn. 17th & 18th sts.). ☎ 800/685-1447. www.innatirving.com. 12 units. Doubles $325–$645. AE, DC, MC, V. Subway: N/R/4/5/6 to 14th St./Union Sq. Map p 150.*

★★ kids The Inn on 23rd CHELSEA One of Manhattan's few full-service B&Bs, this inn has individualized, spacious guest rooms decorated with a personal touch. *131 W. 23rd St. (btwn. Sixth & Seventh aves.). ☎ 877/387-2323. www.innon23rd.com. 14 units. Doubles $175–$250. AE, DC, MC, V. Subway: F/1/9 to 23rd St. Map p 150.*

★ The Jane DOWNTOWN With this canny renovation of a grand 1907 waterfront landmark, New York hotel rooms just got a whole lot cheaper, albeit a whole lot smaller. But with such fabulous public spaces—massive lobby bar with fireplace, turreted rooftop lounge overlooking the Hudson River, pool and spa—who needs a big, pricey room to rattle around in? Two-thirds of the units in this "micro hotel" are 50-square-foot spaces complete with bed, flatscreen TV, Wi-Fi, and A/C—all yours for just $99 a night. *113 Jane St. (West Side Hwy.). ☎ 212/924-6700. www.thejanenyc.com. 210 units. Rooms $99–$260. AE MC, V. Subway: A/C/E to 14th St. Map p 149.*

★ La Quinta Inn MIDTOWN WEST Friends of mine have stayed here and loved it. The location is ideal (close to sights on a nice street), and the decent-size rooms have amenities you wouldn't expect from a budget hotel, such as free high-speed Internet access. *17 W. 32nd St. (btwn. Fifth Ave. & Broadway). ☎ 800/551-2303. www.applecorehotels.com or www.lq.com. 182 units. Doubles start at $109. AE, DC, DISC, MC, V. Subway: B/D/F/V/N/R to 34th St. Map p 150.*

★ Larchmont Hotel GREENWICH VILLAGE If you're willing to share a bathroom, it's hard to find a better priced option than this charming European-style hotel. *27 W. 11th St. (btwn. Fifth & Sixth aves.). ☎ 212/989-9333. www.larchmonthotel.com. 58 units. Doubles $109–$145. AE,*

MC, V. Subway: A/B/C/D/E/F/V to W. 4th St.; F to 14th St. Map p 149.

★★ **The Library Hotel** MIDTOWN EAST Each of the 10 floors is dedicated to a major category of the Dewey Decimal System. It's lovely, even if it's unlikely you'll have time to read the books in your room. *299 Madison Ave. (at 41st St.). ☎ 877/793-7323. www.libraryhotel.com. 60 units. Doubles $409–$559. AE, DC, MC, V. Subway: 4/5/6/7/S to 42nd St. Map p 150.*

★★ **The Mark** UPPER EAST SIDE After a bold new redesign by France's most celebrated interior designer, Jacques Grange, this 1927 classic hotel was scheduled to reopen for business in summer 2008 as a combination hotel/co-op with a smaller number of hotel rooms. The smart, playful new look has already garnered fevered press. *25 E. 77th St. (btwn. Madison & Fifth aves.). ☎ 212/772-1600. www.themarkhotel.com. 118 units. Check website for rates. AE, DC, MC, V. Subway: 6 to 77th St. Map p 150.*

★ **The Mercer** SOHO So hip it hurts. Forget the celebs and enjoy the high-ceilinged guest rooms, lush linens, and tile-and-marble bathrooms. *147 Mercer St. (at Prince St.). ☎ 888/918-6060. www.mercerhotel.com. 75 units. Doubles $595–$820. AE, DC, DISC, MC, V. Subway: N/R to Prince St. Map p 149.*

★★ **The Peninsula—New York** MIDTOWN Housed in a 1905 landmark building, the Peninsula is now a state-of-the-art stunner with some of the priciest rooms in town. Guest rooms come with high-speed wiring and fabulous bathrooms. *700 Fifth Ave. (at 55th St.). ☎ 800/262-9467. www.peninsula.com. 239 units. Doubles $775–$1,125; suites $1,275–$18,000. AE, DC, DISC, MC, V. Subway: E/F to Fifth Ave. Map p 150.*

★ **Ramada Inn Eastside** MIDTOWN EAST My brother-in-law was skeptical about staying at a Manhattan Ramada, but one visit converted him. The neighborhood is a big selling point, as are the 24-hour business center and the 24-hour fitness center. And while the rooms are small, they are well organized. *161 Lexington Ave. (at 30th St.). ☎ 800/625-5980. www.applecorehotels.com/ramada-inn-eastside. 95 units. $109–$459. AE, DC, DISC, MC, V. Subway: 6 to 28th St. Map p 150.*

The Mercer.

The Loews Regency.

★ kids **Red Roof Inn** HERALD SQUARE This former office building has relatively spacious rooms and bathrooms, given the budget price. *6 W. 32nd St. (btwn. Broadway & Fifth Ave.). ☎ 800/567-7720. www.applecorehotels.com/red-roof-inn-manhattan. 171 units. Doubles $109–$459 w/breakfast. AE, DC, DISC, MC, V. Subway: B/D/F/V/N/R to 34th St. Map p 150.*

★★ kids **The Loews Regency** UPPER EAST SIDE A stay at the Regency can make you feel like a star: Guest rooms are big, service is grand, and there's even a kids' concierge. *540 Park Ave. (at 61st St.). ☎ 212/759-4100. www.loewshotels.com. 351 units. Doubles $419–$699. AE, DC, MC, V. Subway: 4/5/6/N/R to 59th St. Map p 150.*

★★★ kids **Ritz-Carlton New York** BATTERY PARK Divinely luxurious with large guest rooms, the Ritz has one drawback—its location on the extreme southern tip of Manhattan. Magnificent views of New York Harbor and Lady Liberty, however, help to compensate. *2 West St. (at 1st Place). ☎ 800/241-3333. www.ritzcarlton.com. 298 units. Doubles $495–$795. AE, DC, DISC, MC, V. Subway: 4/5 to Bowling Green. Map p 149.*

★★ **The Sherry-Netherland** MIDTOWN This 1927 neo-Romanesque property is both a hotel and a residential building. The grandly proportioned rooms have high ceilings, big bathrooms, and walk-in closets. *781 Fifth Ave. (at 59th St.). ☎ 800/247-4377. www.sherrynetherland.com. 77 units. Doubles $599–$1,159. AE, DC, DISC, MC, V. Subway: N/R to Fifth Ave. Map p 150.*

★★ **Sofitel New York** MIDTOWN WEST Built in 2000, the Sofitel blends Old World elegance with New World amenities. Rooms are spacious, adorned with art, and soundproofed. *45 W. 44th St. (btwn. Fifth & Sixth aves.). ☎ 212/354-8844. www.sofitel.com. 398 units. Doubles $380–$685. AE, DC, MC, V. Subway: B/D/F/V to 42nd St. Map p 150.*

★ **Soho Grand Hotel** SOHO Built as a modern ode to SoHo's cast-iron past, the Soho Grand attracts an entertainment-industry crowd. Rooms are small but packed with state-of-the-art amenities. *310 W. Broadway (at Grand St.). ☎ 800/965-3000. www.sohogrand.com. 369 units. Doubles $481–$711. AE, DC, DISC, MC, V. Subway: A/C/E/N/R/1/9 to Canal St. Map p 149.*

The Ritz-Carlton New York.

Budget-Friendly Hotels

New York is one of the most expensive cities in the country—a fact you'll comprehend when you try to book a hotel. To get the best price, follow these rules. **Schedule carefully,** because prices climb sky-high when events such as the Marathon are on. **Don't feel you have to be in the center of town**—you can save money and get more space by staying uptown or downtown. **Look for deals online** on sites like www.orbitz.com, www.expedia.com, www.hotels.com, www.quikbook.com, and www.priceline.com, but don't overlook the hotels' own websites, which can offer exclusive deals. And **be flexible**—so what if your room is tiny, you're going to be too busy to spend much time there anyway.

★★ **The St. Regis** MIDTOWN This swellegant spot is a throwback to Gilded Age luxury. Built in 1904, it has beautifully appointed rooms and your own 24-hour butler service. *2 E. 55th St. (at Fifth Ave.). ☎ 212/753-4500. www.starwoodhotels.com/stregis. 256 units. Doubles $695–$995; suites $1,150 and up. AE, DC, DISC, MC, V. Subway: E/V to Fifth Ave. Map p 150.*

Thirty Thirty MURRAY HILL This is a good bet for travelers who want a budget hotel that also has a sense of style. The rooms, however, are small. *30 E. 30th St. (btwn. Madison & Park aves.). ☎ 800/497-6028. www.thirtythirty-nyc.com. 243 units. Doubles $249–$499. AE, DC, DISC, MC, V. Subway: 6 to 28th St. Map p 150.*

Tribeca Grand Hotel TRIBECA This hotel merges high style, luxury comforts, and a hip downtown location. Because guest rooms face the eight-story atrium, they can be loud, so each is equipped with a white-noise machine. *2 Sixth Ave. (btwn. White & Church sts.). ☎ 877/519-6600. www.tribecagrand.com. 203 units. Doubles $491–$891. AE, DC, DISC, MC, V. Subway: 1/9 to Franklin St.; A/C/E to Canal St. Map p 149.*

The Sherry-Netherland Hotel.

★ **Waldorf=Astoria** MIDTOWN EAST This massive Art Deco masterpiece is a genuine New York landmark. But with 1,000-plus rooms, the pace can be hectic, and the check-in lines daunting. *301 Park Ave. (btwn. 49th & 50th sts.). ☎ 800/WALDORF. www.waldorfastoria.com. 1,245 units. Doubles $339–$519. AE, DC, DISC, MC, V. Subway: 6 to 51st St. Map p 150.*

★ **The Wall Street Inn** FINANCIAL DISTRICT This intimate, seven-story Lower Manhattan oasis is warm, comforting, and serene. Friendly, professional, personalized service is the hallmark. *9 S. William St. (at Broad St.). ☎ 212/747-1500. www.thewallstreetinn.com. 46 units. Doubles $199–$395. AE, DC, DISC, MC, V. Subway:*

B&Bs & Apartment Stays

Yes, hotel prices are high in New York, and the costs climb even higher for families paying for extra people in the room or even extra rooms. Oh, and did I mention hotel room taxes? (Tack on 13.375% to your total bill.) Save big bucks, enjoy more room, and live among the locals by staying in a B&B or a short-stay apartment in New York. (Many even let you bring your pet along.) The city has plenty of reliable operators that offer a range of lodgings, from elegant rooms in prewar apartment buildings to sunny, fully furnished apartments in historic brownstones. Fully equipped kitchens help you save big on meals. Prices can start as low as $90 a night. Check out **NY Habitat** (www.nyhabitat.com; $115–$300/night based on a 3-night stay, with weekly and monthly rates available) for furnished apartments; **City Sonnet** (www.citysonnet.com; $135–$700 double) for both hosted and unhosted lodging in apartments and artists' lofts; or **Manhattan Getaways** (www.manhattangetaways.com; $130–$150 rooms; $200–$750 apts.) for furnished rooms or private apartments. The New York page at **BedandBreakfast.com** (www.bedandbreakfast.com/manhattan-new-york.html) lists B&Bs, inns, guesthouses, and apartments for rent.

2/3 to Wall St.; 4/5 to Bowling Green. Map p 149.

Washington Square Hotel GREENWICH VILLAGE The rooms are tiny but pleasant in this affordable hotel facing Washington Square Park. It's worth paying a few extra dollars for a south-facing room on a high floor. *103 Waverly Place (btwn. Fifth & Sixth aves.). ☎ 800/222-0418. www.wshotel.com. 165 units. Doubles $215–$280. AE, MC, V. Subway: A/B/C/D/E/F/V to W. 4th St. (use 3rd St. exit). Map p 149.*

★ **W Times Square** TIMES SQUARE Most rooms afford magnificent views; thankfully, shades block out most of the neon at night and double-paned windows keep them relatively quiet. *1547 Broadway (at 47th St.). ☎ 888/625-5144. www.starwoodhotels.com/whotels. 509 units. Doubles from $319. AE, DC, DISC, MC, V. Subway: N/R to 49th St. Map p 150.*

★ **W Union Square** UNION SQUARE The 1911 Guardian Life Beaux Arts building has been revived with bold, clean-lined modernism. *201 Park Ave. S. (at 17th St.). ☎ 212/253-9119. www.starwoodhotels.com/whotels. 270 units. Doubles $349–$550. AE, DC, DISC, MC, V. Subway: N/R/W/6/5/4 to Union Sq. Map p 150.*

The Washington Square Hotel has been hosting travelers for more than a century.

The
Savvy Traveler

Before You Go

Government Tourist Offices

In the U.S.: NYC & Company, 810 Seventh Ave., New York, NY 10019 ☎ 800/NYC-VISIT; www.nycvisit.com. **In the U.K.:** NYCVB Visitor Information Center, 36 Southwark Bridge Rd., London, SE1 9EU, ☎ 020/7202-6368.

The Best Time to Go

July and August are hot and humid, but because the local population tries to escape, the city is far less crowded. There are plenty of free alfresco events too. December brings crowds and the highest prices; January and February are relatively cheap. But there's nothing like New York in spring or fall when the weather is mild.

Festivals & Special Events

WINTER. For information on the lighting of the **Rockefeller Center Christmas Tree** call ☎ 212/332-6868. On New Year's Eve the most famous party of them all takes place in Times Square (☎ 212/768-1560; www.timessquarealliance.org). During Restaurant Week (1 week in Jan and 1 week in June), you can enjoy $20 prix-fixe menus at lunch or $35 for dinner at some of the best restaurants in the city (☎ 212/484-1222; www.nycvisit.com).

SPRING. The **Triple Pier Antiques Show,** the city's largest antiques show takes place in March (☎ 212/255-0020; www.antiqnet.com/Stella for this and additional shows) as does, of course, the **St. Patrick's Day Parade** (☎ 212/484-1222) on the 17th. The **Easter Parade** (☎ 212/484-1222)—not a traditional parade, but a flamboyant fashion display along Fifth Avenue from 48th to 57th streets—is on Easter Sunday.

SUMMER. All summer long, the **Lincoln Center Festival** (☎ 212/546-2656; www.lincolncenter.org) celebrates the best of the performing arts from all over the world (tickets go on sale in late May). **SummerStage** (☎ 212/360-2756; www.summerstage.org) is a summer-long festival of outdoor performances in Central Park, featuring world music, pop, folk, and jazz artists, the New York Grand Opera, and the Chinese Golden Dragon Acrobats, among others. At the same time and also in Central Park, well-known actors take on the Bard in the Public Theater's long-running **Shakespeare in the Park** series (☎ 212/539-8750; www.publictheater.org). The **Independence Day Harbor Festival and Fourth of July Fireworks Spectacular** (☎ 212/484-1222, or Macy's Visitor Center at 212/494-2922) takes place on July 4. Dance till you drop at **Midsummer Night Swing** (☎ 212/875-5456; www.lincolncenter.org), 3 weeks of outdoor dance parties held in Lincoln Center's Damrosch Park.

FALL. The **West Indian–American Day Parade** (☎ 718/467-1797; www.wiadca.org), an annual Brooklyn event on Labor Day, is New York's best street festival. The **Greenwich Village Halloween Parade** (☎ 212/475-3333, ext. 14044; www.halloween-nyc.com) on October 31 is a flamboyant parade that everyone is welcome to join. Something everyone should do at least once is see the **Radio City Music Hall Christmas Spectacular** (☎ 212/247-4777 or 212/307-1000 [Ticketmaster]; www.radiocity.com) and watch the **Macy's Thanksgiving Day Parade** (☎ 212/484-1222).

Previous page: The Theatre District lit up after dark.

NEW YORK'S AVERAGE TEMPERATURE & RAINFALL

	JAN	FEB	MAR	APR	MAY	JUNE
Daily Temp. (°F)	38	40	48	61	71	80
Daily Temp. (°C)	3	4	9	16	22	27
Days of Precip.	11	10	11	11	11	10
	JULY	AUG	SEPT	OCT	NOV	DEC
Daily Temp. (°F)	85	84	77	67	54	42
Daily Temp. (°C)	29	29	25	19	12	6
Days of Precip.	11	10	8	8	9	10

The Weather

The worst weather in New York is during that long week or 10 days that arrive between mid-July and August when the temperatures go up to 100°F (38°C) with 90% humidity. Another time when you might not want to stroll around the city is mid-winter when temperatures drop to around 20°F (–7°C) and the winds whip through the concrete canyons. If you want to know how to pack just before you go, check CNN's online 5-day forecast at www.cnn.com/weather. You can also get the local weather by calling ☎ **212/976-1212.**

Useful Websites

- **www.nycvisit.com:** A wealth of free information about the city.
- **http://nymag.com and www.villagevoice.com:** Good coverage of arts and events from *New York* magazine and the *Village Voice,* respectively.
- **www.timeout.com/newyork:** Full listings, restaurant reviews, shopping, and nightlife.
- **www.broadway.com, www.playbill.com, www.theatermania.com:** Offer membership programs that save you money on Broadway tickets.
- **www.panynj.gov and www.mta.nyc.ny.us:** Transit info.
- **www.weather.com:** Up-to-the-minute worldwide weather.

Restaurant & Theater Reservations

I can't say it enough: Book well in advance if you're determined to eat at a particular spot or see a certain show. For popular restaurants, if you didn't call in advance, try asking for early or late hours—often tables are available before 6:30pm and after 9pm. You could also call the day before or first thing in the morning, when you may be able to take advantage of a cancellation.

If you're interested in a popular show, call or go online for tickets well before your trip. Try **TeleCharge** (☎ 212/239-6200) or **Ticketmaster** (☎ 212/307-4100; www.ticketmaster.com). For last-minute theater seats, **TKTS** in the "Getting Tickets" box on p 145.

Cellphones (Mobiles)

In general it's a good bet that your phone will work in New York, although if you're not from the U.S., you'll be appalled at the poor reach of the **GSM (Global System for Mobiles) wireless network,** which is used by much of the rest of the world. (To see where GSM phones work in the U.S., check out www.t-mobile.com/coverage/national_popup.asp). And you may or may not be able to send SMS (text messages) overseas. Assume nothing—call your wireless provider and get the full scoop.

You can always rent a phone from **InTouch USA** (☎ 800/872-7626; www.intouchglobal.com), but beware that you'll pay $1 a minute or more for airtime.

Getting **There**

By Plane

Three major airports serve New York City: **John F. Kennedy International Airport** (☎ 718/244-4444) in Queens, is about 15 miles (24km; 1 hr. driving time) from Midtown Manhattan; **LaGuardia Airport** (☎ 718/533-3400), also in Queens, is about 8 miles (13km; 30 min.) from Midtown; and **Newark International Airport** (☎ 973/961-6000) in nearby New Jersey, is about 16 miles (26km; 45 min.) from Midtown. Always allow extra time, though, especially during rush hour, peak holiday travel times, and if you're taking a bus. Information on all three is available online at **www.panynj.gov.**

Your best bet is to stay away from public transportation when traveling to and from the airport. **Taxis** are a quick and convenient alternative. They're available at designated taxi stands outside the terminals. Fares, whether fixed or metered, do not include bridge and tunnel tolls ($4–$6) or a tip for the cabbie (15%–20% is customary). They do include all passengers in the cab and luggage (from 8pm–6am, a $1 surcharge also applies on New York yellow cabs). **From JFK:** A flat rate of $45 to Manhattan (plus tolls and tip) is charged. **From LaGuardia:** $24 to $28, metered, plus tolls and tip. **From Newark:** The dispatcher for New Jersey taxis gives you a slip of paper with a flat rate ranging from $30 to $38 (toll and tip extra), depending on where you're going in Manhattan. The yellow-cab fare from Manhattan to Newark is the meter amount plus $15 and tolls (about $69–$75, perhaps a few dollars more with tip).

Private car and limousine companies provide convenient 24-hour door-to-door airport transfers. They are a little more expensive than taxis, but they're a good idea if you're traveling at rush hour because they charge flat fees. Call at least 24 hours in advance and a driver will meet you near baggage claim. I use **Allstate** (☎ 800/453-4099 or 212/333-3333) and **Carmel** (☎ 800/922-7635 or 212/666-6666).

AirTrains ($7–$14) are available at Newark and JFK and will certainly save you money, but skip it if you have mobility issues, mountains of luggage, or small children. You'll find it easier to rely on a taxi, car service, or shuttle service that can offer you door-to-door transfers. For information, check out **AirTrain JFK** (www.airtrainjfk.com) and **Newark AirTrain** (☎ 888/EWR-INFO; www.airtrainnewark.com). The latter will deposit you at a NJ Transit station, where you then take another train to Penn Station.

Bus and shuttle services provide a comfortable and less expensive (but usually more time-consuming) option for airport transfers than taxis and car services. The blue vans of **Super Shuttle** (☎ 212/258-3826; www.supershuttle.com) serve all three airports; fares are $13 to $22 per person. **The New York Airport Service** (☎ 718/875-8200; www.nyairportservice.com) buses travel from JFK and LaGuardia to the Port Authority Bus Terminal (42nd St. and Eighth Ave.), Grand Central Terminal (Park Ave. btwn. 41st and 42nd sts.), and to select Midtown hotels. One-way fares run between $12 and $15 per person.

By Car

From the **New Jersey Turnpike** (I-95) and points west, there are three Hudson River crossings into the city's west side: the **Holland Tunnel** (lower Manhattan), the **Lincoln Tunnel** (Midtown), and the **George Washington Bridge** (upper Manhattan). From **upstate New York,** take the **New York State Thruway** (I-87), which crosses the Hudson on the Tappan Zee Bridge and becomes the **Major Deegan Expressway** (I-87) through the Bronx. For the east side, continue to the Triborough Bridge and then down the FDR Drive. For the west side, take the Cross Bronx Expressway (I-95) to the Henry Hudson Parkway or the Taconic State Parkway to the Saw Mill River Parkway to the Henry Hudson Parkway south. From New England, **the New England Thruway** (I-95) connects with the **Bruckner Expressway** (I-278), which leads to the Triborough Bridge and the FDR Drive on the east side. Note that you'll have to pay tolls along some of these roads and at most crossings.

Once you arrive in Manhattan, park your car in a garage (expect to pay $20–$45 per day) and leave it there. Don't use your car for traveling within the city.

By Train

Amtrak (☎ 800/USA-RAIL; www.amtrak.com) runs frequent service to New York City's **Penn Station,** on Seventh Avenue between 31st and 33rd streets, where you can easily pick up a taxi, subway, or bus to your hotel. To get the best rates, book early (as much as 6 months in advance) and travel on weekends.

Getting **Around**

By Subway

Run by the **Metropolitan Transit Authority (MTA),** the subway system is the fastest way to travel around New York, especially during rush hours. The subway runs 24 hours a day, 7 days a week. The rush-hour crushes are roughly from 8 to 9:30am and from 5 to 6:30pm on weekdays. The fare is $2 (half-price for seniors and those with disabilities); children under 44 inches (111 cm) tall ride free. Fares are paid with a **MetroCard,** a magnetically encoded card that debits the fare when swiped through the turnstile (or the fare box on any city bus). MetroCards also allow you free transfers between the bus and subway within a 2-hour period. There are Pay-Per-Ride and Unlimited Ride MetroCards; both can be purchased at any subway station, and from many drugstores.

Once you're in town, you can stop at the MTA desk at the **Times Square Information Center,** 1560 Broadway, between 46th and 47th streets (where Broadway meets Seventh Ave.) to pick up the latest subway map. (You can also ask for one at any token booth, but they might not always be available.)

Less expensive than taxis, with better views than subways—buses would be the perfect alternative if they didn't sometimes get stuck in traffic. They're best for shorter distances or when you're not in a rush. Like the subway fare, bus fare is $2, payable with a **MetroCard** or **exact change.** Bus drivers don't make change, and fare boxes don't accept dollar bills or pennies. If you pay with a MetroCard, you can transfer to another bus or to the subway for free within 2 hours. If you pay cash, you must request a **free transfer** slip that allows you to change to an intersecting bus route only (legal transfer points are listed on the transfer paper) within 1 hour of issue. Transfer slips cannot be used to enter the subway.

Yellow **taxi cabs** are licensed by the Taxi and Limousine Commission (TLC). Base fare on entering the cab is $2.50. The cost is 40¢ for every ⅕ mile or 40¢ per 2 minutes in stopped or very slow-moving traffic (or for waiting time). There's no extra charge for each passenger or for luggage, but you must pay bridge or tunnel tolls. You'll also pay a $1 night surcharge after 8pm and before 6am. A 15% to 20% tip is customary. You can hail a taxi on any street. *Never* accept a ride from any other car except an official city yellow cab (private livery cars are not allowed to pick up fares on the street).

Fast **Facts**

APARTMENT RENTALS Your best bets are **Manhattan Getaways** (☎ **212/956-2010;** manhattangetaways.com) with a network of unhosted apartments around the city that start at $145 per night, or **City Sonnet** (www.citysonnet.com; $135–$700 double) for both hosted and unhosted lodging in apartments and artists' lofts.

ATMS (CASHPOINTS) You'll find **automated teller machines (ATMs)** on just about every block in Manhattan. Some ATMs will allow you to draw U.S. currency against your bank and credit cards. Check with your bank before leaving home and remember that you will need your personal identification number (PIN) to do so.

BABYSITTING The first place to check is with your hotel. Many hotels have babysitting services or will provide you with lists of reliable sitters. If this doesn't pan out, call the **Baby Sitters' Guild** (☎ **212/682-0227;** www.babysittersguild.com). The sitters are licensed, insured, and bonded, and can even take your child on outings.

BANKING HOURS Banks tend to be open Monday through Friday from 9am to 3pm and sometimes Saturday mornings.

B&BS In addition to **Manhattan Getaways** (see "Apartment Rentals" above) you can try **As You Like It** (☎ **800/277-0413** or 212/695-0191; www.furnapts.com) or **Manhattan Lodgings** (☎ **212/677-7616;** www.manhattanlodgings.com).

BUSINESS HOURS In general, retail stores are open Monday through Saturday from 10am to 6 or 7pm, Thursday from 10am to 8:30 or 9pm, and Sunday from noon to 5pm.

CLIMATE See "The Weather" on p 161.

CONCERTS See "Tickets" below.

CONSULATES & EMBASSIES All embassies are located in Washington,

D.C. All the countries listed below have consulates in New York, and most nations have a mission to the United Nations (also in New York). If your country isn't listed, call for directory information in Washington, D.C. (☎ **202/555-1212**), for the number of your national embassy. The embassy of **Australia** is at 1601 Massachusetts Ave. NW, Washington, DC 20036 (☎ **202/797-3000;** www.austemb.org). The embassy of **Canada** is at 501 Pennsylvania Ave. NW, Washington, DC 20001 (☎ **202/682-1740;** www.canadianembassy.org). The embassy of **Ireland** is at 2234 Massachusetts Ave. NW, Washington, DC 20008 (☎ **202/462-3939;** www.irelandemb. org). The embassy of the **United Kingdom** is at 3100 Massachusetts Ave. NW, Washington, DC 20008 (☎ **202/588-7800;** www.britainusa.com/consular/embassy).

CREDIT CARDS Credit cards are a safe way to "carry" money, they provide a convenient record of all your expenses, and they generally offer good exchange rates. You can also withdraw cash advances from your credit cards at banks or ATMs, provided you know your PIN.

CUSTOMS Visitors arriving by air, no matter what the port of entry, should cultivate patience and resignation before setting foot on U.S. soil. Getting through immigration control can take as long as 2 hours on some days, especially on summer weekends. People traveling by air from Canada, Bermuda, and certain countries in the Caribbean can sometimes clear Customs and Immigration at the point of departure, which is much quicker.

DENTISTS If you have dental problems, a nationwide referral service known as **1-800-DENTIST** (☎ **800/336-8478**) will provide the name of a nearby dentist or clinic.

DINING With a few exceptions at the high end of the scale, dining attire is fairly casual. It's a good idea to make reservations in advance if you plan to dine between 7 and 9pm.

DOCTORS The **NYU Downtown Hospital** offers physician referrals at ☎ **888/698-3362.**

ELECTRICITY Like Canada, the United States uses 110 to 120 volts AC (60 cycles), compared to 220 to 240 volts AC (50 cycles) in most of Europe, Australia, and New Zealand. If your small appliances use 220 to 240 volts, you'll need a 110-volt transformer and a plug adapter with two flat parallel pins to operate them here. Downward converters that change 220–240 volts to 110–120 volts are difficult to find in the United States, so bring one with you.

EMBASSIES See "Consulates & Embassies," above.

EMERGENCIES Dial ☎ **911** for fire, police, and ambulance. The **Poison Control Center** can be reached at ☎ **800/222-1222** toll-free from any phone. If you encounter serious problems, contact **Traveler's Aid International** (☎ **202/546-1127;** www.travelersaid.org) to help direct you to a local branch. This nationwide, nonprofit, social-service organization geared to helping travelers in difficult straits offers services that might include reuniting families separated while traveling, providing food and/or shelter to people stranded without cash, or even emotional counseling.

EVENT LISTINGS Good sources include the ***New York Times*** (www.nytimes.com) with excellent arts and entertainment coverage, ***Time Out New York*** (www.timeout.com/newyork) with extensive weekly listings, and the weekly ***Village Voice*** (www.villagevoice.com), which you can pick up for free all over the city.

FAMILY TRAVEL Good bets for timely information include the

"Weekend" section of Friday's ***New York Times,*** which has a section dedicated to the week's best kid-friendly activities; the weekly ***New York*** magazine, which has a full calendar of children's events in its "Cue" section; and ***Time Out New York Kids.*** For more extensive recommendations, you might want to purchase a copy of ***Frommer's New York City with Kids,*** an entire guidebook dedicated to family visits to the Big Apple.

GAY & LESBIAN TRAVELERS All over Manhattan, but especially in neighborhoods such as the **West Village** and **Chelsea,** shops, services, and restaurants cater to a gay and lesbian clientele. The **Lesbian, Gay & Transgender Community Services Center** is at 208 W. 13th St., between Seventh and Eighth avenues (☎ **212/620-7310;** www.gaycenter.org).

HOLIDAYS Banks, government offices, post offices, and many stores, restaurants, and museums are closed on the following legal national holidays: January 1 (New Year's Day), the third Monday in January (Martin Luther King Jr. Day), the third Monday in February (Presidents' Day, Washington's Birthday), the last Monday in May (Memorial Day), July 4th (Independence Day), the first Monday in September (Labor Day), the second Monday in October (Columbus Day), November 11 (Veterans' Day/Armistice Day), the fourth Thursday in November (Thanksgiving Day), and December 25 (Christmas). Also, the Tuesday following the first Monday in November is Election Day and is a federal government holiday in presidential-election years (held every 4 years, and next in 2008).

INSURANCE **Trip-Cancellation Insurance** helps you get your money back if you have to back out of a trip, if you have to go home early, or if your travel supplier goes bankrupt. Allowed reasons for cancellation can range from sickness to natural disasters to the State Department declaring your destination unsafe for travel. In this unstable world, trip-cancellation insurance is a good buy if you're getting tickets well in advance. Insurance policy details vary, so read the fine print—and especially make sure that your airline or cruise line is on the list of carriers covered in case of bankruptcy. For information, contact one of the following insurers: **Access America** (☎ **800/284-8300;** www.accessamerica.com); **AIG Travel Guard** (☎ **800/826-4919;** www.travelguard.com); **Travel Insured International** (☎ **800/243-3174;** www.travelinsured.com); and **Travelex Insurance Services** (☎ **888/457-4602;** www.travelex-insurance.com).

Although it's not required of travelers, **health insurance** is highly recommended. The United States does not usually offer free or low-cost medical care to its citizens or visitors. Doctors and hospitals are expensive, and in most cases will require advance payment or proof of coverage before they render their services. Though lack of health insurance may prevent you from being admitted to a hospital in non-emergencies, don't worry about being left on a street corner to die: The American way is to fix you now and bill the living daylights out of you later.

Insurance for British Travelers: Most big travel agents offer their own insurance and will probably try to sell you their package when you book a holiday. Think before you sign. **Britain's Consumers' Association** recommends that you review the policy and read the fine print before buying. **The Association of British Insurers** (☎ **020/7600-3333;** www.abi.org.uk) gives advice by phone and publishes *Holiday*

Insurance, a free guide to policy provisions and prices.

Insurance for Canadian Travelers: You should check with their provincial health plan offices or call **Health Canada** (☎ **613/957-2991;** www.hc-sc.gc.ca) to find out the extent of your coverage and what documentation and receipts you must take home in case you are treated in the United States.

Lost-Luggage Insurance: On domestic flights, checked baggage is covered up to $2,500 per ticketed passenger. On international flights (including U.S. portions of international trips), baggage is limited to approximately $9 per pound, up to approximately $635 per checked bag. If you plan to check items more valuable than the standard liability, see if your valuables are covered by your homeowner's policy or get baggage insurance as part of your comprehensive travel-insurance package. Don't buy insurance at the airport, as it's usually overpriced. Be sure to take any valuables with you in your carry-on luggage, since many valuables (including books, money, and electronics) aren't covered by airline policies. If your luggage is lost, immediately file a lost-luggage claim at the airport, detailing the luggage contents. For most airlines, you must report delayed, damaged, or lost baggage within 4 hours of arrival. The airlines are required to deliver luggage, once found, directly to your house or destination for free.

INTERNET CENTERS The **Times Square Visitors Center,** 1560 Broadway, between 46th and 47th streets (☎ **212/768-1560;** open daily 8am–8pm), has computer terminals that you can use to send e-mails courtesy of Yahoo! In Times Square, **easyInternetcafé,** 234 W. 42nd St., between Seventh and Eighth avenues (☎ **212/398-0775;** www.easyeverything.com), is open 24/7. **FedEx Kinko's** (www.kinkos.com) charges 30¢ per minute ($15 per hour) and has numerous locations around town.

LIMOS Try **Allstate** (☎ **800/453-4099**) or **Tel-Aviv** (☎ **800/222-9888**).

LOST PROPERTY **Travelers Aid** (www.travelersaid.org) helps distressed travelers with all kinds of problems, including lost or stolen luggage. There are locations in Terminals 1, 3, 4, 6, 7, 8 & 9 at JFK Airport (☎ **718/656-4870**), and in Newark Airport's Terminals A, B & C (☎ **973/623-5052**).

MAIL & POSTAGE The main post office is at 421 Eighth Ave. (33rd St.); other branches can be found by calling ☎ **800/275-8777** or logging onto www.usps.gov. Mail can be sent to you, in your name, c/o General Delivery at the main post office. Most post offices will hold your mail for up to 1 month, and are open Monday to Friday from 8am to 6pm, and Saturday from 9am to 3pm. At press time, domestic postage rates were 27¢ for a postcard and 42¢ for a letter. For international mail, a first-class letter of up to 1 ounce costs 94¢ (72¢ to Canada and Mexico); and a first-class postcard costs 94¢ (72¢ to Canada and Mexico).

MONEY Don't carry a lot of cash in your wallet, but always have $20 in small bills on hand for taxi fare. A few small restaurants won't accept credit cards, so ask up front if you plan to pay with plastic.

PASSPORTS Keep a photocopy of your passport with you when you're traveling. If your passport is lost or stolen, having a copy will significantly speed up the reissuing process at your consulate. Keep your passport and other valuables in your room's safe or in the hotel safe.

PHARMACIES **Duane Reade** (www.duanereade.com) has 24-hour pharmacies in Midtown at 224 W. 57th

St., at Broadway (☎ **212/541-9708**); on the Upper West Side at 253 W. 72nd St., between Broadway and West End Avenue (☎ **212/580-0497**); and on the Upper East Side at 1279 Third Ave., at 74th Street (☎ **212/744-2668**).

SAFETY New York is one of the safest large cities in the United States, but crime most definitely exists here. Trust your instincts because they're usually right. You'll rarely be hassled, but it's always best to walk with a sense of purpose and self-confidence. Don't stop in the middle of the sidewalk to pull out and peruse your map. Anywhere in the city, if you find yourself on a deserted street that feels unsafe, it probably is; leave as quickly as possible. If you do find yourself accosted by someone with or without a weapon, remember to keep your anger in check and that the most reasonable response (maddening though it may be) is not to resist.

SENIOR TRAVELERS New York subway and bus fares are half price ($1) for people 65 and older. Many museums and sights (and some theaters and performance halls) offer discounted admittance and tickets to seniors, so don't be shy about asking and always bring an ID card. Many hotels offer senior discounts; **Choice Hotels** (www.hotelchoice.com) gives 30% off their published rates to anyone over 50, provided you book your room through their nationwide toll-free reservations number (that is, not directly with the hotels or through a travel agent). Members of **AARP,** 601 E St. NW, Washington, DC 20049 (☎ **888/687-2277** or 202/434-2277; www.aarp.org), get discounts on hotels, airfares, and car rentals. Anyone over 50 can join.

SMOKING Smoking is prohibited on public transportation, in hotel and office buildings, lobbies, in taxis, bars, restaurants, and in most shops.

SPECTATOR SPORTS You've got your choice of baseball teams, the **Yankees** (☎ **718/293-6000;** www.yankees.com) and the **Mets** (☎ **718/507-TIXX;** www.mets.com). For basketball there's the **Knicks** (☎ **877/NYK-DUNK;** www.nyknicks.com) and the **New York Liberty** (☎ **212/465-6080;** www.wnba.com/liberty).

TAXES **Sales tax** is 8.375% on meals, most goods, and some services. **Hotel tax** is 13.375% plus $2 per room per night (including sales tax). **Parking garage tax** is 18.375%.

TAXIS See "Limos" and "Getting Around" above.

TELEPHONE For directory assistance, dial ☎ **411;** for long-distance information, dial 1, then the appropriate area code and 555-1212. Pay phones cost 25¢ for local calls. There are four area codes in the city: two in Manhattan, the original **212** and the new **646,** and two in the outer boroughs, the original **718** and the new **347.** The **917** area code is assigned to cellphones, pagers, and the like. Calls between these area codes are local, but you'll have to dial 1 + the area code + the 7 digits, even within your area code.

TICKETS Tickets for concerts at all larger theaters can be purchased through **Ticketmaster** (☎ **212/307-7171;** www.ticketmaster.com). For advance tickets at smaller venues contact **Ticketweb** (☎ **866/468-7619;** www.ticketweb.com). For theater tickets you can buy tickets in advance from **TeleCharge** (☎ **212/239-6200;** www.telecharge.com) or **Ticketmaster** (☎ **212/307-4100;** www.ticketmaster.com). If you want last-minute tickets, check the "Getting Tickets" box on p 145.

TIPPING In hotels, tip **bellhops** at least $1 per bag ($2–$3 if you have a lot of luggage) and tip the **chamber**

staff $1 to $2 per day (more if you've left a disaster area for him or her to clean up, or if you're traveling with kids and/or pets). Tip the **doorman** or **concierge** only if he or she has provided you with some specific service (like calling a cab). In restaurants, bars, and nightclubs, tip **service staff** 15% to 20% of the check, tip **bartenders** 10% to 15%, and tip **checkroom attendants** $1 per garment. Tipping is not expected in cafeterias and fast-food restaurants. Tip **cab drivers** 15% of the fare and tip **skycaps** at airports at least $1 per bag ($2–$3 if you have a lot of luggage).

TOILETS Public restrooms are available at the **visitor centers** in Midtown (1560 Broadway, btwn. 46th and 47th sts.; and 810 Seventh Ave., btwn. 52nd and 53rd sts.). Grand Central Terminal, at 42nd Street between Park and Lexington avenues, also has clean restrooms. Your best bet on the street is **Starbucks** or another city java chain—you can't walk more than a few blocks without seeing one. The big **chain bookstores** are good for this, too. Also head to **hotel lobbies** (especially the big Midtown ones) and **department stores** such as Macy's and Bloomingdale's. On the Lower East Side, stop into the **Lower East Side BID Visitor Center,** 261 Broome St., between Orchard and Allen streets (open Sun–Fri 10am–4pm, sometimes later).

TOURIST OFFICE NYC & Company, 810 Seventh Ave., New York, NY 10019 (☎ **800/NYC-VISIT;** www.nycvisit.com).

TOURS **Big Apple Greeter** (☎ **212/669-8159;** www.bigapplegreeter.org) provides free neighborhood walking tours. Or try one of the hop-on, hop-off bus tours offered by **Gray Line** (☎ **800/669-0051;** www.graylinenewyork.com). They also have a host of other options—helicopter flights, museum admission, and guided visits of sights.

TRAVELERS WITH DISABILITIES **Hospital Audiences, Inc.** (☎ **212/575-7676;** www.hospitalaudiences.org) arranges attendance and provides details about accessibility at cultural institutions as well as cultural events adapted for people with disabilities. Services include "Describe!," which allows visually impaired theatergoers to enjoy theater events; and the invaluable **HAI Hot Line** (☎ **212/575-7676**), which offers accessibility information for hotels, restaurants, attractions, cultural venues, and much more. This nonprofit organization also publishes ***Access for All,*** a guidebook on accessibility, available by calling ☎ **212/575-7663** or by sending a $5 check to 548 Broadway, third floor, New York, NY 10012-3950.

Another terrific source for travelers with disabilities who are coming to New York City is **Big Apple Greeter** (☎ **212/669-8159;** www.bigapplegreeter.org). Its employees are well versed in accessibility issues. They can provide a resource list of agencies that serve the city's community with disabilities, and sometimes have special discounts available to theater and music performances. Big Apple Greeter even offers one-to-one tours that pair volunteers with visitors with disabilities; they can even introduce you to the public transportation system. Reserve at least 1 week ahead.

Public buses are an inexpensive and easy way to get around New York. All buses' back doors are supposed to be equipped with wheelchair lifts (though the city has had complaints that not all are in working order). Buses also "kneel," lowering their front steps for people who have difficulty boarding. Passengers with disabilities pay half-price fares ($1). The **subway** isn't yet fully wheelchair accessible, but a list of about 30 accessible subway stations and a guide to wheelchair-accessible subway itineraries are on the MTA website. Call ☎ **718/596-8585** for bus and subway transit info or go online to www.mta.nyc.ny.us/nyct and click on the wheelchair symbol.

A Brief **History**

1524 Giovanni da Verrazano sails into New York Harbor.

1609 Henry Hudson sails up the Hudson River.

1621 The Dutch West India Company begins trading from New York City.

1626 The Dutch pay 60 guilders ($24) to the Lenape Tribe for the island of New Amsterdam.

1664 The Dutch surrender New Amsterdam to the British and the island is renamed after the brother of King Charles II, The Duke of York.

1765 The Sons of Liberty burn the British Governor in effigy.

1776 Independence from England is declared.

1789 The first Congress is held at Federal Hall on Wall Street, and George Washington is inaugurated.

1792 The first stock exchange is established on Wall Street.

1820 New York City is the nation's largest city with a population of 124,000.

1863 The draft riots rage throughout New York; 125 people die including 11 African Americans who are lynched by mobs of Irish immigrants.

1883 The Brooklyn Bridge opens.

1886 The Statue of Liberty is completed.

1892 Ellis Island opens and begins processing over a million immigrants yearly.

1904 The first subway departs from City Hall.

1920 Babe Ruth joins the New York Yankees.

1929 The stock market crashes.

1931 The Empire State Building opens and is the tallest building in the world.

1939 The New York World's Fair opens in Flushing Meadows, Queens.

1947 The Brooklyn Dodgers sign Jackie Robinson, the first African American to play in the Major Leagues.

1957 Elvis Presley performs live in New York on *The Ed Sullivan Show.*

1969 The Gay Rights movement begins with the Stonewall Rebellion in Greenwich Village.

1990 David Dinkins is elected as the first African-American mayor of New York City.

2000 The New York Yankees beat the New York Mets in the first Subway Series in 44 years. New York's population exceeds eight million.

2001 Terrorists use hijacked planes to crash into the Twin Towers of the World Trade Center, which brings both towers down and kills more than 3,000 people.

2003 Smoking is banned in all restaurants and bars.

2004 Ground breaks on the Freedom Tower, to be built on the site of the World Trade Center.

2005 Michael Bloomberg wins a second term for mayor of New York City.

2008 The New York Giants win the Super Bowl with Eli Manning leading the way.

Art & Architecture

New York is famous for its great buildings, but the truth is that the most interesting thing about its architecture is its diversity. From elegant Greek Revival row houses to soaring skyscrapers, the city contains excellent examples of every style. Constructed over 300 years, these buildings represent the changing tastes of the city's residents from Colonial times to the present.

Georgian (1700–76)

This style reflects Renaissance ideas made popular in England, and later in the United States, through the publication of books on 16th-century Italian architects. Georgian houses are characterized by a formal arrangement of parts employing a symmetrical composition enriched with classical details, such as columns and pediments.

St. Paul's Chapel (p 8), the only pre-Revolutionary building in Manhattan, is an almost perfect example of the Georgian style, with a pediment, colossal columns, Palladian window, quoins, and balustrade above the roofline.

Federal (1780–1820)

Federal was the first American architectural style. It was an adaptation of a contemporaneous English style called Adamesque, which included ornate, colorful interior decoration. Federal combined Georgian architecture with the delicacy of the French rococo and the classical architecture of Greece and Rome. The overall effect is one of restraint and dignity, and may appear delicate when compared to the more robust Georgian style.

In the **West Village,** near and along Bedford Street between Christopher and Morton streets, are more original Federal-style houses than anywhere else in Manhattan. House nos. 4 through 10 (1825–34) on Grove Street, just off Bedford, present one of the most authentic groups of late Federal–style houses in America. See p 79.

Greek Revival (1820–60)

The Greek Revolution in the 1820s, in which Greece won its independence from the Turks, recalled to American intellectuals the democracy of ancient Greece and its elegant architecture. At the same time, the War of 1812 diminished American affection for the British influence. With many believing America to be the spiritual successor of Greece, the use of classical Greek forms came to dominate residential, commercial, and government architecture.

Perhaps the city's finest Greek Revival building is **Federal Hall National Memorial** (1834–42), at 26 Wall St., at Nassau Street. The structure has a Greek temple front, with Doric columns and a simple pediment, resting on a high base,

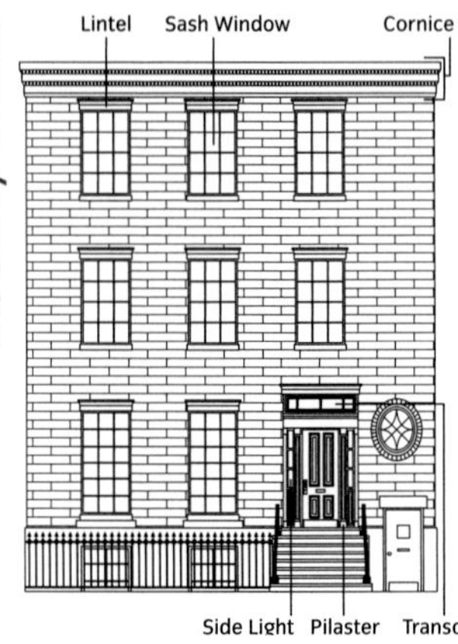

Typical Federal Exterior.

called a plinth, with a steep flight of steps. See p 67.

Gothic Revival (1830–60)

The term "Gothic Revival" refers to a literary and aesthetic movement of the 1830s and 1840s that occurred in England and the United States. Adherents believed that the wickedness of modern times could benefit with a dose of "goodness" presumed to have been associated with the Christian medieval past. Architecture was chosen as one of the vehicles to bring this message to the people. Some structures had only one or two Gothic features, while others, usually churches, were copies of English Gothic structures.

Trinity Church, at Broadway and Wall Street (Richard Upjohn, 1846), is one of the most celebrated, authentic Gothic Revival structures in the United States. Here you see all the features of a Gothic church: a steeple, battlements, pointed arches, Gothic tracery, stained-glass windows, flying buttresses (an external bracing system for supporting a roof or vault), and medieval sculptures. See p 8.

Italianate (1840–80)

The architecture of Italy served as the inspiration for this building style, which could be as picturesque as the Gothic or as restrained as the classical. In New York, the style was used for urban row houses and commercial buildings. The development of cast iron at this time permitted the inexpensive mass production of decorative features that few could have afforded in carved stone. This led to the creation of cast-iron districts in nearly every American city.

New York's **SoHo–Cast Iron Historic District** has 26 blocks jammed with cast-iron facades, many in the Italianate manner. The single richest section is **Greene Street** between Houston and Canal streets.

Early Skyscraper (1880–1920)

The invention of the skyscraper can be traced directly to the use of cast iron in the 1840s for storefronts, such as those seen in New York's SoHo. Experimentation with cast and wrought iron in the construction of interior skeletons eventually allowed buildings to rise higher. These buildings were spacious, cost-effective, efficient, and quickly erected—in short, the perfect architectural solution for America's growing downtowns. But solving the technical problems of the skyscraper did not resolve how the buildings should look. Most solutions relied on historical precedents, including decoration reminiscent of the Gothic, Romanesque (a style characterized by the use of rounded arches), or Beaux Arts.

Examples include the **American Surety Company,** at 100 Broadway (Bruce Price, 1895). The triangular **Flatiron Building,** at Fifth Avenue and 23rd Street (Daniel H. Burnham & Co., 1902), has strong tripartite divisions and Renaissance Revival detail, see p 42. And, the **Woolworth**

Building (Cass Gilbert, 1913), on Broadway at Park Place, see p 7.

Second Renaissance Revival (1890–1920)

Buildings in this style show a studied formalism. A relative faithfulness to Italian Renaissance precedents of window and doorway treatments distinguishes it from the looser adaptations of the Italianate. Scale and size, in turn, set the Second Renaissance Revival apart from the first, which occurred from 1840 to 1890. The style was used for banks, swank town houses, government buildings, and private clubs.

New York's Upper East Side has two fine examples of this building type, each exhibiting most of the style's key features: the **Racquet and Tennis Club,** 370 Park Ave. (McKim, Mead & White, 1918), based on the style of an elegant Florentine palazzo; and the **Metropolitan Club,** 1 E. 60th St. (McKim, Mead & White, 1891–94).

Beaux Arts (1890–1920)

This style takes its name from the Ecole des Beaux-Arts in Paris, where a number of prominent American architects trained, beginning around the mid–19th century. These architects adopted the academic design principles of the Ecole, which emphasized the study of Greek and Roman structures, composition, and symmetry, and the creation of elaborate presentation drawings. Because of the idealized origins and grandiose use of classical forms, the Beaux Arts in America was seen as the ideal style for expressing civic pride. Grandiose compositions, an exuberance of detail, and a variety of stone finishes typify most Beaux Arts structures.

The **New York Public Library** (p 43), at Fifth Avenue and 42nd Street (Carrère & Hastings, 1911), is perhaps the best example. Others of note are **Grand Central Terminal** (p 43), at 42nd Street and Park Avenue (Reed & Stem and Warren & Whetmore, 1903–13), and the **U.S. Custom House** (Cass Gilbert, 1907) on Bowling Green between State and Whitehall streets.

International Style (1920–45)

In 1932, the Museum of Modern Art hosted its first architecture exhibit, titled simply "Modern Architecture." Displays included images of International Style buildings from around the world. The structures all share a stark simplicity and vigorous functionalism, a definite break from historically based, decorative styles. The International Style was popularized in the United States through the teachings and designs of **Ludwig Mies van der Rohe** (1886–1969), a German émigré based in Chicago. Interpretations of the "Miesian" International Style were built in most U.S. cities, as late as 1980.

Two famous examples of this style in New York are the **Seagram Building,** at 375 Park Ave. (Ludwig Mies van der Rohe, 1958), and the **Lever House,** at 390 Park Ave., between 53rd and 54th streets (Skidmore, Owings & Merrill, 1952).

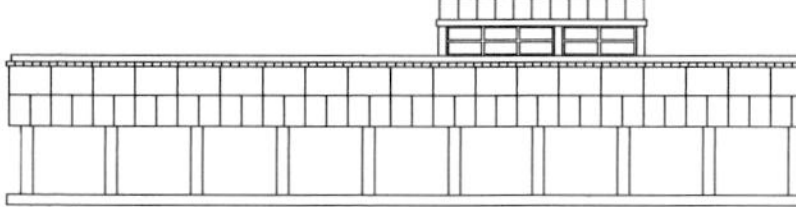

Lever House.

Art Deco (1925–40)

Art Deco is a decorative style that took its name from a Paris exposition in 1925. The jazzy style embodied the idea of modernity. One of the first widely accepted styles not based on historic precedents, it influenced all areas of design from jewelry and household goods to cars, trains, and ocean liners. Art Deco buildings are characterized by a linear, hard edge, or angular composition, often with a vertical emphasis and highlighted with stylized decoration.

Despite the effects of the Depression, several major Art Deco structures were built in New York in the 1930s, often providing crucial jobs. **Rockefeller Center** (Raymond Hood, 1932–40), p 44, includes 30 Rockefeller Plaza, a tour de force of Art Deco style, with a soaring, vertical shaft and aluminum details. The **Chrysler Building's** needlelike spire (William Allen, 1930; p 43) with zigzag patterns in glass and metal is a distinctive feature on the city's skyline. The famous **Empire State Building,** p 43 (Shreve, Lamb & Harmon, 1931), contains a black- and silver-toned lobby among its many Art Deco features.

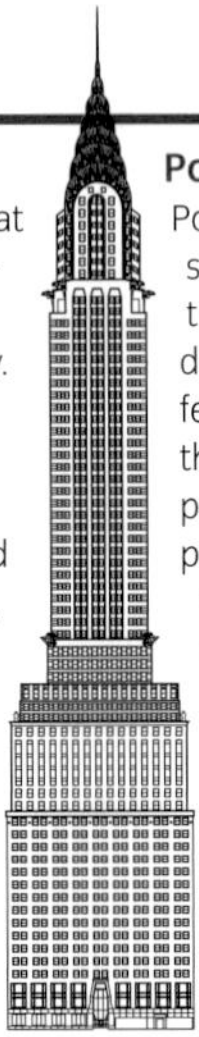

Chrysler Building.

Art Moderne (1930–45)

Art Moderne strove for modernity and an artistic expression for the sleekness of the machine age. Unbroken horizontal lines and smooth curves visually distinguish it from Art Deco and give it a streamlined effect. It was popular with movie theaters, and was often applied to cars, trains, and boats to suggest the idea of speed.

Radio City Music Hall, on Sixth Avenue at 50th Street (Edward Durrell Stone and Donald Deskey, 1932), has a sweeping Art Moderne marquee. See p 16.

Postmodern (1975–90)

Postmodernism burst on the scene in the 1970s with the reintroduction of historical precedents in architecture. With many feeling that the office towers of the previous style were too cold, postmodernists began to incorporate classical details and recognizable forms into their designs—often applied in outrageous proportions.

The **Sony Building,** at 550 Madison Ave. (Philip Johnson/John Burgee, 1984), brings the distinctive shape of a Chippendale cabinet to the New York skyline.

Sony Building.

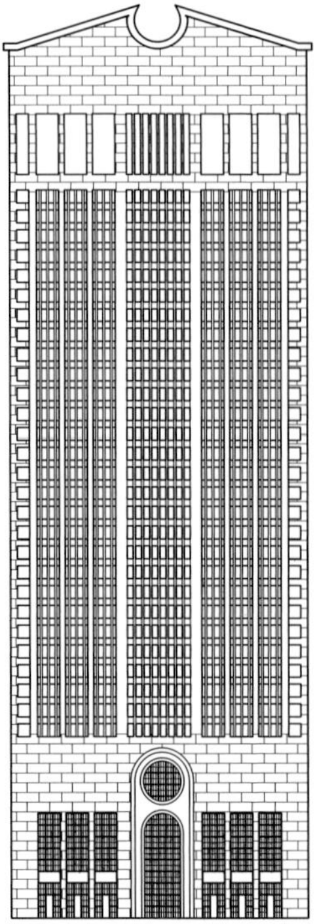

Index

See also Accommodations and Restaurant indexes, below.

Accommodations

Restaurants

Photo **Credits**

p viii: © Mitchell Funk/Getty Images; p 3 top: © Martin Shields/Alamy; p 4 top: © Courtesy the Gramercy Park Hotel; p 5: © Michael Howell/PhotoLibrary; p 7 bottom: © Amanda Hall/Robert Harding Travel/PhotoLibrary; p 8 top: © Norman Tomalin/Alamy; p 9 bottom: © M.Flynn/Alamy; p 11 bottom: © Peter Hendrie/Lonely Planet Images; p 12 bottom: © Louie Psihoyos/Corbis; p 13 top: © Alan Schein Photography/Corbis; p 15 bottom: © Kevin Foy/Alamy Images; p 16 top: © Richard I'Anson/Lonely Planet Images; p 16 bottom: © SCPhotos/Alamy; p 17 bottom: © Eric Kamp/PhotoLibrary ; p 18 top: © Louie Psihoyos/Corbis; p 19: © Digital Vision/AGE Fotostock; p 21 bottom: © Courtesy Café des Artistes; p 22 bottom: © Klaus Lucka/Lincoln Center for the Performing Arts; p 23 top: © SuperStock/AGE Fotostock; p 25 bottom: © Paul Katz/PhotoLibrary ; p 26 top: © Richard Bryant/Arcaid/Alamy; p 26 bottom: Harold Pestana's Soldiers of the Queen, © The Forbes Collection, New York All Rights Reserved; p 27 top: © Rudy Sulgan/AGE Fotostock; p 27 bottom: © Kevin Foy/Alamy; p 29 bottom: Carrie Walter Stettheimer, Stettheimer Doll House, left side 1920's, © Museum of the City of New York, Gift of Miss Ettie Stettheimer; p 30 bottom: © AM Corporation/Alamy; p 33 bottom: © Andrew H. Walker/Getty Images; p 34 top: © Comstock Images/Alamy; p 34 bottom: © Heungman Kwan/PhotoLibrary; p 35 top: © Heungman Kwan/PhotoLibrary; p 37 bottom: © Marc Asnin/Corbis; p 38 top: © Omni Photo Communications Inc./PhotoLibrary; p 38 bottom: © Steve Sands/New York Newswire/Corbis; p 39 bottom: © Barry Winiker/PhotoLibrary; p 41 middle: © Omni Photo Communications Inc./PhotoLibrary; p 42 top: © Keate/Masterfile; p 42 bottom: © Mike Segar/Reuters/Corbis; p 43 bottom: © Eric Kamp/PhotoLibrary; p 44 top: © Eric Kamp/PhotoLibrary; p 45 bottom: © Paul Katz/PhotoLibrary; p 47 top: © Michael Dwyer/Alamy; p 48 top: © Courtesy The Public Theatre; p 48 bottom: © Stuart Kelly/Alamy Images; p 49: © Ellen McKnight/Alamy; p 51 bottom: © Greg Gawlowski/Lonely Planet Images; p 52 bottom: © Michael S. Yamashita/Corbis; p 53 top: © SuperStock, Inc./SuperStock; p 55 top: © Angus Oborn/Lonely Planet Images; p 56 top: © Richard Bryant/Arcaid/Alamy; p 61 bottom: © Michael Kim/Corbis; p 63: © Chuck Pefley/Alamy; p 65 top: © Rick Shupper/Ambient Images/drr.net; p 66 top: © Jeff Greenburg/PhotoLibrary; p 67 bottom: © Peter Bennett/Ambient Images Inc./Alamy; p 69 bottom: © Omni Photo Communications Inc./PhotoLibrary; p 70 top: © Lee Snider/Photo Images/Corbis; p 71 bottom: © Ted Pink/Alamy; p 73 top: © Omni Photo Communications Inc./PhotoLibrary; p 73 bottom: © Brad Barket/Getty Images; p 74 top: © Brian Ach/WireImage/Getty Images; p 75 bottom: © Omni Photo Communications Inc./PhotoLibrary; p 77 top: © Lee Snider/Photo Images/Corbis; p 78 top: © Peter Bennett/Ambient Images Inc./Alamy; p 79 bottom: © Courtesy One If By Land; p 81 bottom: © David Forbert/SuperStock; p 82 top: © Mark Gidson/Photo Library; p 82 bottom: © Lauree Feldman/PhotoLibrary; p 83 top: © SuperStock, Inc./SuperStock; p 86 top: © Jochen Tack/Das Fotoarchiv/Black Star/Alamy; p 86 bottom: © Heungman Kwan/PhotoLibrary; p 87 top: © Ace Stock Limited/Alamy; p 87 bottom: © Lauree Feldman/PhotoLibrary; p 88 bottom: © Robert Holmes/Corbis; p 89: © Bertrand Reiger/AGE Fotostock; p 94 bottom: © Joe Viesti/V1/drr.net; p 96 bottom: © Kevin Foy/Alamy; p 97 top: © Kim Grant/Lonely Planet Images; p 98 top: © Joe Viesti/V1/drr.net; p 100 bottom: © Chris Gascoigne/VIEW Pictures Ltd/Alamy; p 101: © Rudy Sulgan/Corbis; p 103 top: © Rudi Von Briel/PhotoLibrary; p 104 top: © Comstock Images/Alamy; p 105 bottom: © Ambient Images Inc./Alamy; p 107 top: © Jeff Richman, Green-Wood Cemetery Historian; p 108 top: © Lauree Feldman/PhotoLibrary; p 108 bottom: © Jeff Richman, Green-Wood Cemetery Historian; p 109: © Frances Roberts/Alamy; p 114 top: © Owen Franken/Courtesy Restaurant Daniel; p 114 bottom: © Eric Laignel; p 115 top: © Courtesy Jean-Georges; p 115 bottom: © Andy Levin/Alamy; p 116 top: © Courtesy Keens Steakhouse; p 117 top: © Mark Peterson/Corbis; p 117 bottom: © Courtesy One If By Land; p 118 bottom: © Rosa Mexicano Restaurants; p 119 top: © Bebeto Matthews/AP Photo; p 121 bottom: © Courtesy The Spotted Pig; p 122 bottom: © Walter Bibikow/Jon Arnold Images/Alamy; p 123: © Courtesy Bowlmor Lanes & Pressure Lounge; p 128 bottom: © Courtesy Bowlmor Lanes; p 129 top: © Courtesy City Hall; p 130 top: © Dan Herrick/Lonely Planet Images; p 130 bottom: © Thomas A. Kelly/Corbis; p 131 top: © Gail Mooney/Corbis; p 132 top: © PCL/Alamy; p 132 bottom: © Kim Grant/Lonely Planet Images; p 133: © WireImage/Getty Images; p 134 bottom: © Peter Kramer/Getty Images; p 139 top: © Kathy Willens/AP; p 140 bottom: © Bettmann/Corbis; p 141 top: © Barry Winiker/PhotoLibrary; p 142 top: © Viviane Moos/Corbis; p 142 bottom: © Omni Photo Communications Inc./PhotoLibrary; p 143 top: © Angela Jimenez/drr.net; p 143 bottom: © Dan Herrick/Lonely Planet Images; p 144 bottom: © Bojan Brecelj/Corbis; p 145 top: © Bo Zaunders/Corbis; p 147: © Courtesy the St. Regis Hotel; p 152 top: © Rick

Shupper/Ambient Images/drr.net; p 153 top: © Courtesy The Greenwich Hotel; p 153 bottom: © Roy Wright ; p 154 top: © Omni Photo Communications Inc./PhotoLibrary; p 155 bottom: © Courtesy The Mercer Hotel; p 156 top: © Courtesy Loews Regency Hotel; p 156 bottom: © The Ritz-Carlton New York, Battery Park; p 157 bottom: © Lauree Feldman/PhotoLibrary; p 158 bottom: © Washington Square Hotel; p 159: © picturescolourlibrary.com/Stock Connection/drr.net